INDIANA JONES™

and the

KINGDOM OF
THE CRYSTAL SKULL™

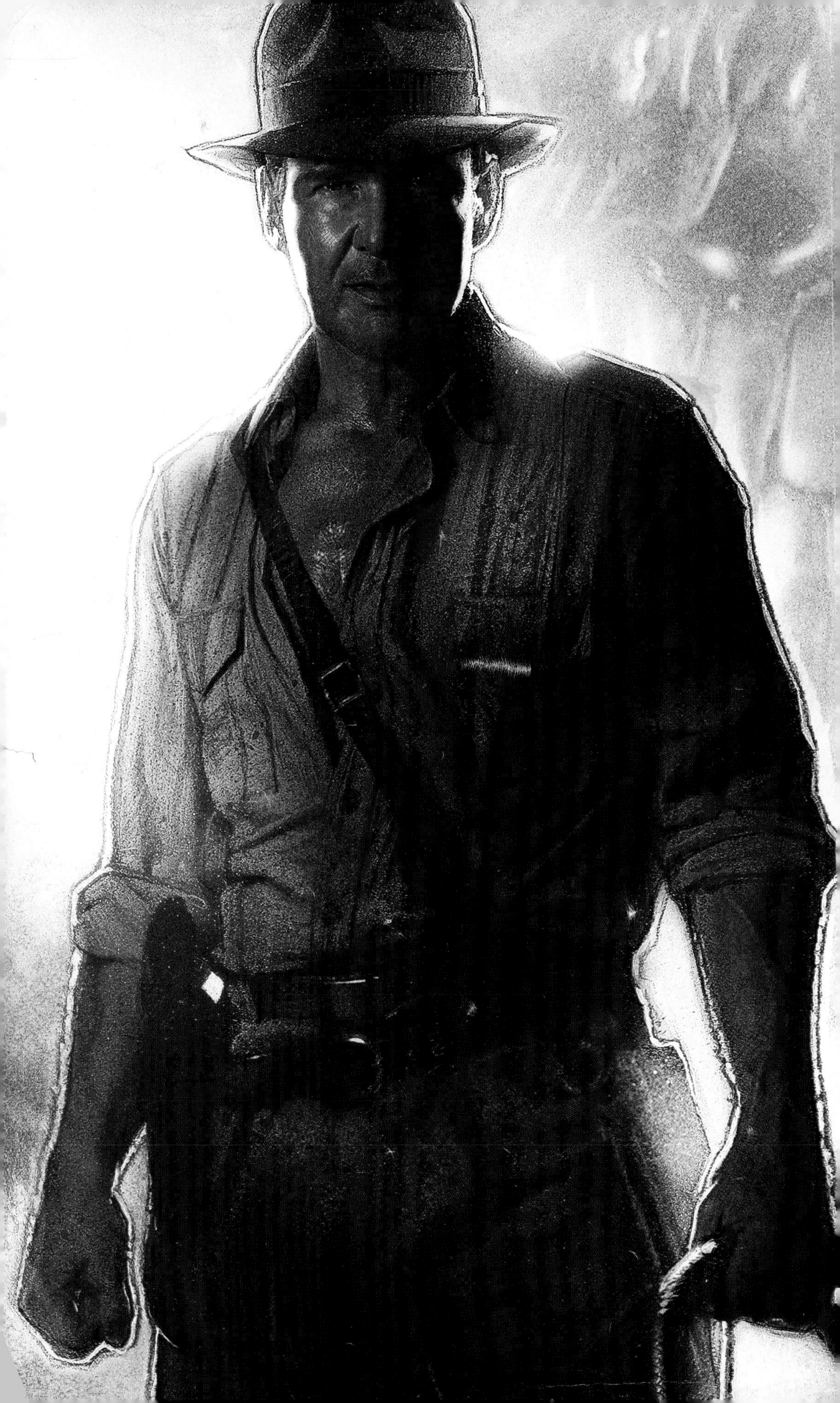

INDIANA JONES

and the
KINGDOM OF THE CRYSTAL SKULL

BASED ON THE STORY BY
GEORGE LUCAS
and **JEFF NATHANSON**

AND THE SCREENPLAY BY
DAVID KOEPP

ADAPTATION
JOHN JACKSON MILLER

PENCILS
LUKE ROSS
CLIFF RICHARDS

INKS
FABIO LAGUNA
EBER FERREIRA

COLORS
DAN JACKSON
PAMELA RAMBO

LETTERS
MICHAEL HEISLER

COVER
DREW STRUZAN

DARK HORSE BOOKS®

PUBLISHER
MIKE RICHARDSON

COLLECTION DESIGNER
STEPHEN REICHERT

ART DIRECTOR
LIA RIBACCHI

EDITOR
JEREMY BARLOW

ASSISTANT EDITORS
FREDDYE LINS and **DAVE MARSHALL**

Special thanks to Sue Rostoni, Frank Parisi, Leland Chee, Troy Alders, Carol Roeder, Elaine Mederer, Jann Moorehead, and David Anderman at Lucas Licensing

Indiana Jones and the Kingdom of the Crystal Skull, May 2008. Published by Dark Horse Comics, Inc., 10956 SE Main St, Milwaukie, OR 97222. Indiana Jones © 2008 Lucasfilm Ltd. & TM. All rights reserved. Used under authorization. Text and illustrations for Indiana Jones are © 2008 Lucasfilm Ltd. Dark Horse Books® and the Dark Horse logo are registered trademarks of Dark Horse Comics, Inc. All rights reserved. No portion of this publication may be reproduced or transmitted, in any form or by any means, without the express written permission of Dark Horse Comics, Inc. Names, characters, places, and incidents featured in this publication either are the product of the author's imagination or are used fictitiously. Any resemblance to actual persons (living or dead), events, institutions, or locales, without satiric intent, is coincidental.

This volume collects issues one and two of the Dark Horse comic-book series
Indiana Jones and the Kingdom of the Crystal Skull.

Published by
Dark Horse Books
A division of Dark Horse Comics, Inc.
10956 SE Main Street
Milwaukie, OR 97222

darkhorse.com
indianajones.com

To find a comics shop in your area, call the Comic Shop Locator Service toll-free at 1-888-266-4226

First edition: May 2008
ISBN: 978-1-59307-952-9

10 9 8 7 6 5 4 3 2 1
Printed in Canada

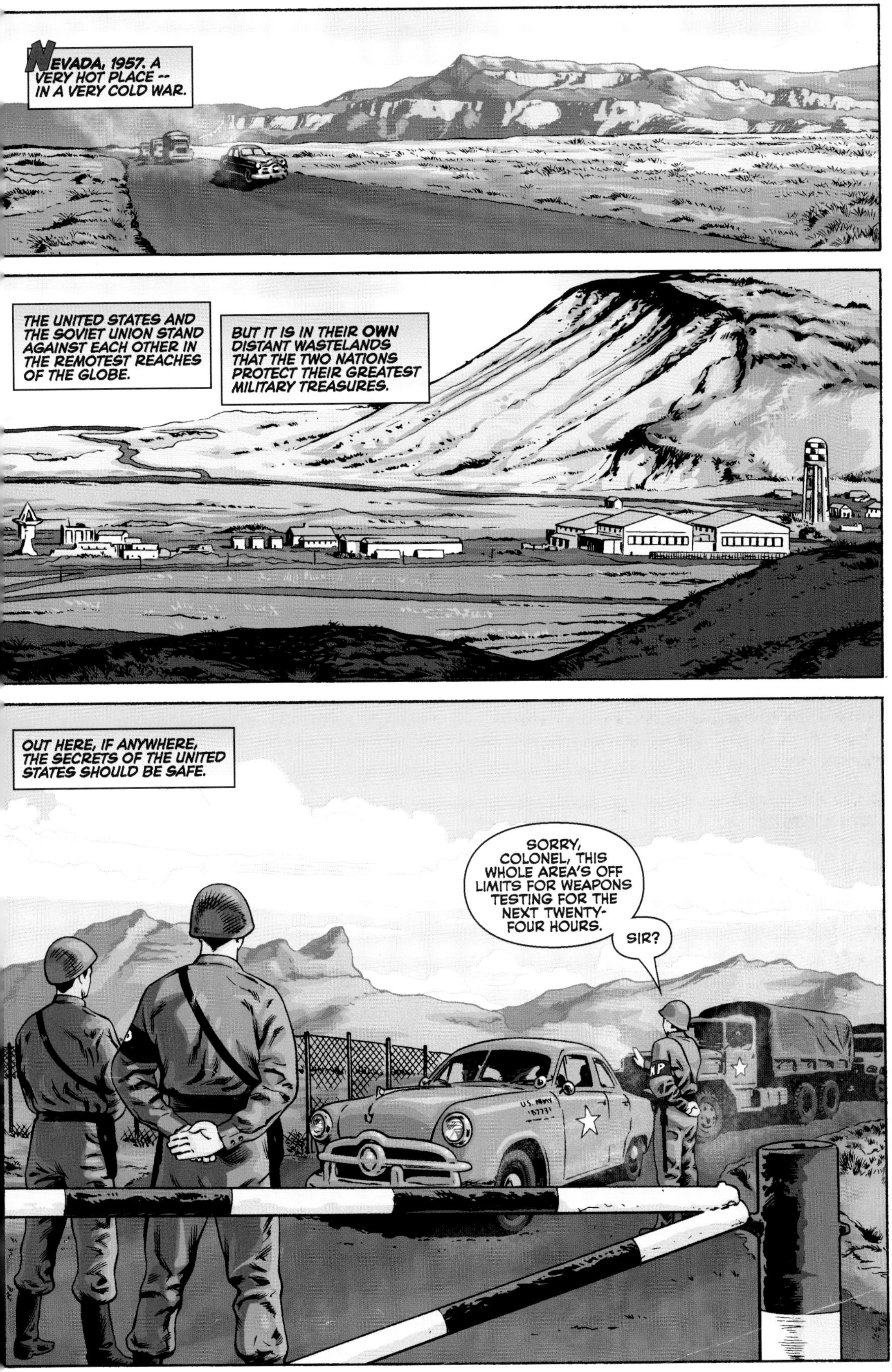
NEVADA, 1957. A VERY HOT PLACE -- IN A VERY COLD WAR.
THE UNITED STATES AND THE SOVIET UNION STAND AGAINST EACH OTHER IN THE REMOTEST REACHES OF THE GLOBE.
BUT IT IS IN THEIR OWN DISTANT WASTELANDS THAT THE TWO NATIONS PROTECT THEIR GREATEST MILITARY TREASURES.
OUT HERE, IF ANYWHERE, THE SECRETS OF THE UNITED STATES SHOULD BE SAFE.
SORRY, COLONEL, THIS WHOLE AREA'S OFF LIMITS FOR WEAPONS TESTING FOR THE NEXT TWENTY-FOUR HOURS.
SIR?
MP
U.S. NAVY

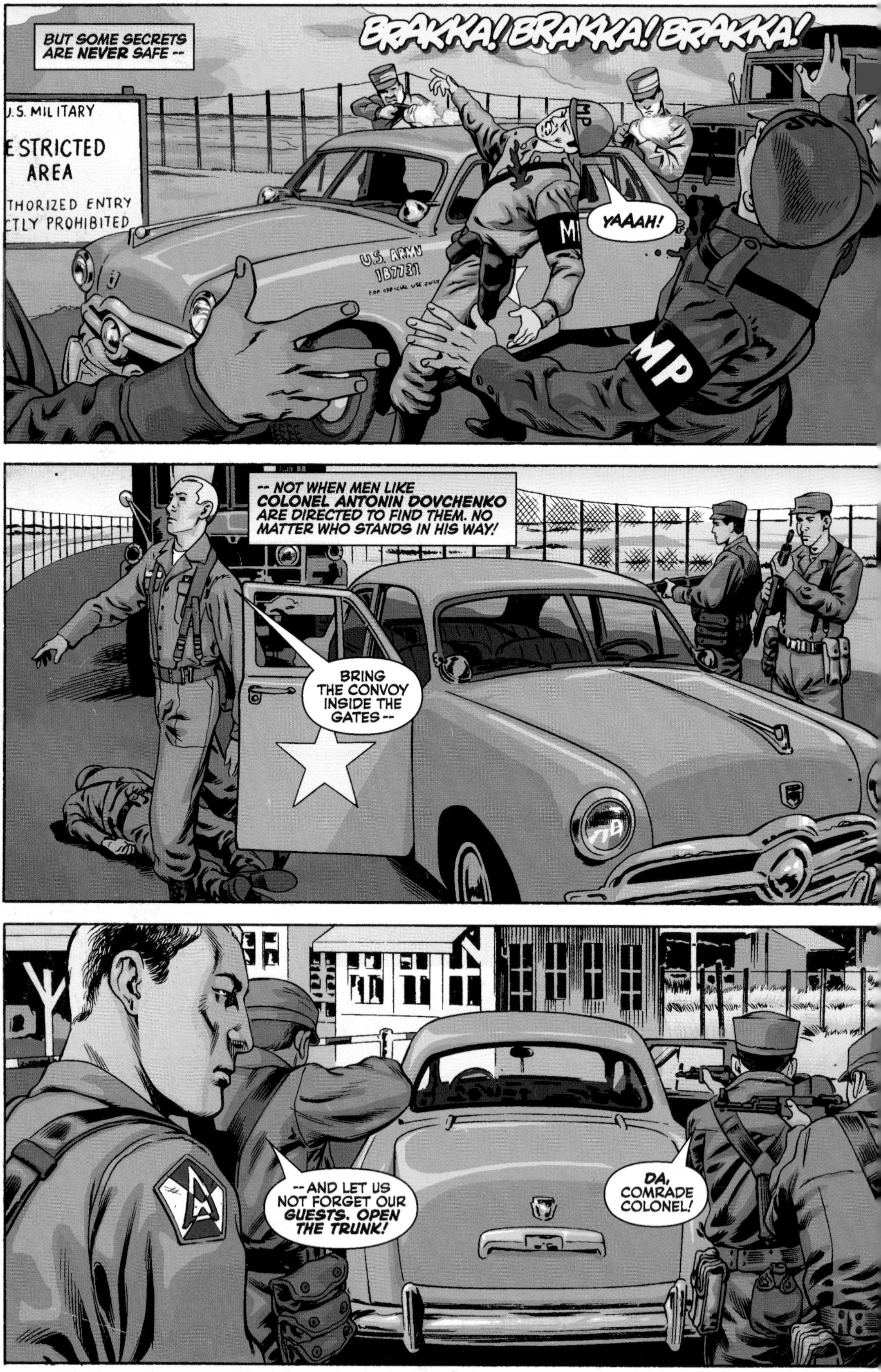
BUT SOME SECRETS ARE NEVER SAFE --
BRAKKA! BRAKKA! BRAKKA!
YAAAH!
U.S. ARMY 1B7731
-- NOT WHEN MEN LIKE COLONEL ANTONIN DOVCHENKO ARE DIRECTED TO FIND THEM. NO MATTER WHO STANDS IN HIS WAY!
BRING THE CONVOY INSIDE THE GATES --
-- AND LET US NOT FORGET OUR GUESTS. OPEN THE TRUNK!
DA, COMRADE COLONEL!

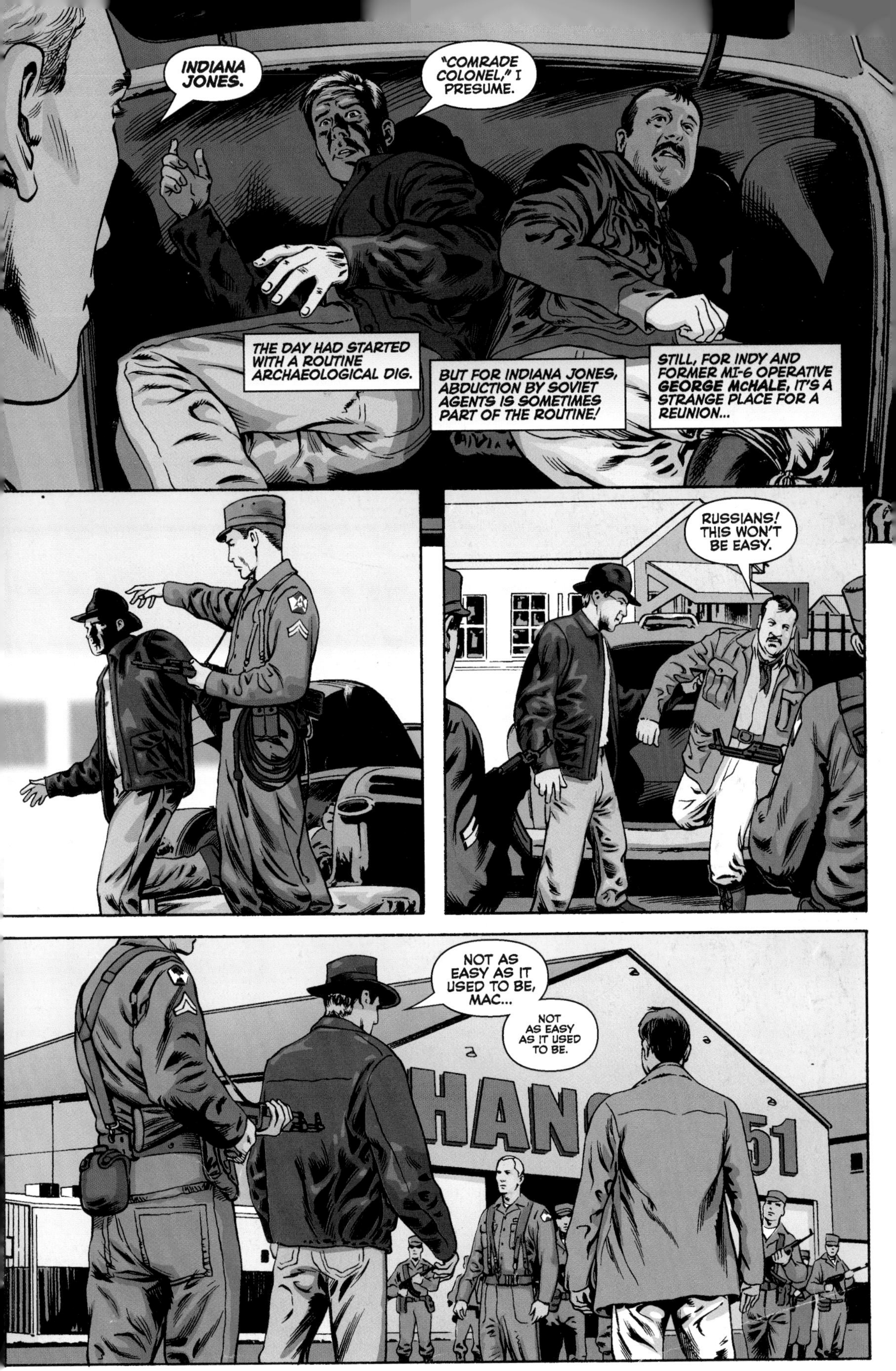

INDIANA JONES.
"COMRADE COLONEL," I PRESUME.
THE DAY HAD STARTED WITH A ROUTINE ARCHAEOLOGICAL DIG.
BUT FOR INDIANA JONES, ABDUCTION BY SOVIET AGENTS IS SOMETIMES PART OF THE ROUTINE!
STILL, FOR INDY AND FORMER MI-6 OPERATIVE GEORGE MCHALE, IT'S A STRANGE PLACE FOR A REUNION...
RUSSIANS! THIS WON'T BE EASY.
NOT AS EASY AS IT USED TO BE, MAC...
NOT AS EASY AS IT USED TO BE.

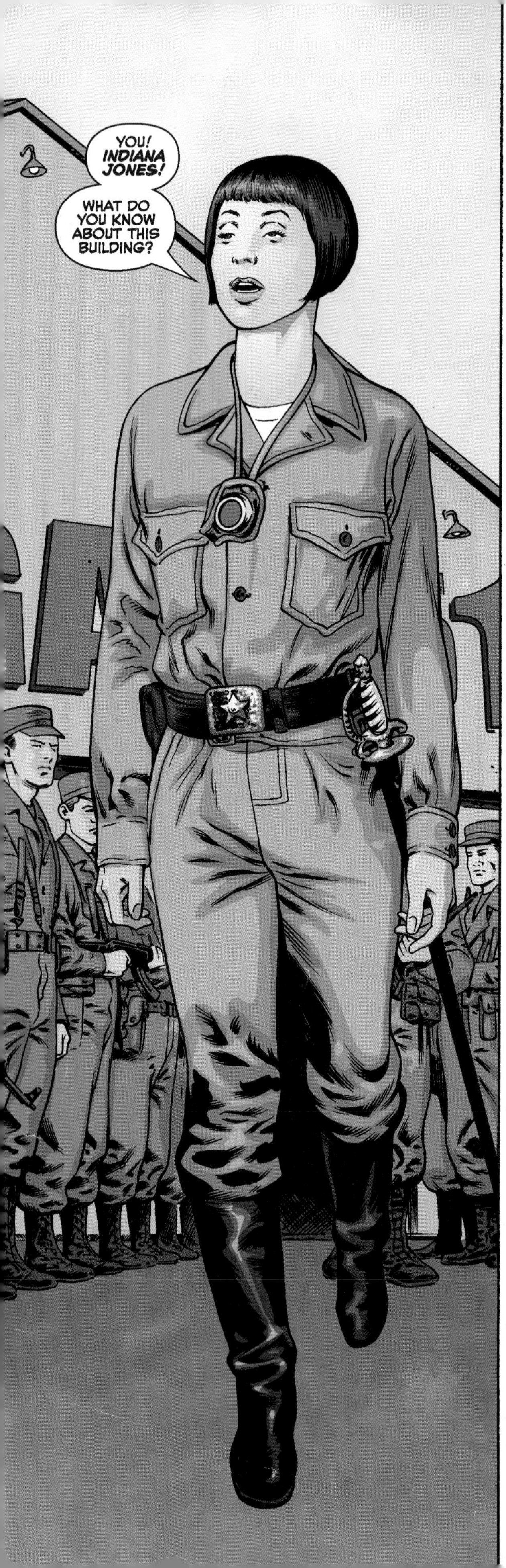
YOU! *INDIANA JONES!*
WHAT DO YOU KNOW ABOUT THIS BUILDING?

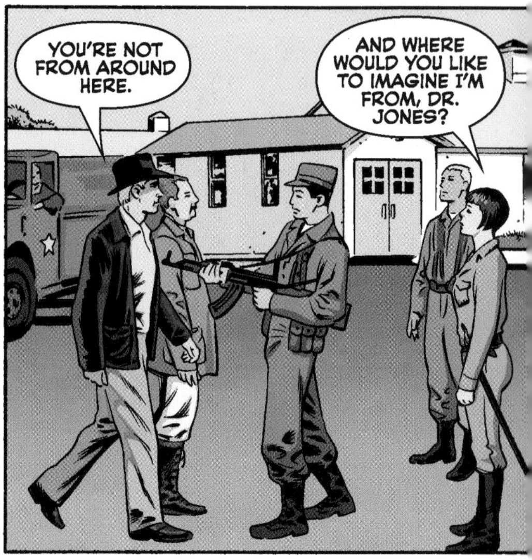
YOU'RE NOT FROM AROUND HERE.
AND WHERE WOULD YOU LIKE TO IMAGINE I'M FROM, DR. JONES?

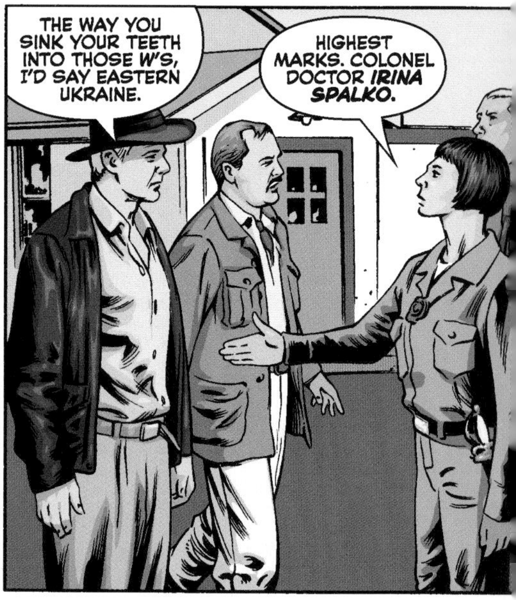
THE WAY YOU SINK YOUR TEETH INTO THOSE *W'S*, I'D SAY EASTERN UKRAINE.
HIGHEST MARKS. COLONEL DOCTOR *IRINA SPALKO.*

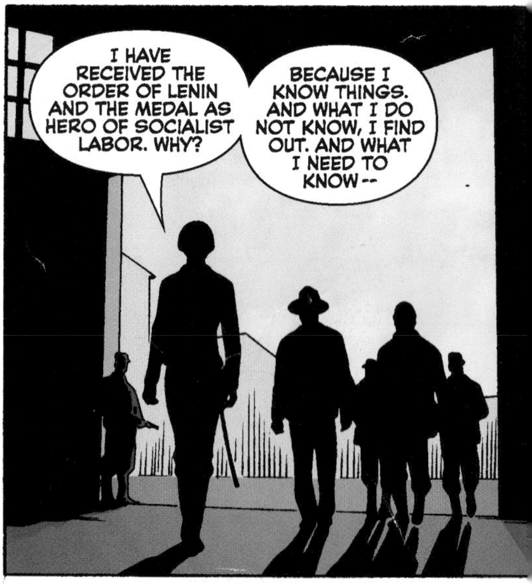
I HAVE RECEIVED THE ORDER OF LENIN AND THE MEDAL AS HERO OF SOCIALIST LABOR. WHY?
BECAUSE I KNOW THINGS. AND WHAT I DO NOT KNOW, I FIND OUT. AND WHAT I NEED TO KNOW --

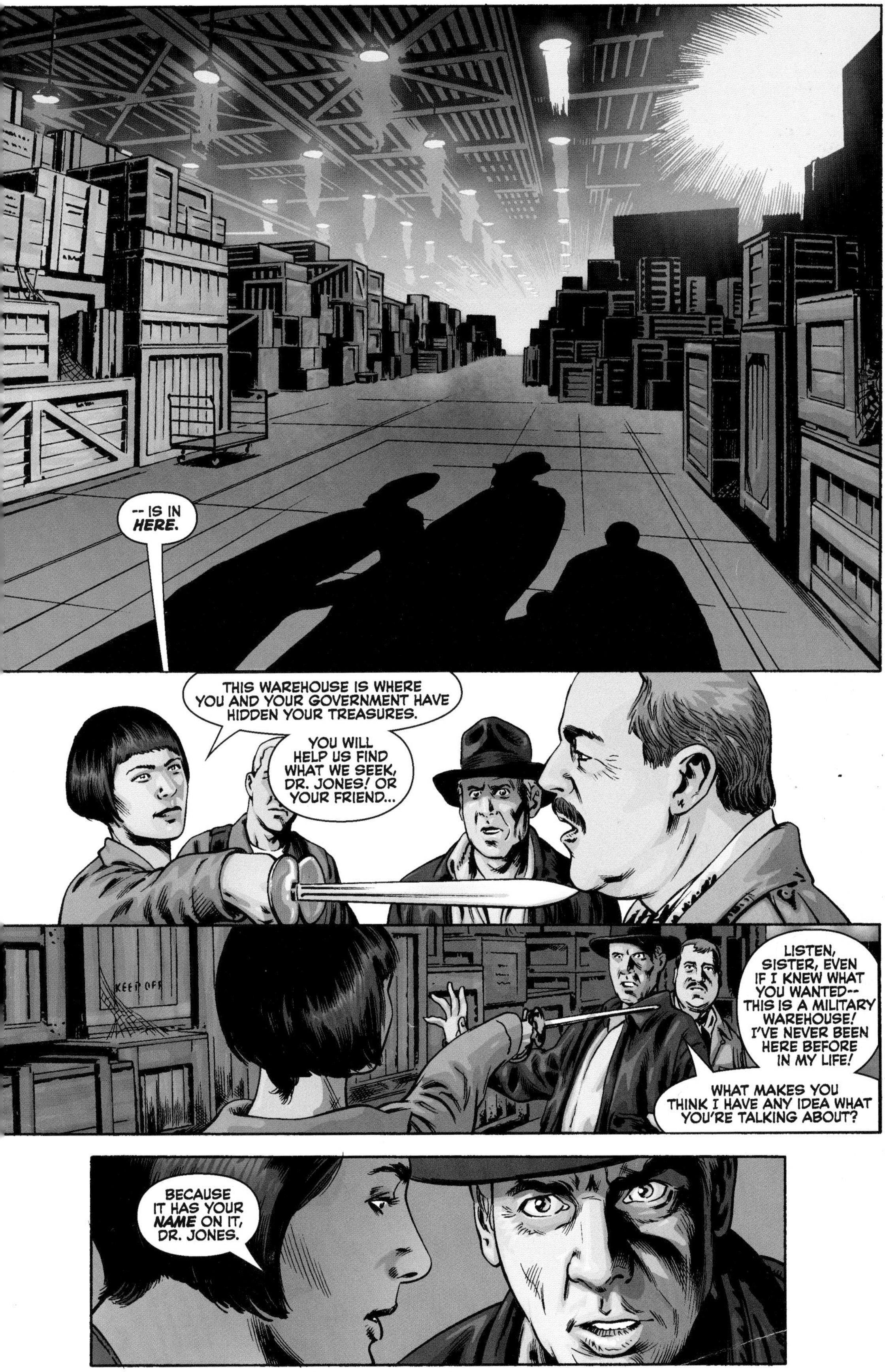

-- IS IN *HERE*.
THIS WAREHOUSE IS WHERE YOU AND YOUR GOVERNMENT HAVE HIDDEN YOUR TREASURES.
YOU WILL HELP US FIND WHAT WE SEEK, DR. JONES! OR YOUR FRIEND...
KEEP OFF
LISTEN, SISTER, EVEN IF I KNEW WHAT YOU WANTED-- THIS IS A MILITARY WAREHOUSE! I'VE NEVER BEEN HERE BEFORE IN MY LIFE!
WHAT MAKES YOU THINK I HAVE ANY IDEA WHAT YOU'RE TALKING ABOUT?
BECAUSE IT HAS YOUR *NAME* ON IT, DR. JONES.

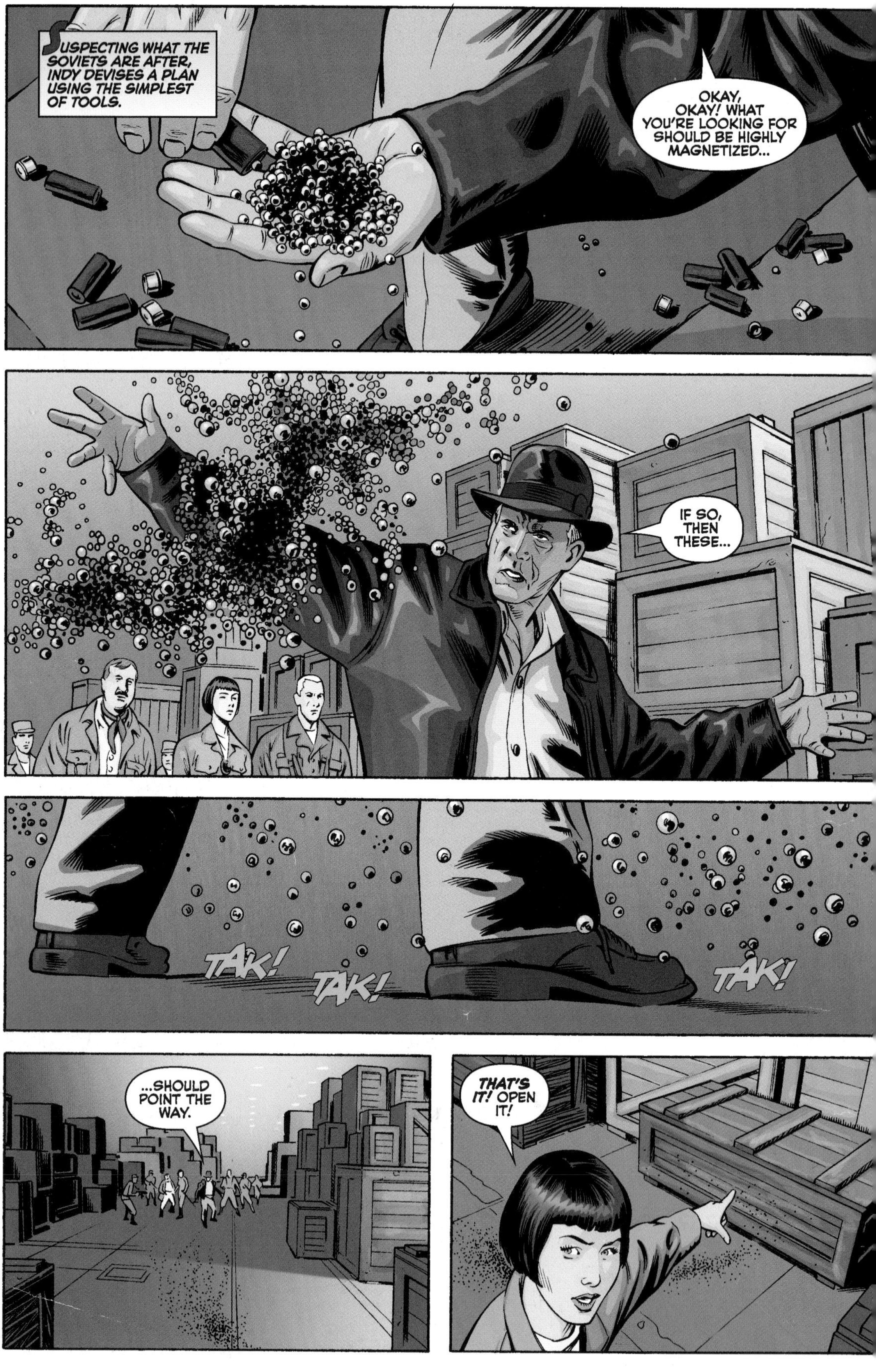
SUSPECTING WHAT THE SOVIETS ARE AFTER, INDY DEVISES A PLAN USING THE SIMPLEST OF TOOLS.
OKAY, OKAY! WHAT YOU'RE LOOKING FOR SHOULD BE HIGHLY MAGNETIZED...
IF SO, THEN THESE...
TAK!
TAK!
TAK!
...SHOULD POINT THE WAY.
THAT'S IT! OPEN IT!

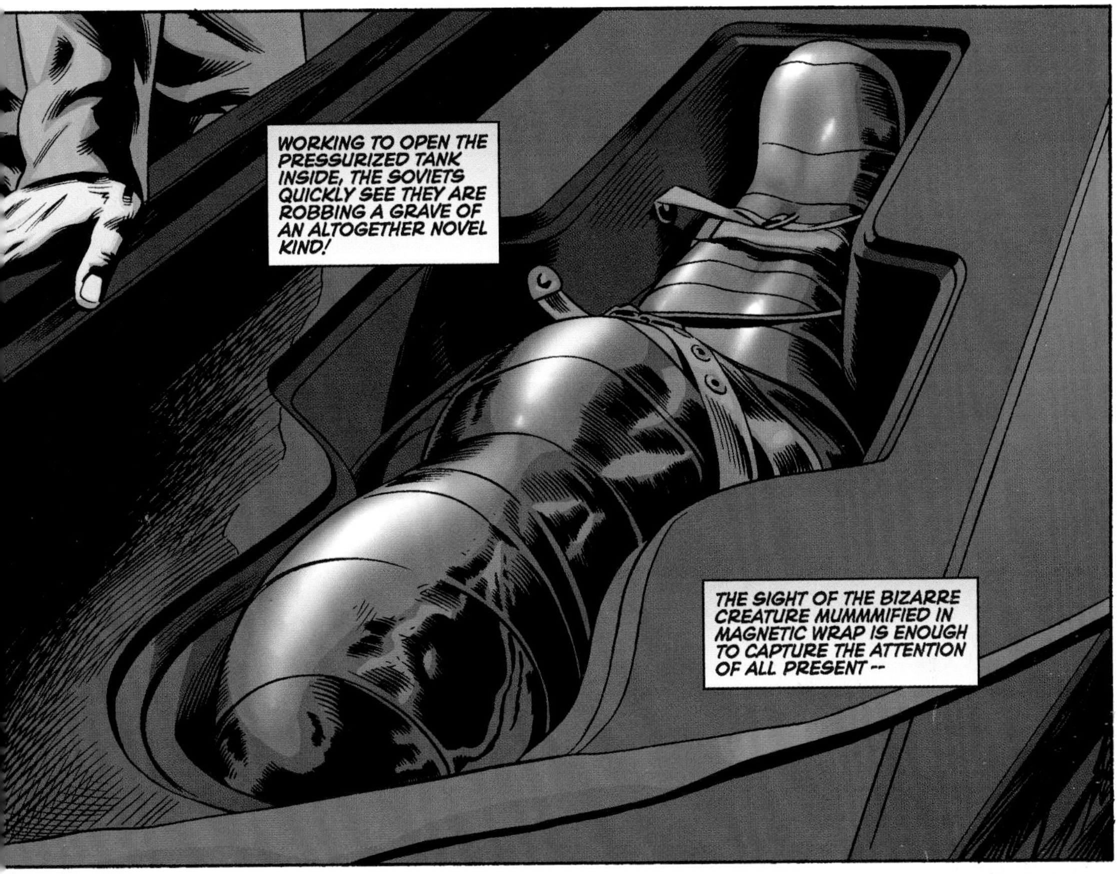
WORKING TO OPEN THE PRESSURIZED TANK INSIDE, THE SOVIETS QUICKLY SEE THEY ARE ROBBING A GRAVE OF AN ALTOGETHER NOVEL KIND!
THE SIGHT OF THE BIZARRE CREATURE MUMMMIFIED IN MAGNETIC WRAP IS ENOUGH TO CAPTURE THE ATTENTION OF ALL PRESENT --

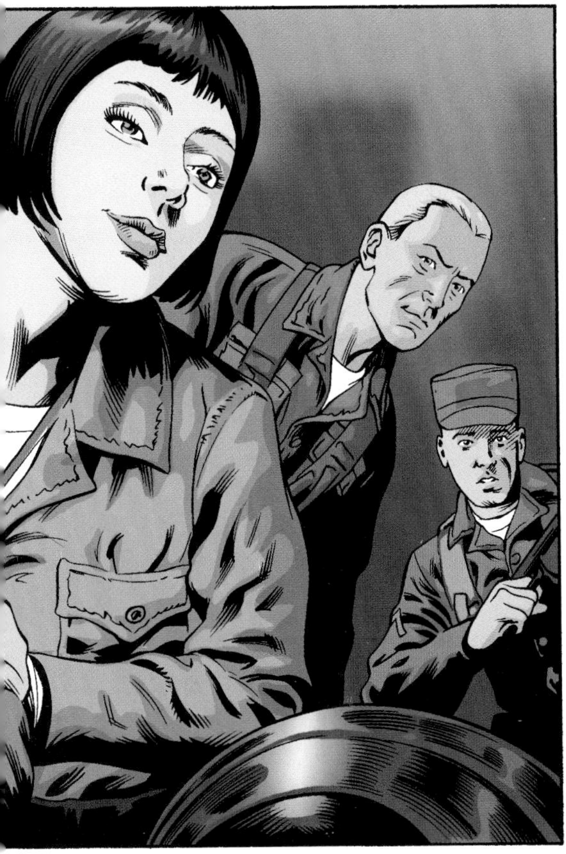

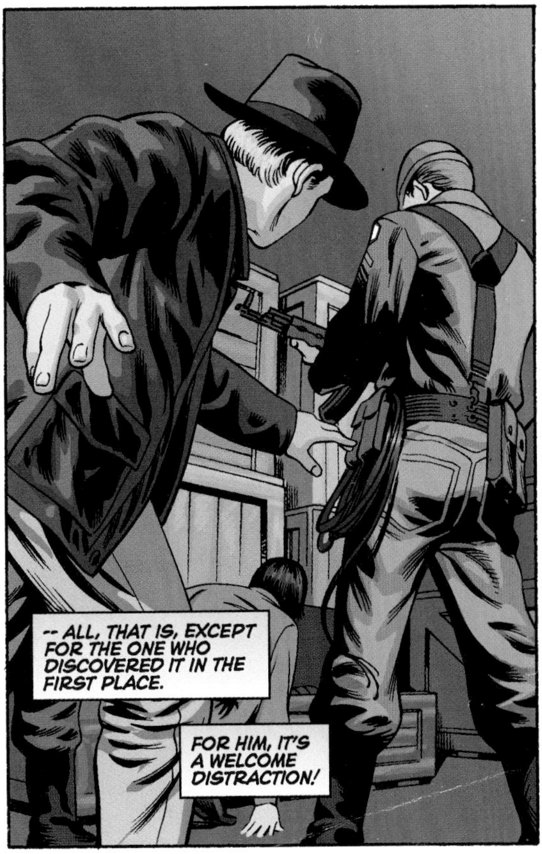
-- ALL, THAT IS, EXCEPT FOR THE ONE WHO DISCOVERED IT IN THE FIRST PLACE.
FOR HIM, IT'S A WELCOME DISTRACTION!

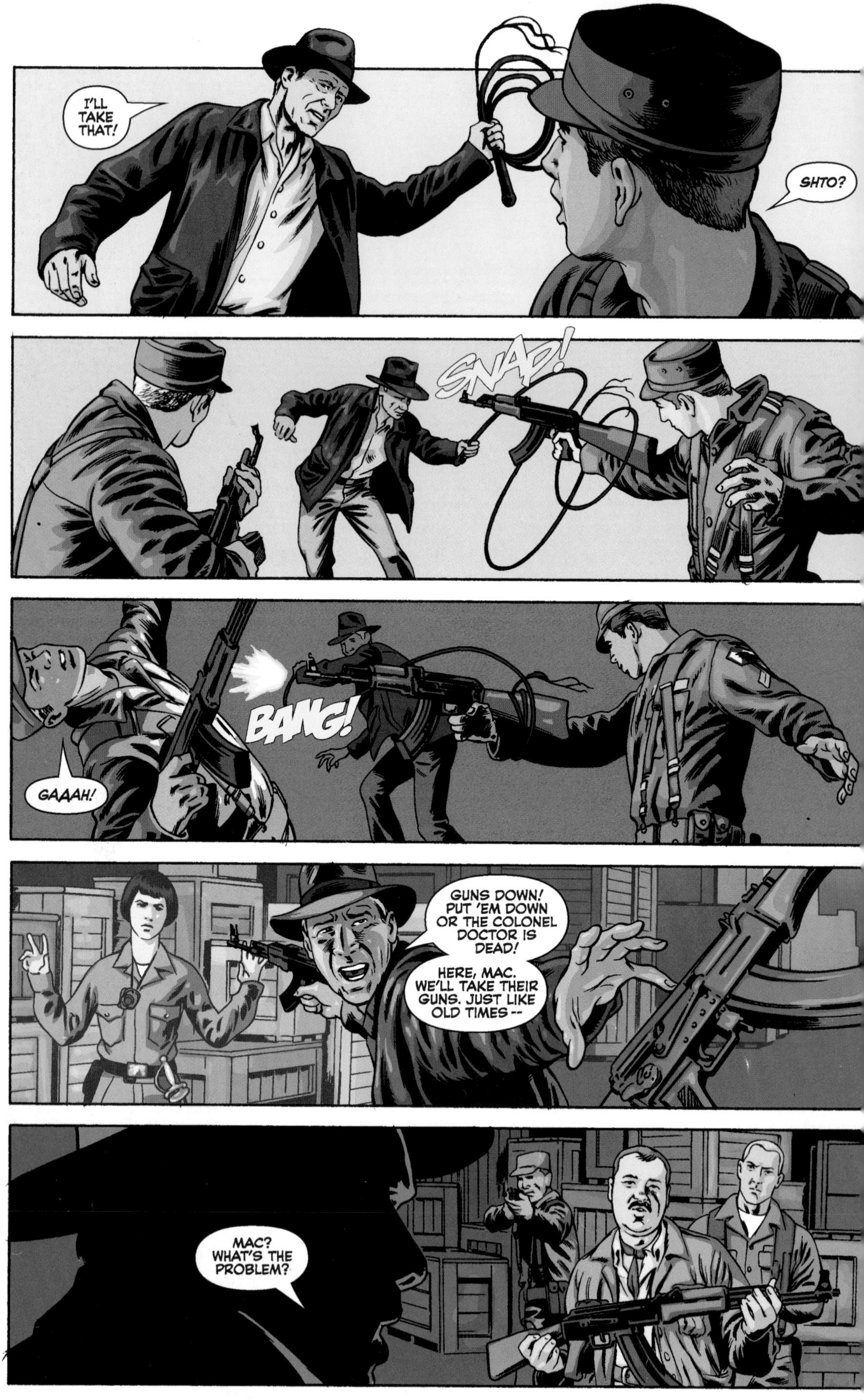
I'LL TAKE THAT!
SHTO?
SNAP!
BANG!
GAAAH!
GUNS DOWN! PUT 'EM DOWN OR THE COLONEL DOCTOR IS DEAD!
HERE, MAC. WE'LL TAKE THEIR GUNS. JUST LIKE OLD TIMES --
MAC? WHAT'S THE PROBLEM?

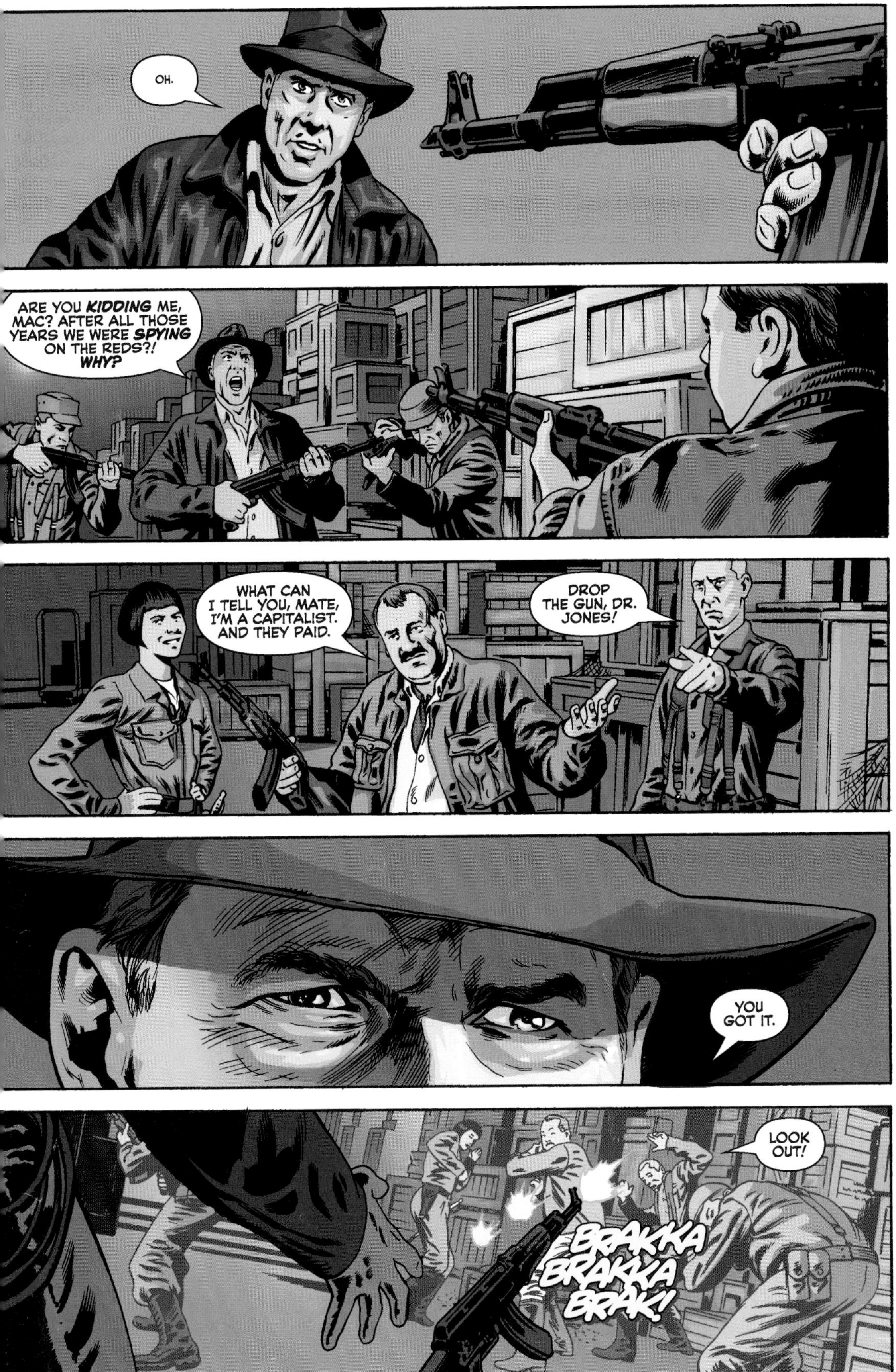
OH.
ARE YOU KIDDING ME, MAC? AFTER ALL THOSE YEARS WE WERE SPYING ON THE REDS?! WHY?
WHAT CAN I TELL YOU, MATE, I'M A CAPITALIST. AND THEY PAID.
DROP THE GUN, DR. JONES!
YOU GOT IT.
LOOK OUT!
BRAKKA BRAKKA BRAK!

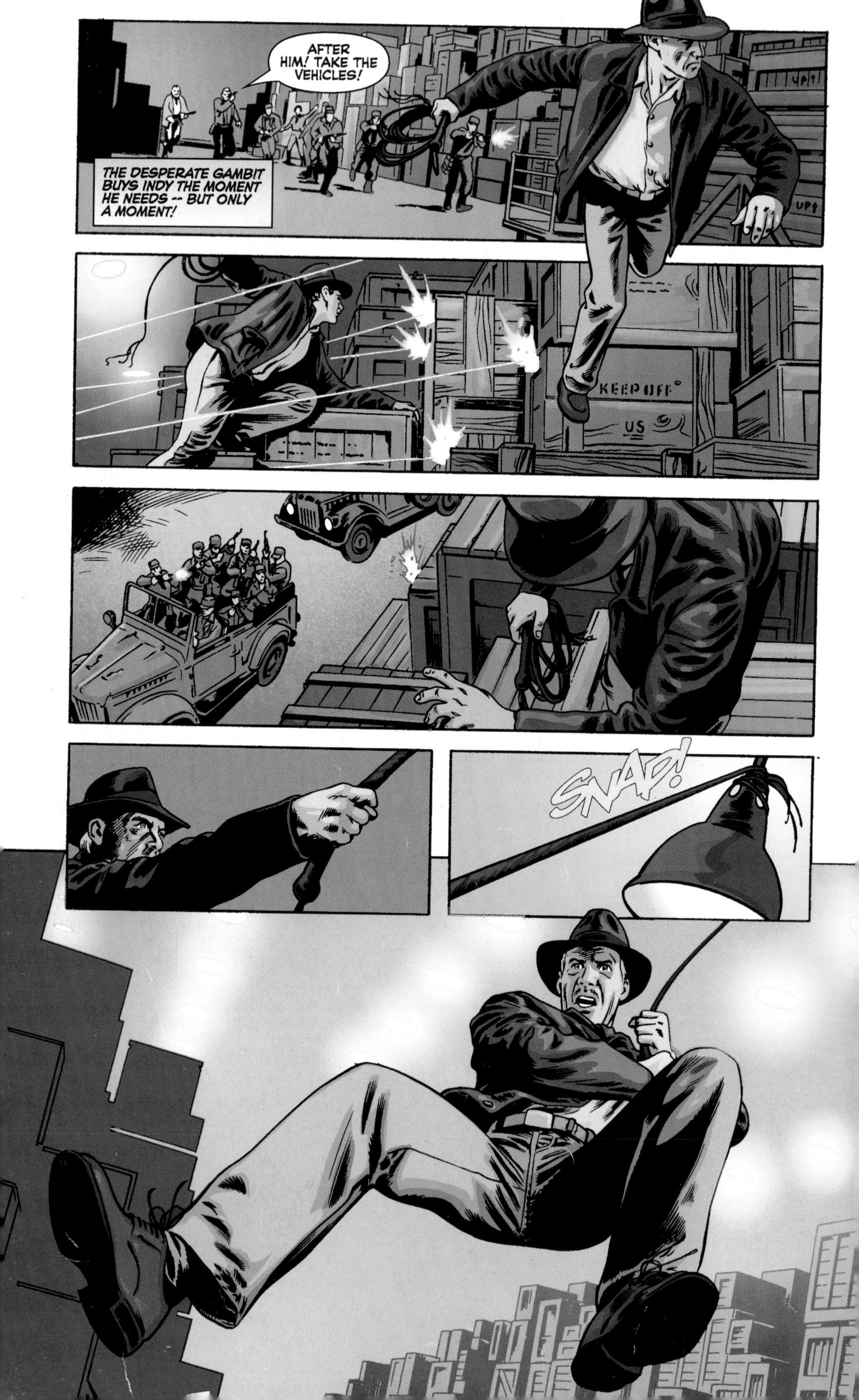
AFTER HIM! TAKE THE VEHICLES!
THE DESPERATE GAMBIT BUYS INDY THE MOMENT HE NEEDS -- BUT ONLY A MOMENT!
UP
UP
KEEP OFF
US
SNAP!

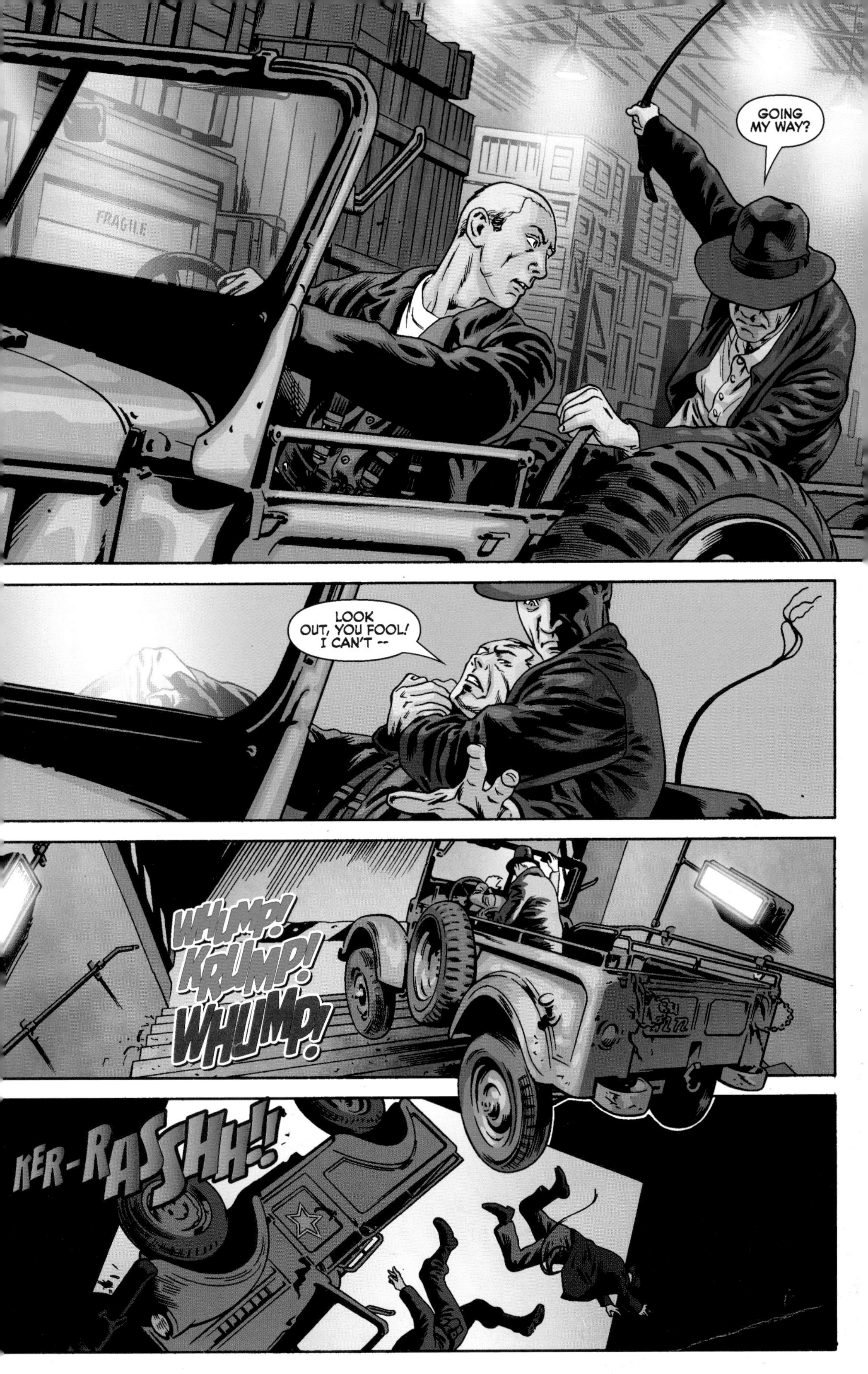
GOING MY WAY?
FRAGILE
LOOK OUT, YOU FOOL! I CAN'T --
WHUMP! KRUMP! WHUMP!
KER-RASHH!!

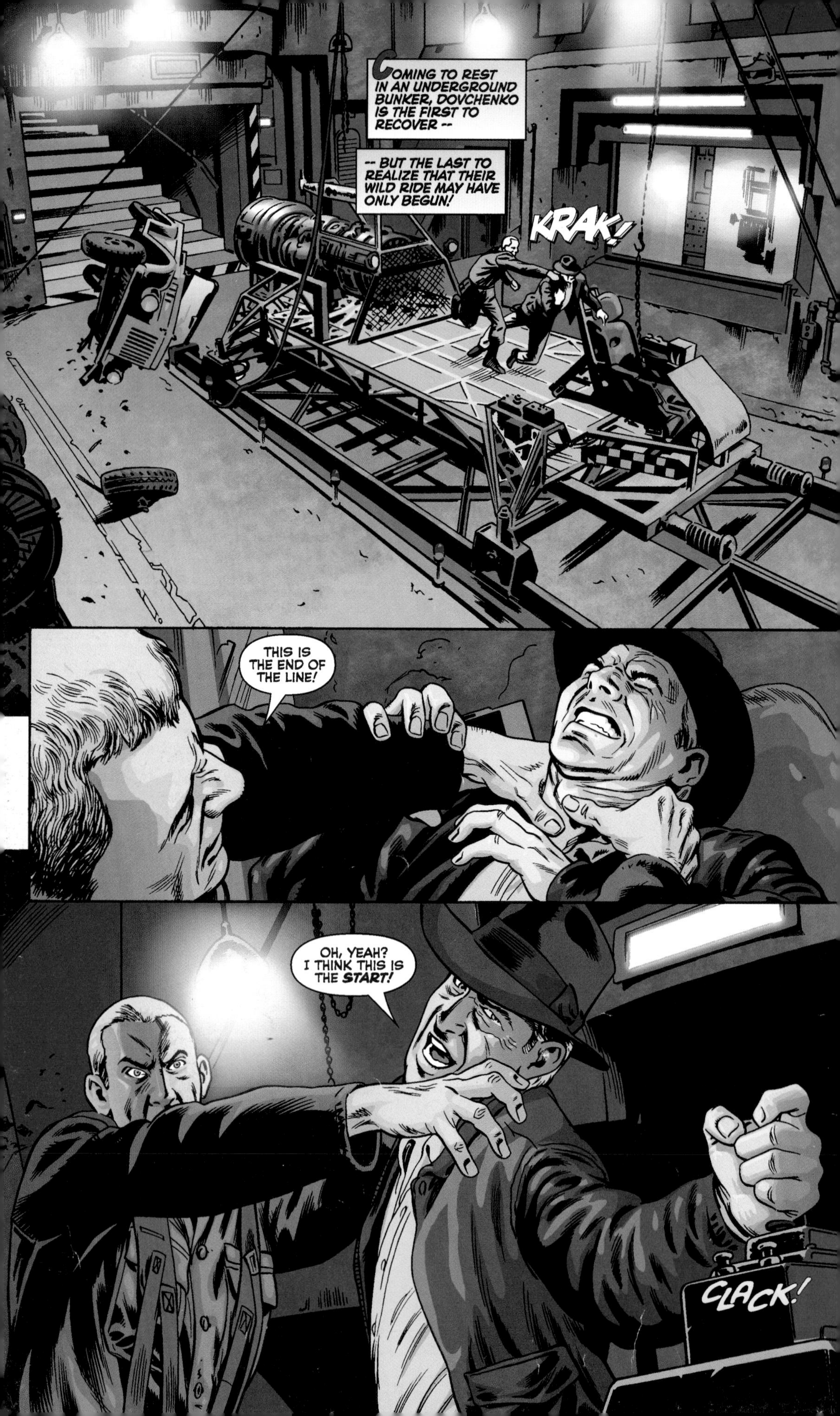
COMING TO REST IN AN UNDERGROUND BUNKER, DOVCHENKO IS THE FIRST TO RECOVER --
-- BUT THE LAST TO REALIZE THAT THEIR WILD RIDE MAY HAVE ONLY BEGUN!
KRAK!
THIS IS THE END OF THE LINE!
OH, YEAH? I THINK THIS IS THE START!
CLACK!

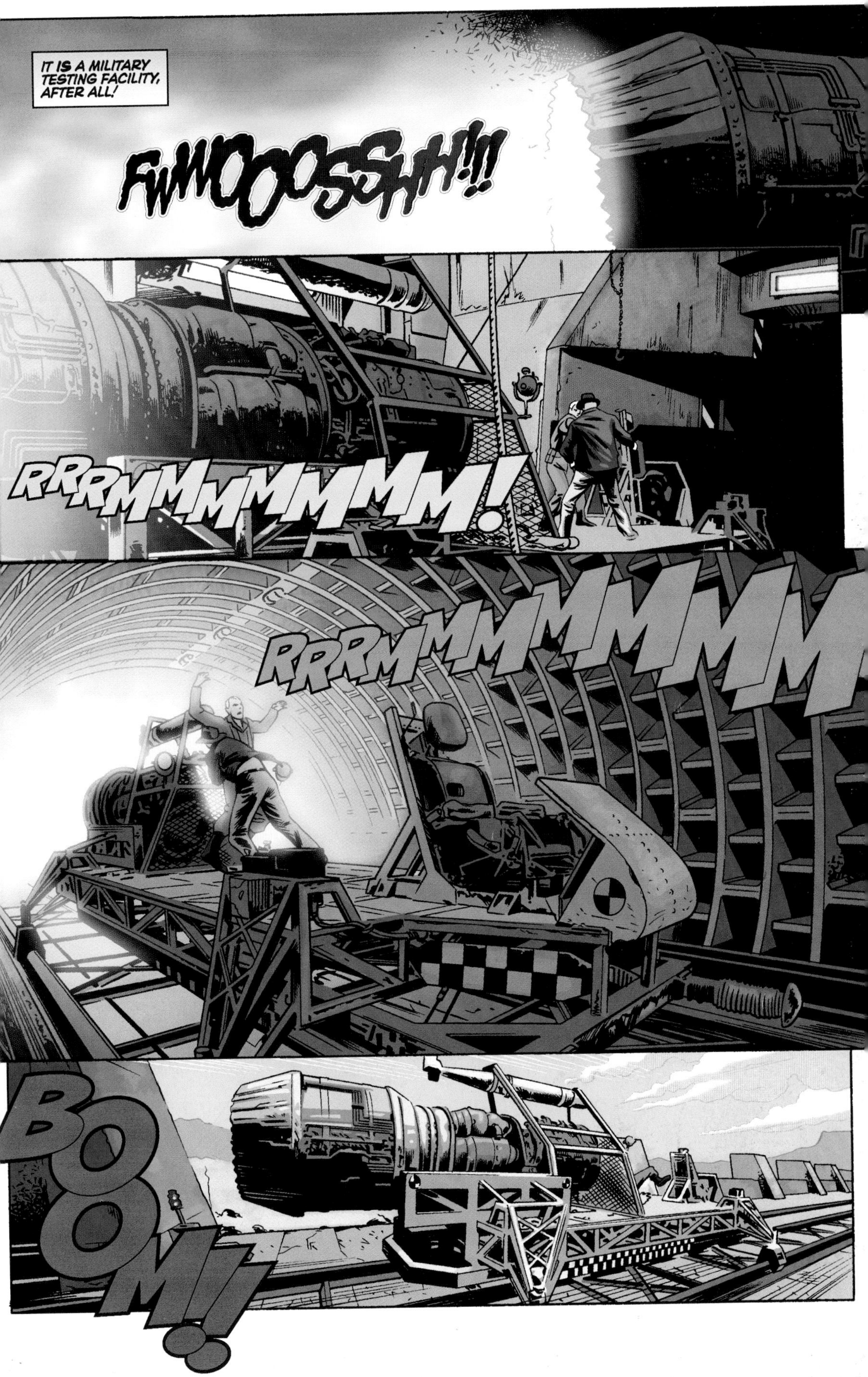
IT IS A MILITARY TESTING FACILITY, AFTER ALL!
FWOOOSSHH!!!
RRRMMMMMMMM!
RRRMMMMMMMM
BOOM!!

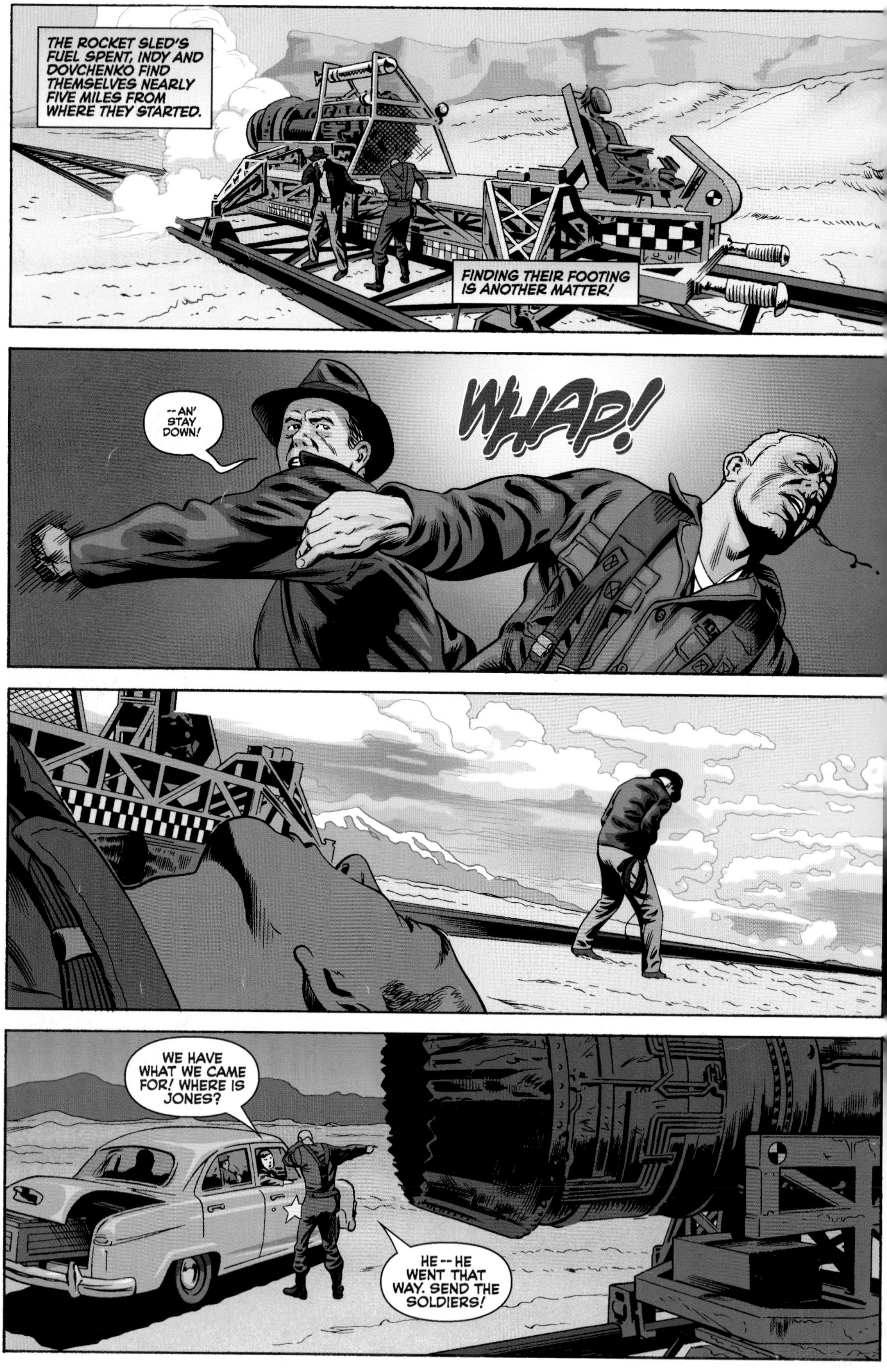
THE ROCKET SLED'S FUEL SPENT, INDY AND DOVCHENKO FIND THEMSELVES NEARLY FIVE MILES FROM WHERE THEY STARTED.
FINDING THEIR FOOTING IS ANOTHER MATTER!
--AN' STAY DOWN!
WHAP!
WE HAVE WHAT WE CAME FOR! WHERE IS JONES?
HE--HE WENT THAT WAY. SEND THE SOLDIERS!

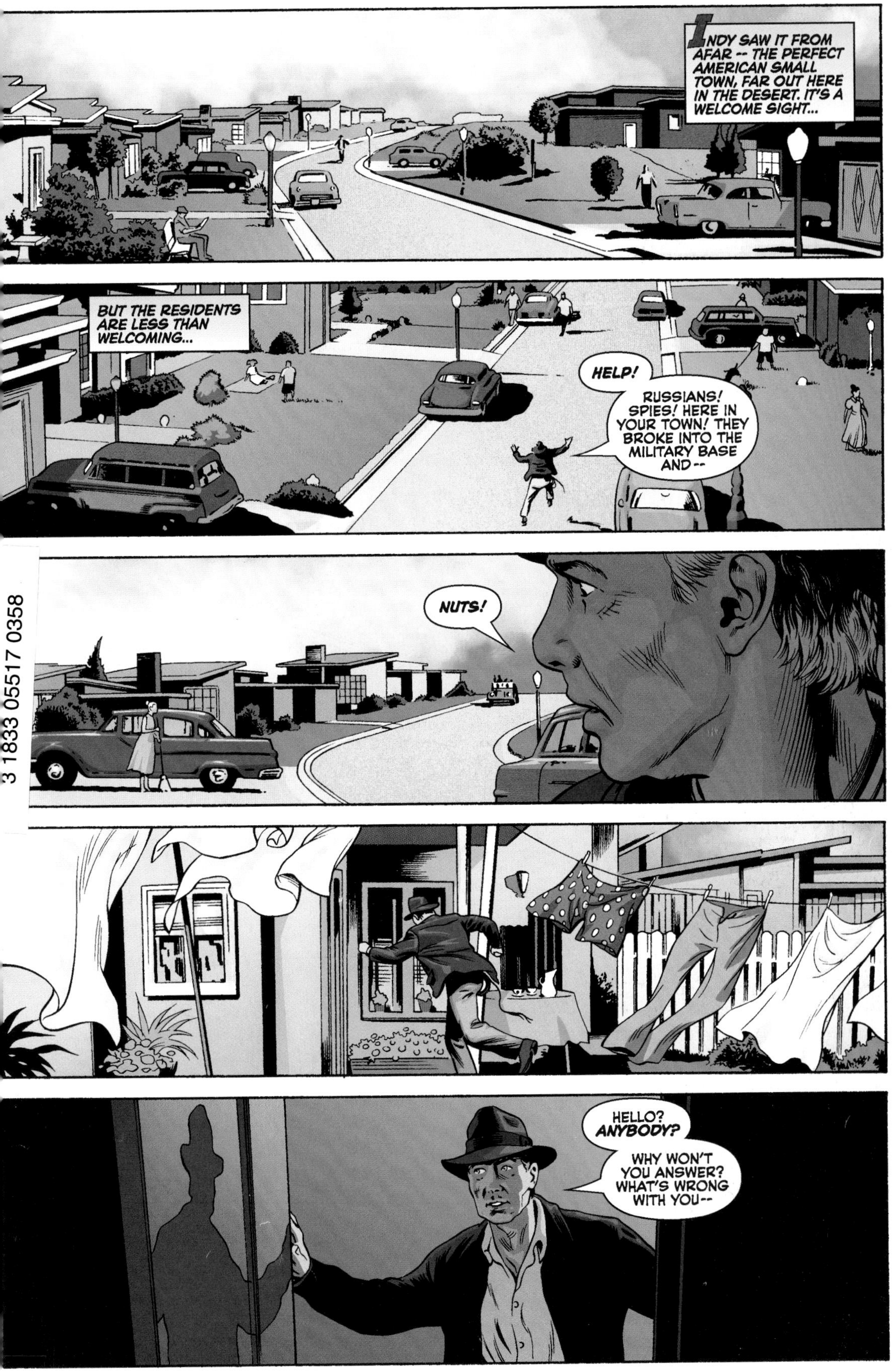
INDY SAW IT FROM AFAR -- THE PERFECT AMERICAN SMALL TOWN, FAR OUT HERE IN THE DESERT. IT'S A WELCOME SIGHT...
BUT THE RESIDENTS ARE LESS THAN WELCOMING...
HELP!
RUSSIANS! SPIES! HERE IN YOUR TOWN! THEY BROKE INTO THE MILITARY BASE AND --
NUTS!
HELLO? ANYBODY?
WHY WON'T YOU ANSWER? WHAT'S WRONG WITH YOU--

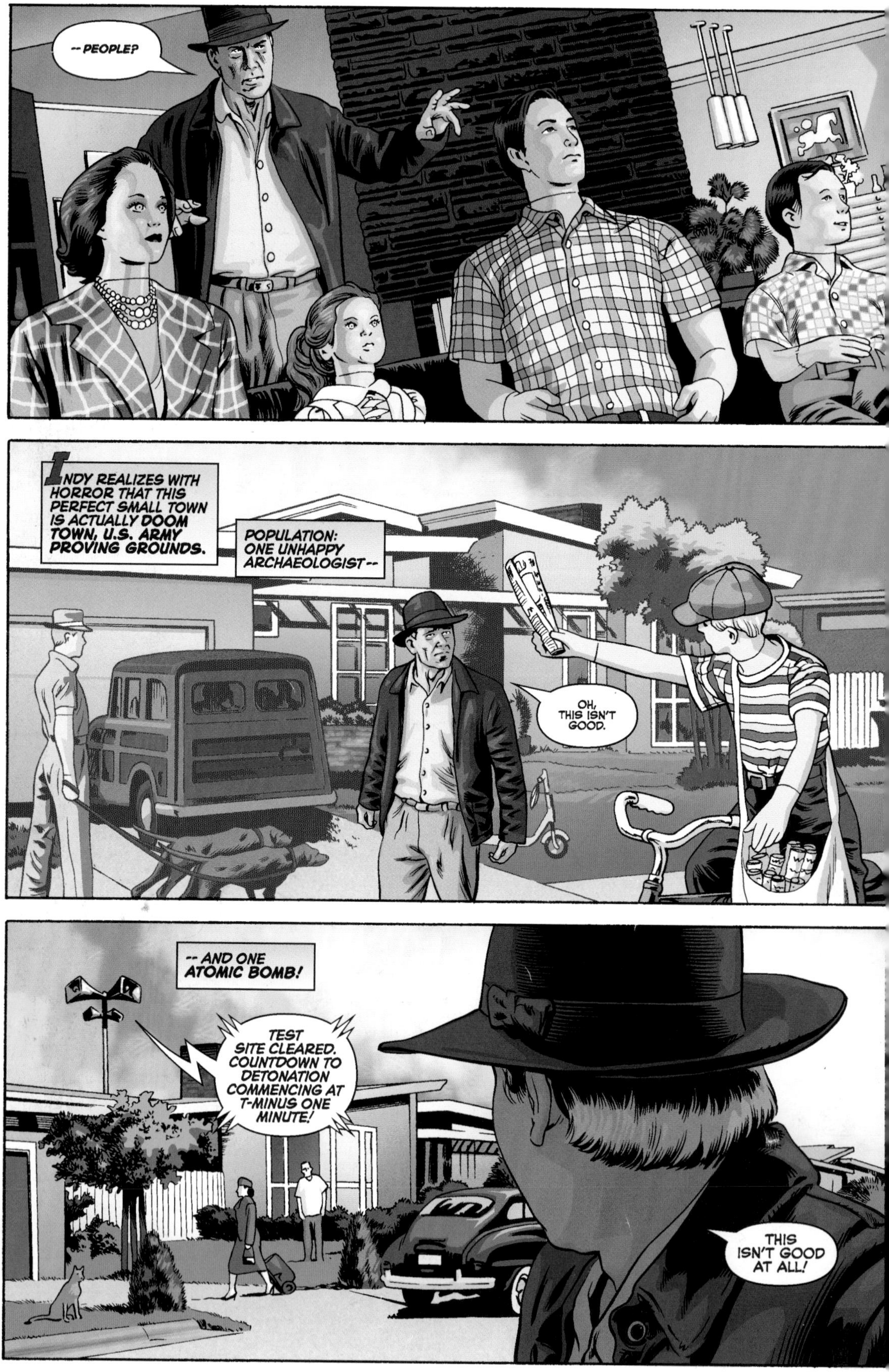
-- PEOPLE?
INDY REALIZES WITH HORROR THAT THIS PERFECT SMALL TOWN IS ACTUALLY DOOM TOWN, U.S. ARMY PROVING GROUNDS.
POPULATION: ONE UNHAPPY ARCHAEOLOGIST --
OH, THIS ISN'T GOOD.
-- AND ONE ATOMIC BOMB!
TEST SITE CLEARED. COUNTDOWN TO DETONATION COMMENCING AT T-MINUS ONE MINUTE!
THIS ISN'T GOOD AT ALL!

DOOM TOWN'S OTHER TOURISTS ALSO GET THE PICTURE. NOTHING BREAKS A LANGUAGE BARRIER LIKE A WARNING SIREN ON A TESTING GROUND!

RRRREEEEEEEEE!!!

VODITAY! VODITAY!

WAIT! WAIT! COME BACK!

T-MINUS THIRTY SECONDS!

I KNOW, I KNOW!

T-MINUS TEN SECONDS!

NINE!

INDY TAKES A LAST, DESPERATE GAMBLE.

ON, OF ALL THINGS, THE LATEST IN HOME APPLIANCES!

NOT THE HEALTHIEST OF CONCEPTS --

King Coal

CLICK!

-- A REFRIGERATOR MARKED LEAD-LINED FOR SUPERIOR INSULATION!

BUT IN DOOM TOWN, "HEALTHY" IS A RELATIVE TERM!

BOOOOM!!!

THE MILITARY TESTERS RECORD THAT THE BLAST STARTS WITH A FLASH -- FOLLOWED BY A SHOCKWAVE AND SOUND.

YAAAAHHH!!!

BY THE TIME THE FIREBALL ARRIVES, IT'S TOO LATE FOR DOOM TOWN.

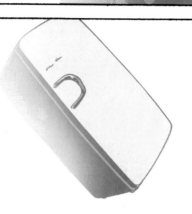

IF ONLY THERE WERE SOME WAY TO RIDE THE SHOCKWAVE, AHEAD OF THE FIREBALL!

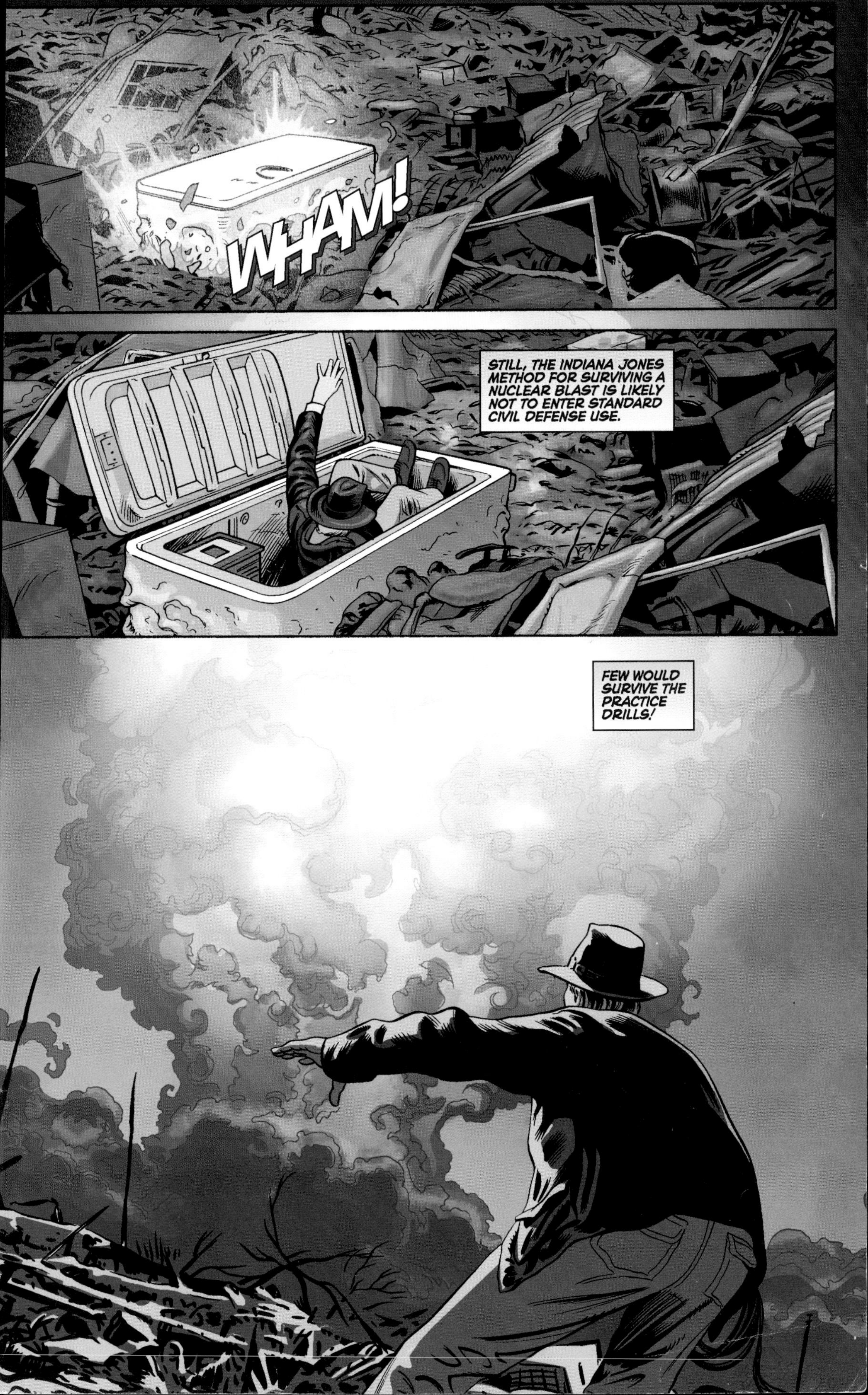
WHAM!
STILL, THE INDIANA JONES METHOD FOR SURVIVING A NUCLEAR BLAST IS LIKELY NOT TO ENTER STANDARD CIVIL DEFENSE USE.
FEW WOULD SURVIVE THE PRACTICE DRILLS!

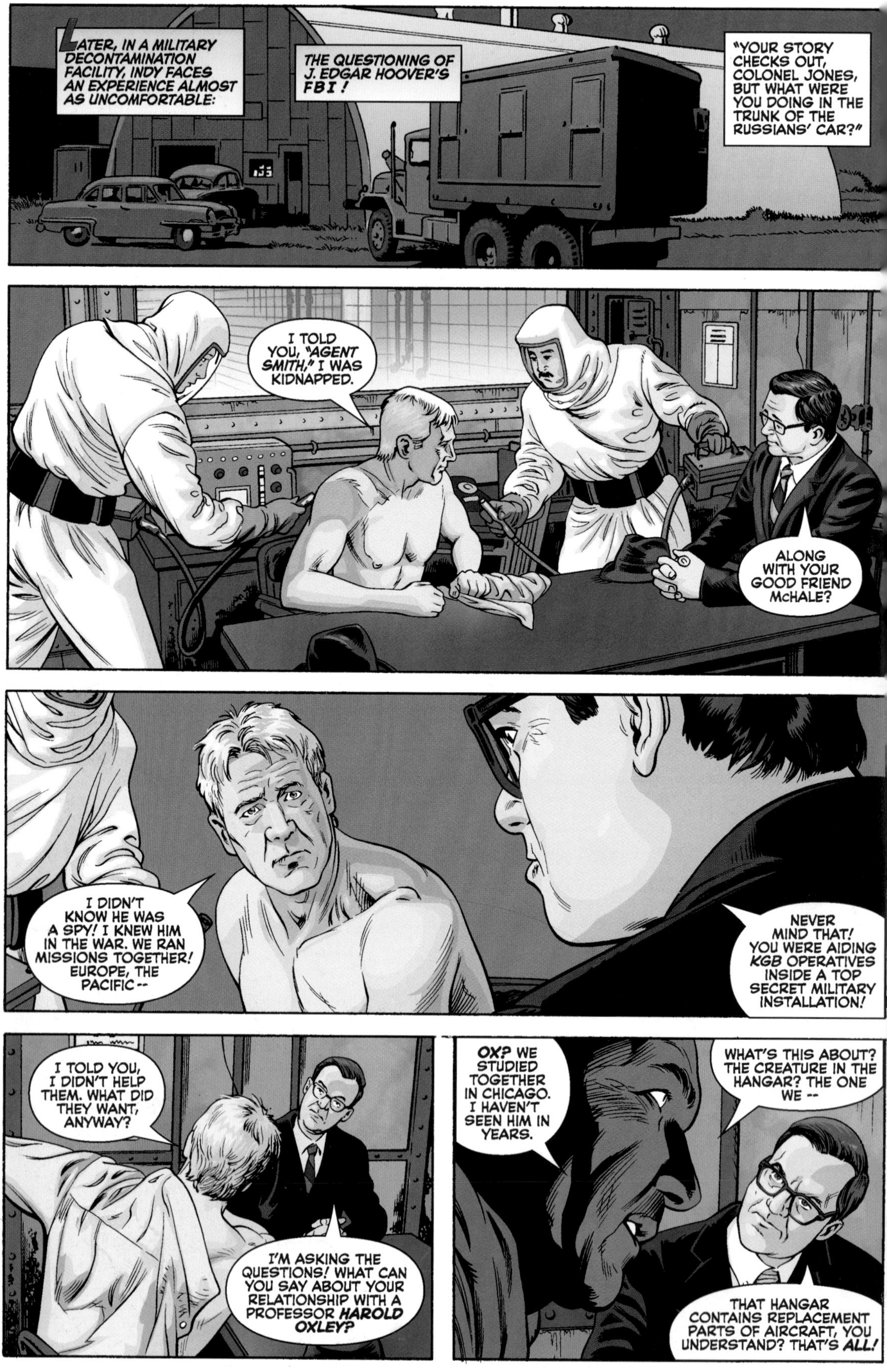
LATER, IN A MILITARY DECONTAMINATION FACILITY, INDY FACES AN EXPERIENCE ALMOST AS UNCOMFORTABLE:
THE QUESTIONING OF J. EDGAR HOOVER'S FBI!
"YOUR STORY CHECKS OUT, COLONEL JONES, BUT WHAT WERE YOU DOING IN THE TRUNK OF THE RUSSIANS' CAR?"
I TOLD YOU, "AGENT SMITH," I WAS KIDNAPPED.
ALONG WITH YOUR GOOD FRIEND McHALE?
I DIDN'T KNOW HE WAS A SPY! I KNEW HIM IN THE WAR. WE RAN MISSIONS TOGETHER! EUROPE, THE PACIFIC --
NEVER MIND THAT! YOU WERE AIDING KGB OPERATIVES INSIDE A TOP SECRET MILITARY INSTALLATION!
I TOLD YOU, I DIDN'T HELP THEM. WHAT DID THEY WANT, ANYWAY?
I'M ASKING THE QUESTIONS! WHAT CAN YOU SAY ABOUT YOUR RELATIONSHIP WITH A PROFESSOR HAROLD OXLEY?
OX? WE STUDIED TOGETHER IN CHICAGO. I HAVEN'T SEEN HIM IN YEARS.
WHAT'S THIS ABOUT? THE CREATURE IN THE HANGAR? THE ONE WE --
THAT HANGAR CONTAINS REPLACEMENT PARTS OF AIRCRAFT, YOU UNDERSTAND? THAT'S ALL!

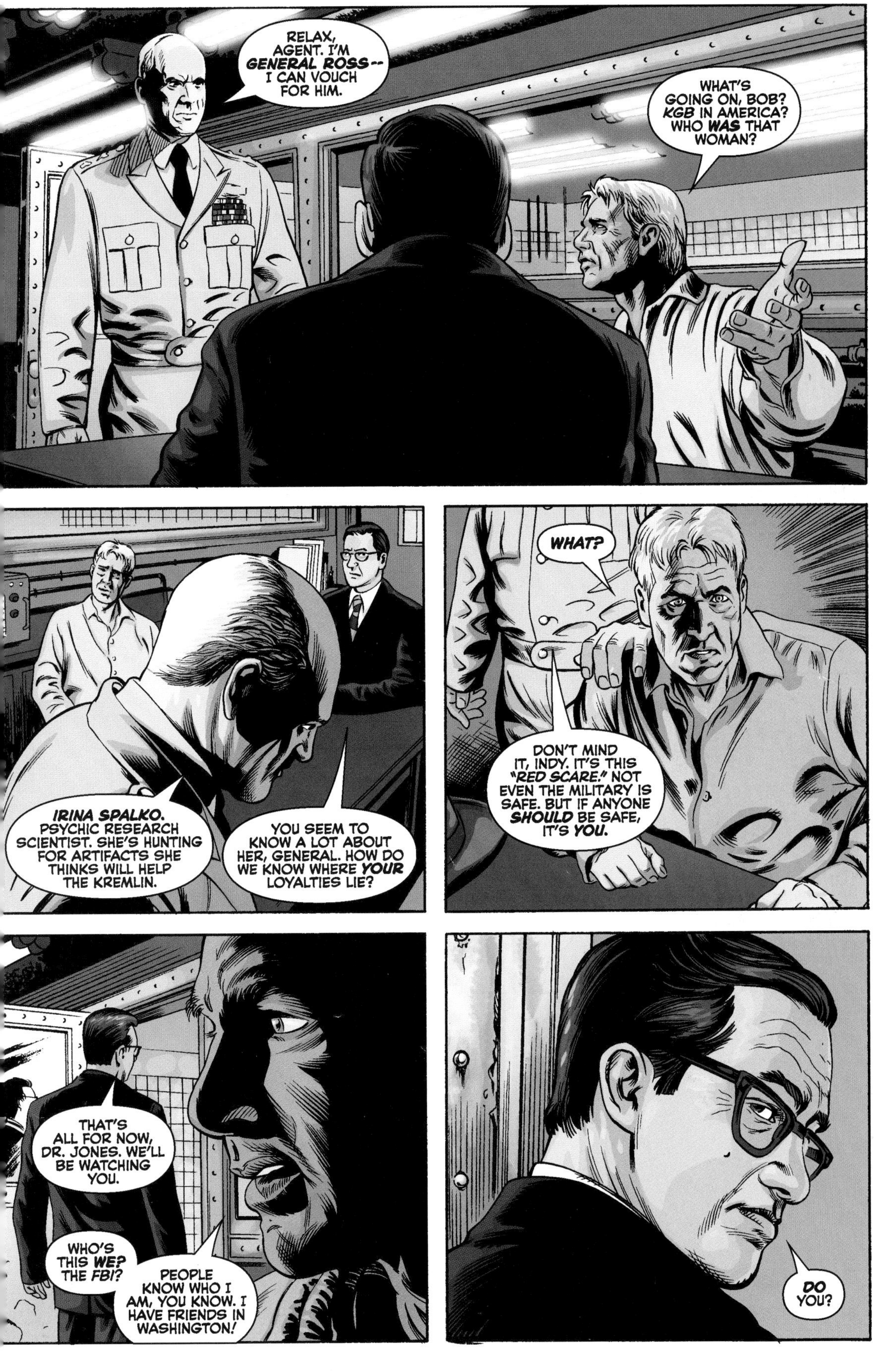

RELAX, AGENT. I'M **GENERAL ROSS**-- I CAN VOUCH FOR HIM.
WHAT'S GOING ON, BOB? **KGB** IN AMERICA? WHO **WAS** THAT WOMAN?
IRINA SPALKO. PSYCHIC RESEARCH SCIENTIST. SHE'S HUNTING FOR ARTIFACTS SHE THINKS WILL HELP THE KREMLIN.
YOU SEEM TO KNOW A LOT ABOUT HER, GENERAL. HOW DO WE KNOW WHERE **YOUR** LOYALTIES LIE?
WHAT?
DON'T MIND IT, INDY. IT'S THIS **"RED SCARE."** NOT EVEN THE MILITARY IS SAFE. BUT IF ANYONE **SHOULD** BE SAFE, IT'S **YOU.**
THAT'S ALL FOR NOW, DR. JONES. WE'LL BE WATCHING YOU.
WHO'S THIS **WE?** THE **FBI?**
PEOPLE KNOW WHO I AM, YOU KNOW. I HAVE FRIENDS IN WASHINGTON!
DO YOU?

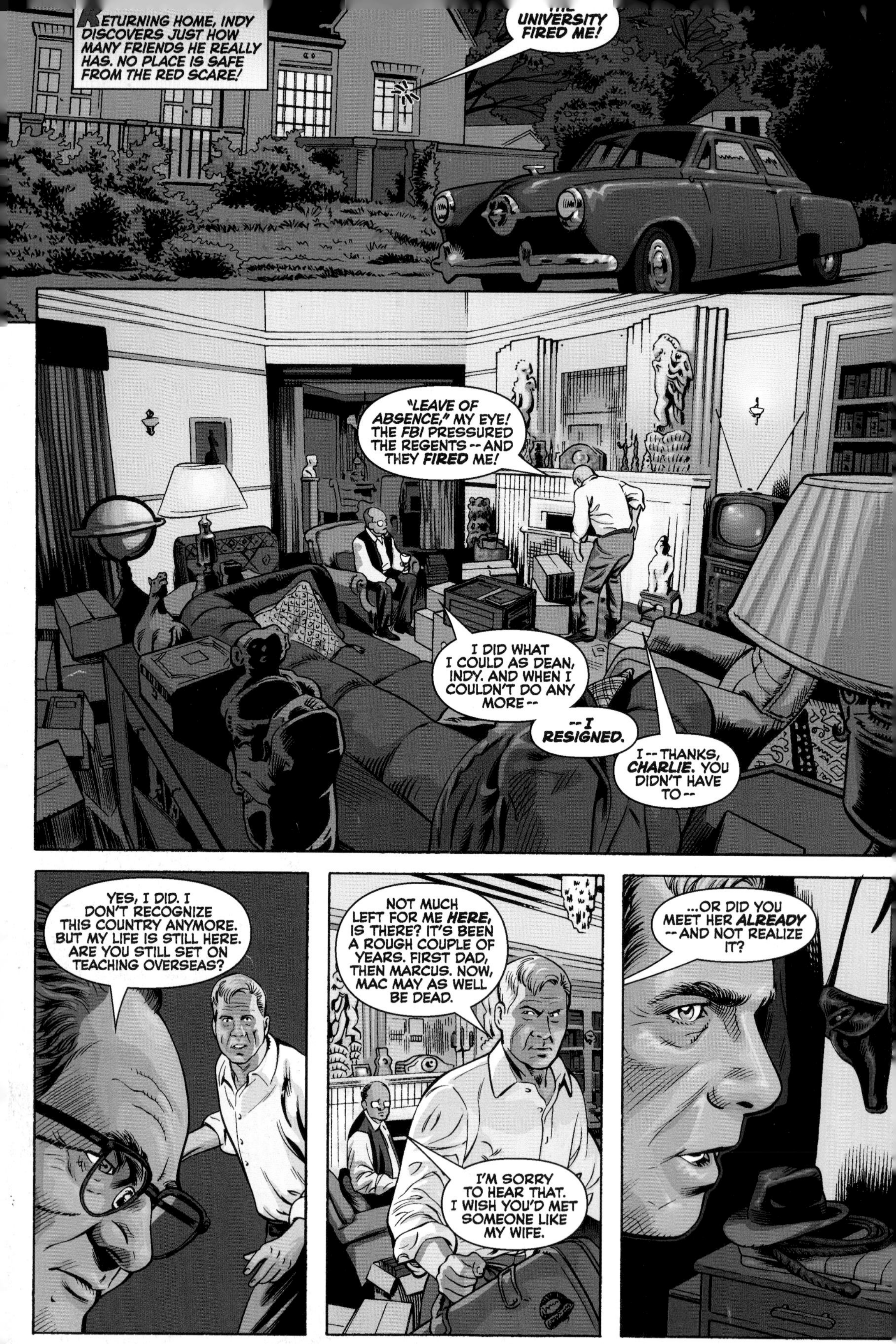
RETURNING HOME, INDY DISCOVERS JUST HOW MANY FRIENDS HE REALLY HAS. NO PLACE IS SAFE FROM THE RED SCARE!
UNIVERSITY FIRED ME!
"LEAVE OF ABSENCE," MY EYE! THE FBI PRESSURED THE REGENTS -- AND THEY FIRED ME!
I DID WHAT I COULD AS DEAN, INDY. AND WHEN I COULDN'T DO ANY MORE --
-- I RESIGNED.
I -- THANKS, CHARLIE. YOU DIDN'T HAVE TO --
YES, I DID. I DON'T RECOGNIZE THIS COUNTRY ANYMORE. BUT MY LIFE IS STILL HERE. ARE YOU STILL SET ON TEACHING OVERSEAS?
NOT MUCH LEFT FOR ME HERE, IS THERE? IT'S BEEN A ROUGH COUPLE OF YEARS. FIRST DAD, THEN MARCUS. NOW, MAC MAY AS WELL BE DEAD.
I'M SORRY TO HEAR THAT. I WISH YOU'D MET SOMEONE LIKE MY WIFE.
...OR DID YOU MEET HER ALREADY -- AND NOT REALIZE IT?

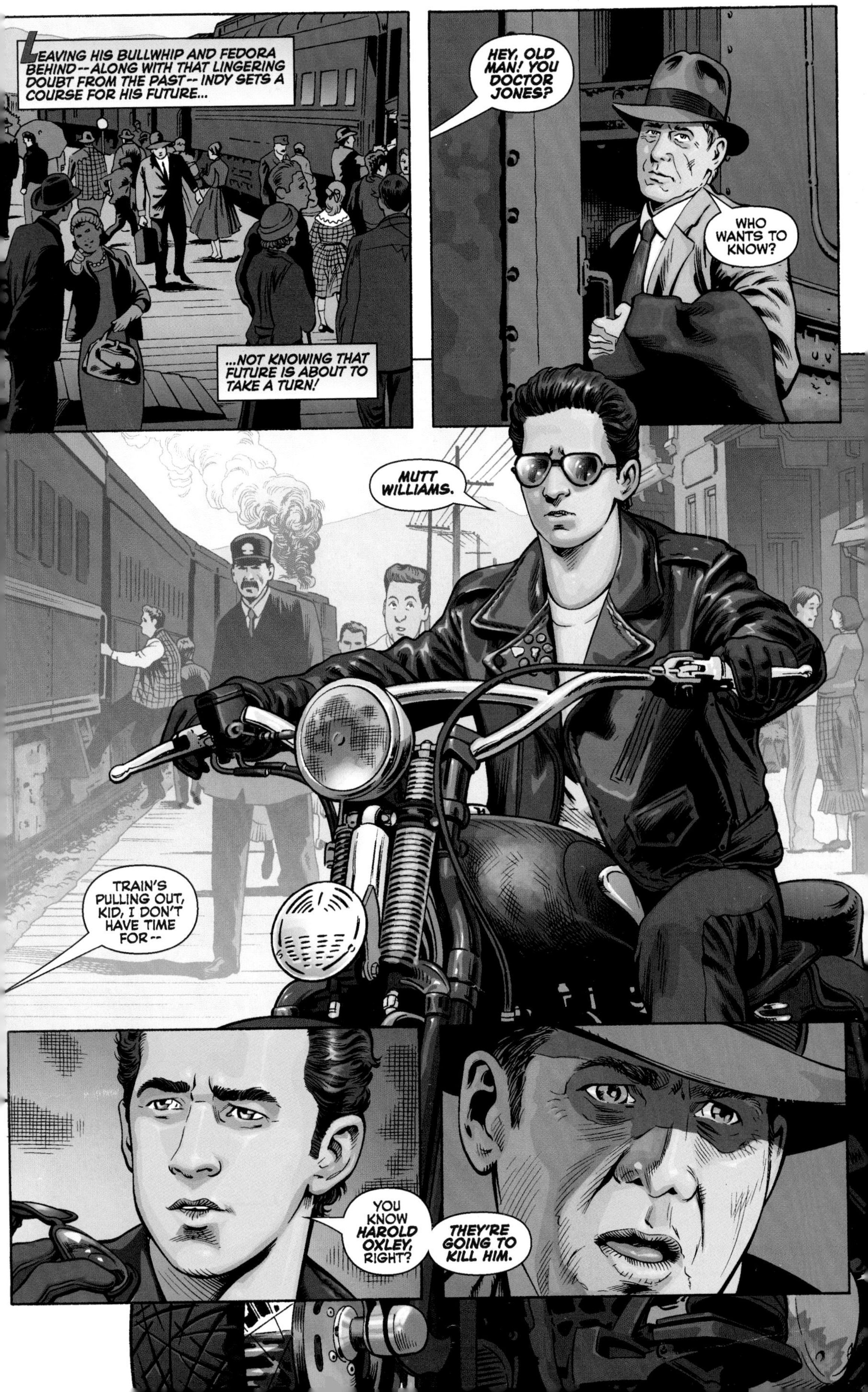

LEAVING HIS BULLWHIP AND FEDORA BEHIND -- ALONG WITH THAT LINGERING DOUBT FROM THE PAST -- INDY SETS A COURSE FOR HIS FUTURE...
...NOT KNOWING THAT FUTURE IS ABOUT TO TAKE A TURN!
HEY, OLD MAN! YOU DOCTOR JONES?
WHO WANTS TO KNOW?
MUTT WILLIAMS.
TRAIN'S PULLING OUT, KID, I DON'T HAVE TIME FOR --
YOU KNOW HAROLD OXLEY, RIGHT?
THEY'RE GOING TO KILL HIM.

INDY HADN'T SEEN "OX" SINCE A FALLING-OUT, YEARS BEFORE. BUT THIS NEWS, FROM SUCH AN UNLIKELY SOURCE, IS WORTH A CHANGE IN PLANS!

WHAT KIND OF NAME IS *MUTT?*

THE ONE I PICKED. YOU GOT A PROBLEM WITH IT?

FORGET IT, KID. HOW DO YOU KNOW OXLEY?

OX HELPED MOM RAISE ME AFTER MY DAD DIED IN THE WAR.

THEN, SIX MONTHS AGO, WE GOT A LETTER FROM HIM IN PERU.

HE FOUND A CRYSTAL SKULL, LIKE THE ONE THAT GUY MITCHELL-HEDGES FOUND. WHAT WAS IT, LIKE AN IDOL?

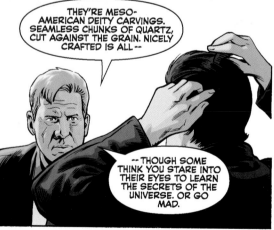

THEY'RE MESO-AMERICAN DEITY CARVINGS. SEAMLESS CHUNKS OF QUARTZ, CUT AGAINST THE GRAIN. NICELY CRAFTED IS ALL --

-- THOUGH SOME THINK YOU STARE INTO THEIR EYES TO LEARN THE SECRETS OF THE UNIVERSE. OR GO MAD.

WHERE DID OX FIND IT?

ON HIS WAY TO SOME PLACE CALLED *AKATOR.*

AKATOR? ARE YOU SURE?

YEAH, WHAT IS IT?

EL DORADO.

THE GODS CHOSE THE UGHA TRIBE MILLENNIA AGO TO BUILD A GREAT CITY OUT OF SOLID GOLD. AQUEDUCTS, ELECTRICITY -- THE WORKS.

FRANCESCO DE ORELLANA DISAPPEARED IN 1546 LOOKING FOR IT. I ALMOST DIED LOOKING FOR IT MYSELF.

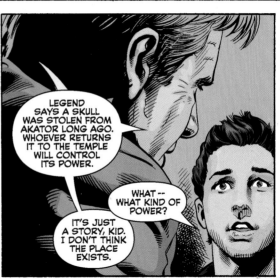

LEGEND SAYS A SKULL WAS STOLEN FROM AKATOR LONG AGO. WHOEVER RETURNS IT TO THE TEMPLE WILL CONTROL ITS POWER.

WHAT -- WHAT KIND OF POWER?

IT'S JUST A STORY, KID. I DON'T THINK THE PLACE EXISTS.

WELL, OX DID. MOM THOUGHT HE WAS GOING CRAZY. SHE WENT TO FIND HIM -- ONLY SOMEONE KIDNAPPED HIM. THEN HER.

IF SHE DOESN'T PRODUCE THE SKULL, THEY'RE BOTH DEAD. SHE SAID YOU'D HELP -- YOU REMEMBER MARY WILLIAMS?

THERE WERE A LOT OF MARY WILLIAMS, KID.

WELL, THIS MARY WILLIAMS GOT AWAY LONG ENOUGH TO SEND THIS --

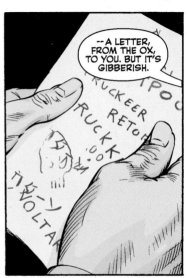

-- A LETTER, FROM THE OX, TO YOU. BUT IT'S GIBBERISH.

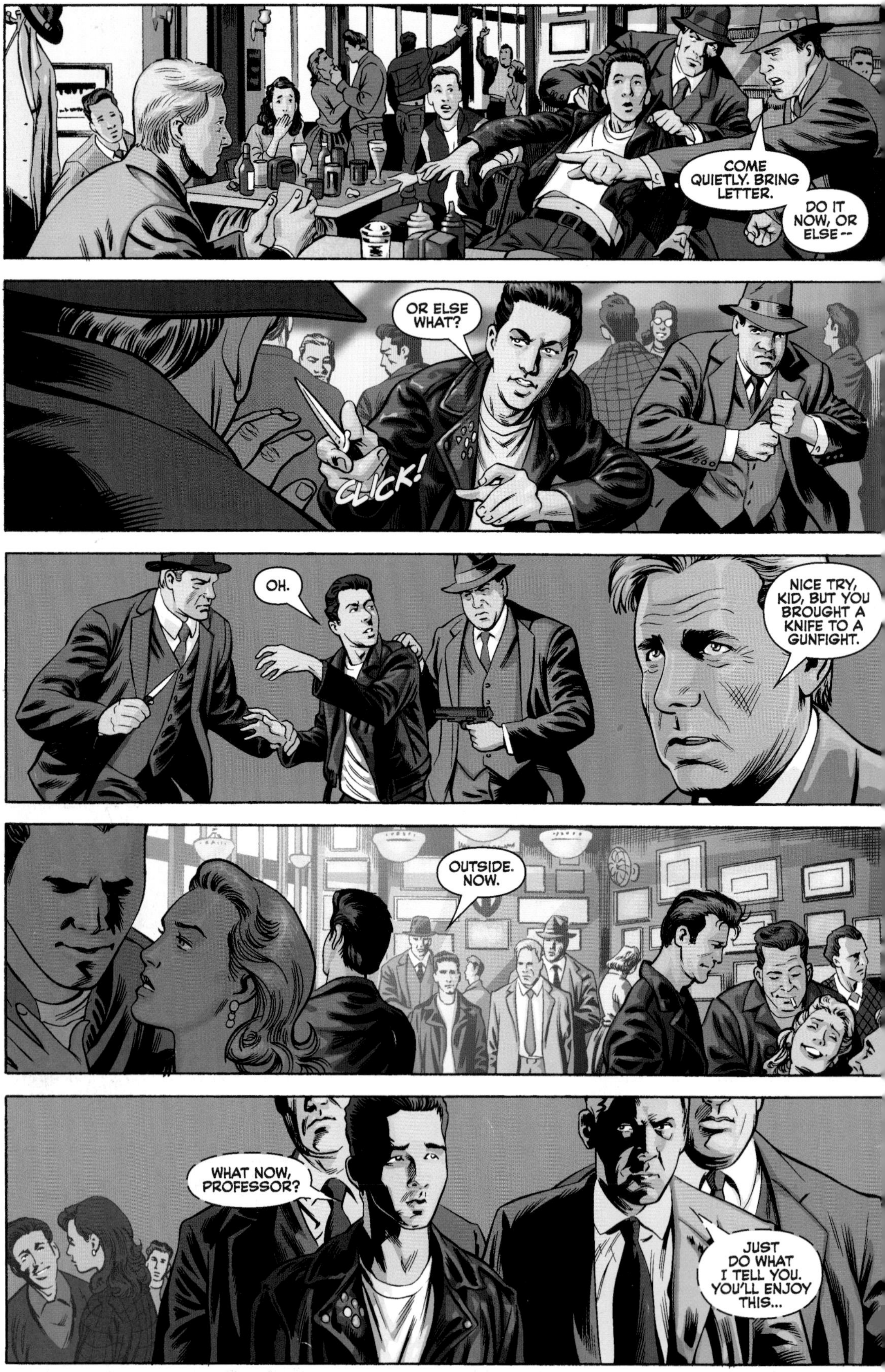
COME QUIETLY. BRING LETTER.
DO IT NOW, OR ELSE--
OR ELSE WHAT?
CLICK!
OH.
NICE TRY, KID, BUT YOU BROUGHT A KNIFE TO A GUNFIGHT.
OUTSIDE. NOW.
WHAT NOW, PROFESSOR?
JUST DO WHAT I TELL YOU. YOU'LL ENJOY THIS...

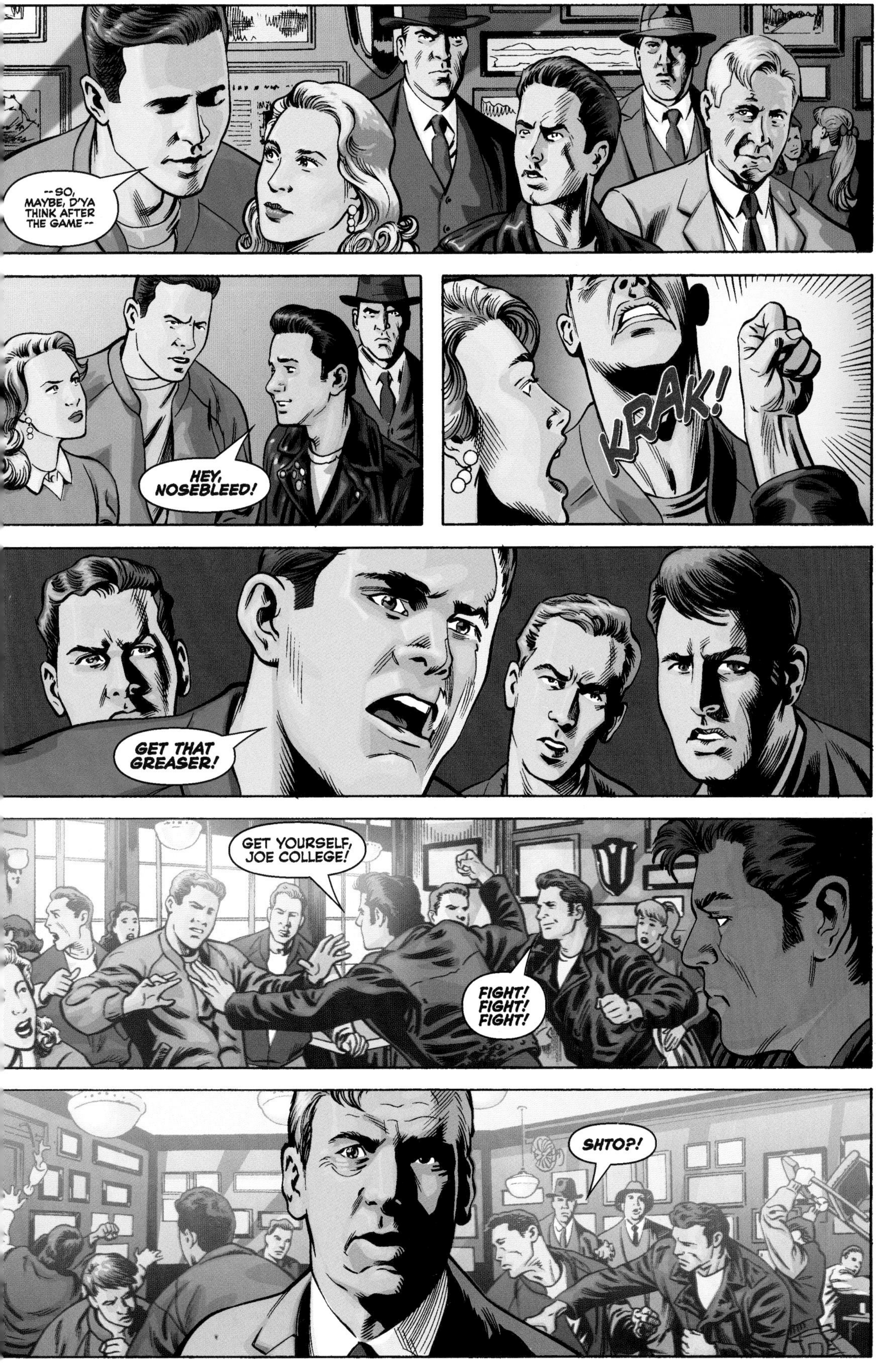
--SO, MAYBE, D'YA THINK AFTER THE GAME--
HEY, NOSEBLEED!
KRAK!
GET THAT GREASER!
GET YOURSELF, JOE COLLEGE!
FIGHT! FIGHT! FIGHT!
SHTO?!

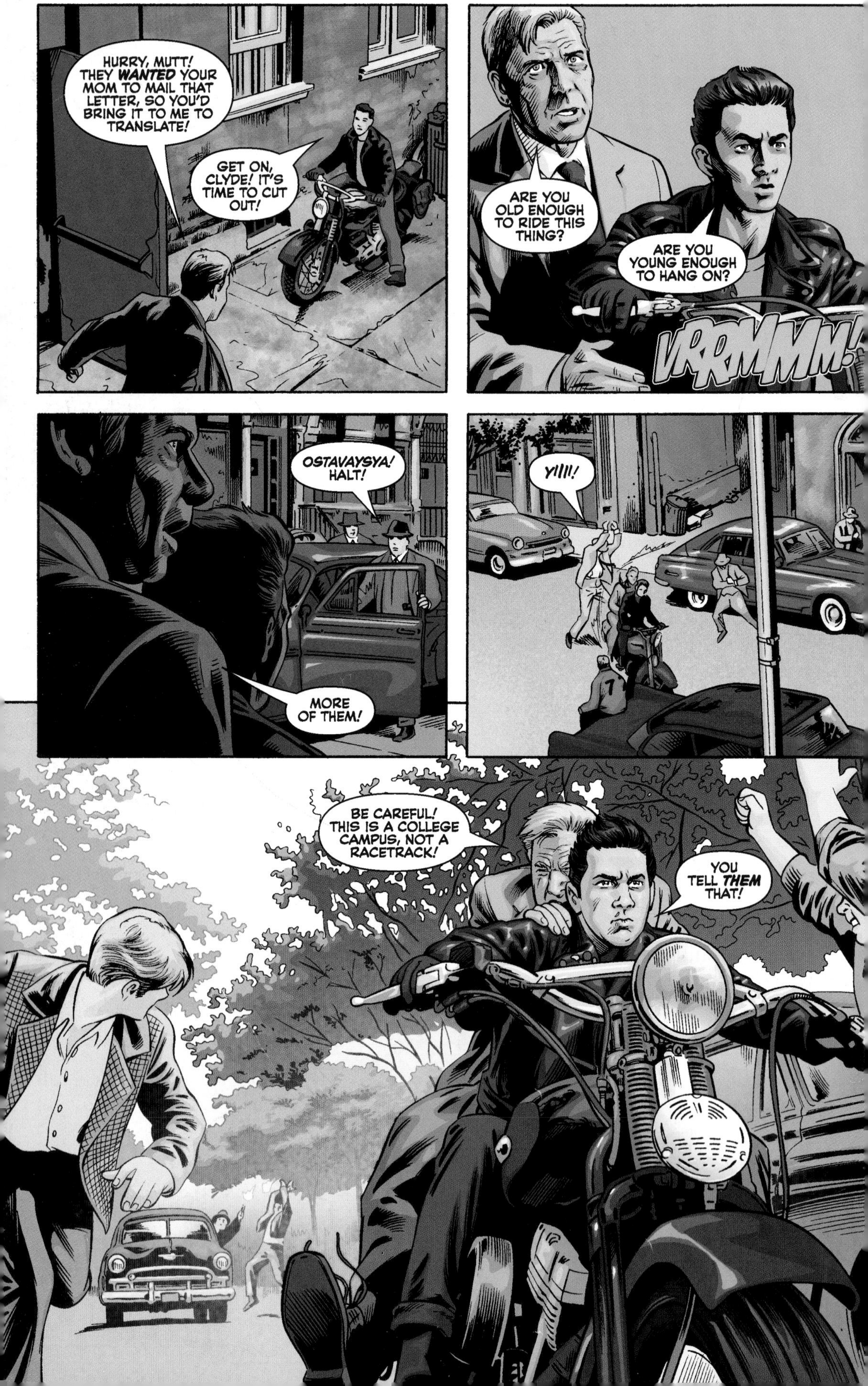
HURRY, MUTT! THEY **WANTED** YOUR MOM TO MAIL THAT LETTER, SO YOU'D BRING IT TO ME TO TRANSLATE!
GET ON, CLYDE! IT'S TIME TO CUT OUT!
ARE YOU OLD ENOUGH TO RIDE THIS THING?
ARE YOU YOUNG ENOUGH TO HANG ON?
VRRMMMM!
OSTAVAYSYA! HALT!
MORE OF THEM!
YIIII!
BE CAREFUL! THIS IS A COLLEGE CAMPUS, NOT A RACETRACK!
YOU TELL ***THEM*** THAT!

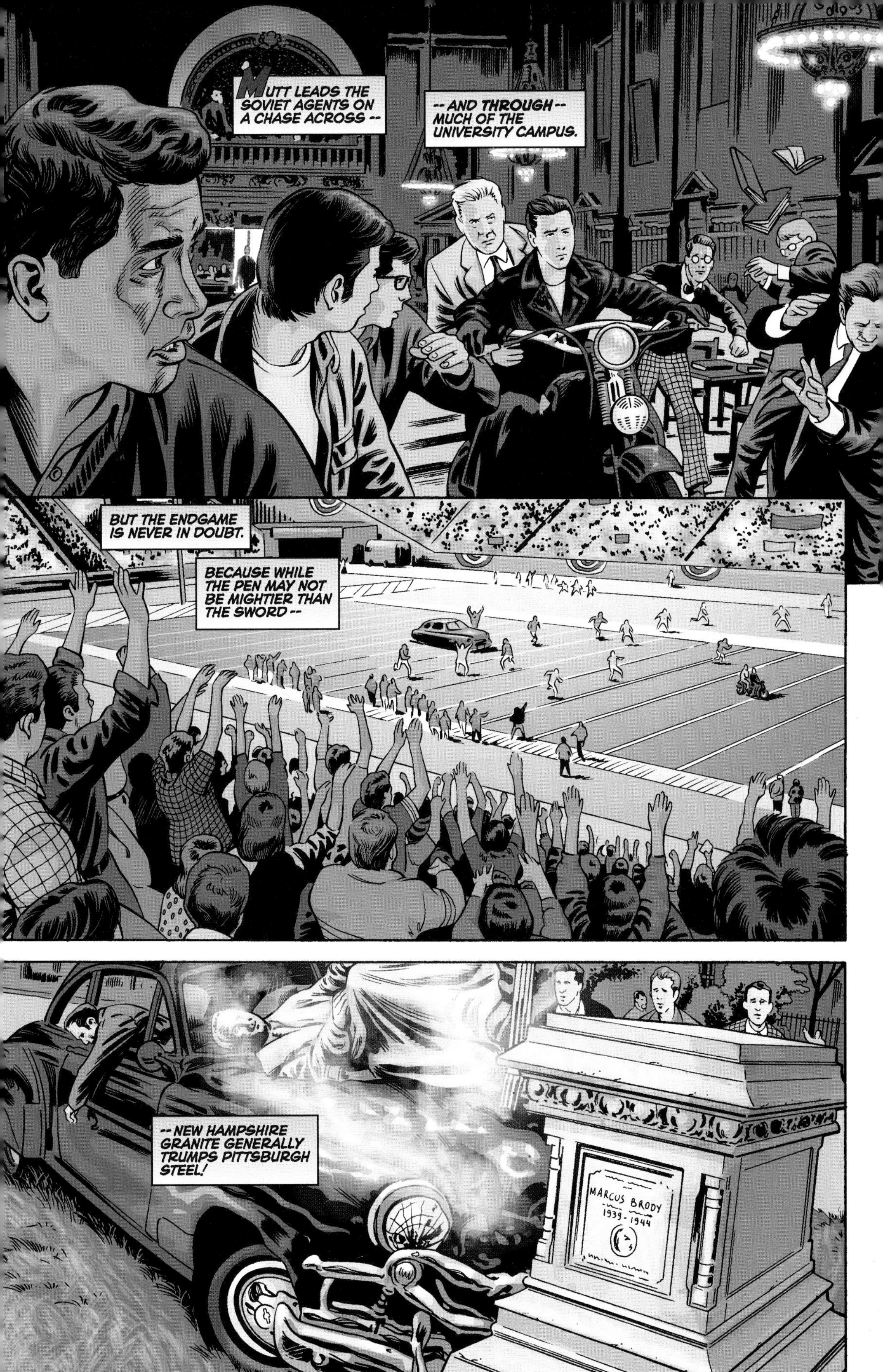
MUTT LEADS THE SOVIET AGENTS ON A CHASE ACROSS --
-- AND THROUGH -- MUCH OF THE UNIVERSITY CAMPUS.
BUT THE ENDGAME IS NEVER IN DOUBT.
BECAUSE WHILE THE PEN MAY NOT BE MIGHTIER THAN THE SWORD --
-- NEW HAMPSHIRE GRANITE GENERALLY TRUMPS PITTSBURGH STEEL!
MARCUS BRODY
1939 - 1944

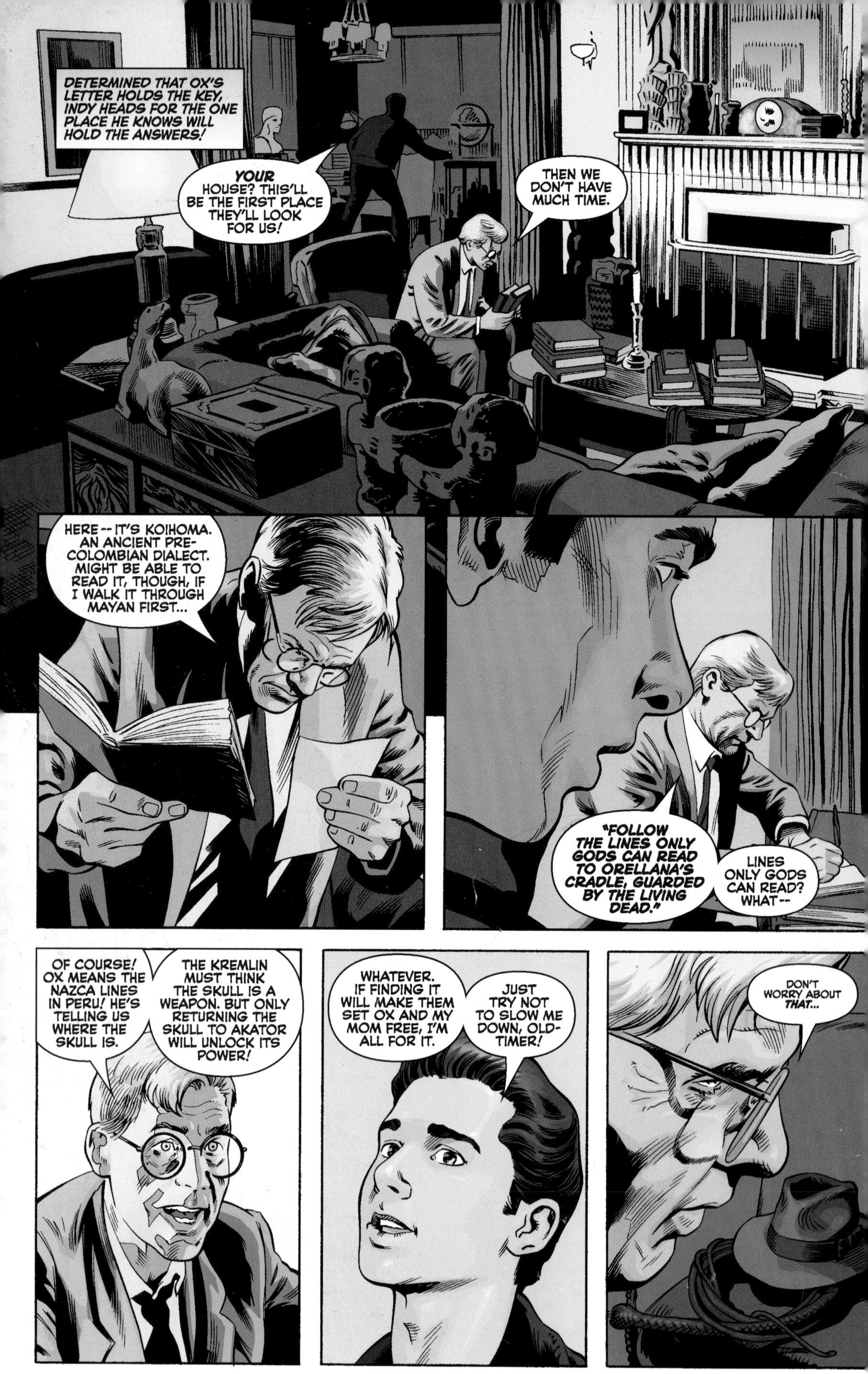
DETERMINED THAT OX'S LETTER HOLDS THE KEY, INDY HEADS FOR THE ONE PLACE HE KNOWS WILL HOLD THE ANSWERS!
YOUR HOUSE? THIS'LL BE THE FIRST PLACE THEY'LL LOOK FOR US!
THEN WE DON'T HAVE MUCH TIME.
HERE -- IT'S KOIHOMA. AN ANCIENT PRE-COLOMBIAN DIALECT. MIGHT BE ABLE TO READ IT, THOUGH, IF I WALK IT THROUGH MAYAN FIRST...
"FOLLOW THE LINES ONLY GODS CAN READ TO ORELLANA'S CRADLE, GUARDED BY THE LIVING DEAD."
LINES ONLY GODS CAN READ? WHAT --
OF COURSE! OX MEANS THE NAZCA LINES IN PERU! HE'S TELLING US WHERE THE SKULL IS.
THE KREMLIN MUST THINK THE SKULL IS A WEAPON. BUT ONLY RETURNING THE SKULL TO AKATOR WILL UNLOCK ITS POWER!
WHATEVER. IF FINDING IT WILL MAKE THEM SET OX AND MY MOM FREE, I'M ALL FOR IT.
JUST TRY NOT TO SLOW ME DOWN, OLD-TIMER!
DON'T WORRY ABOUT THAT...

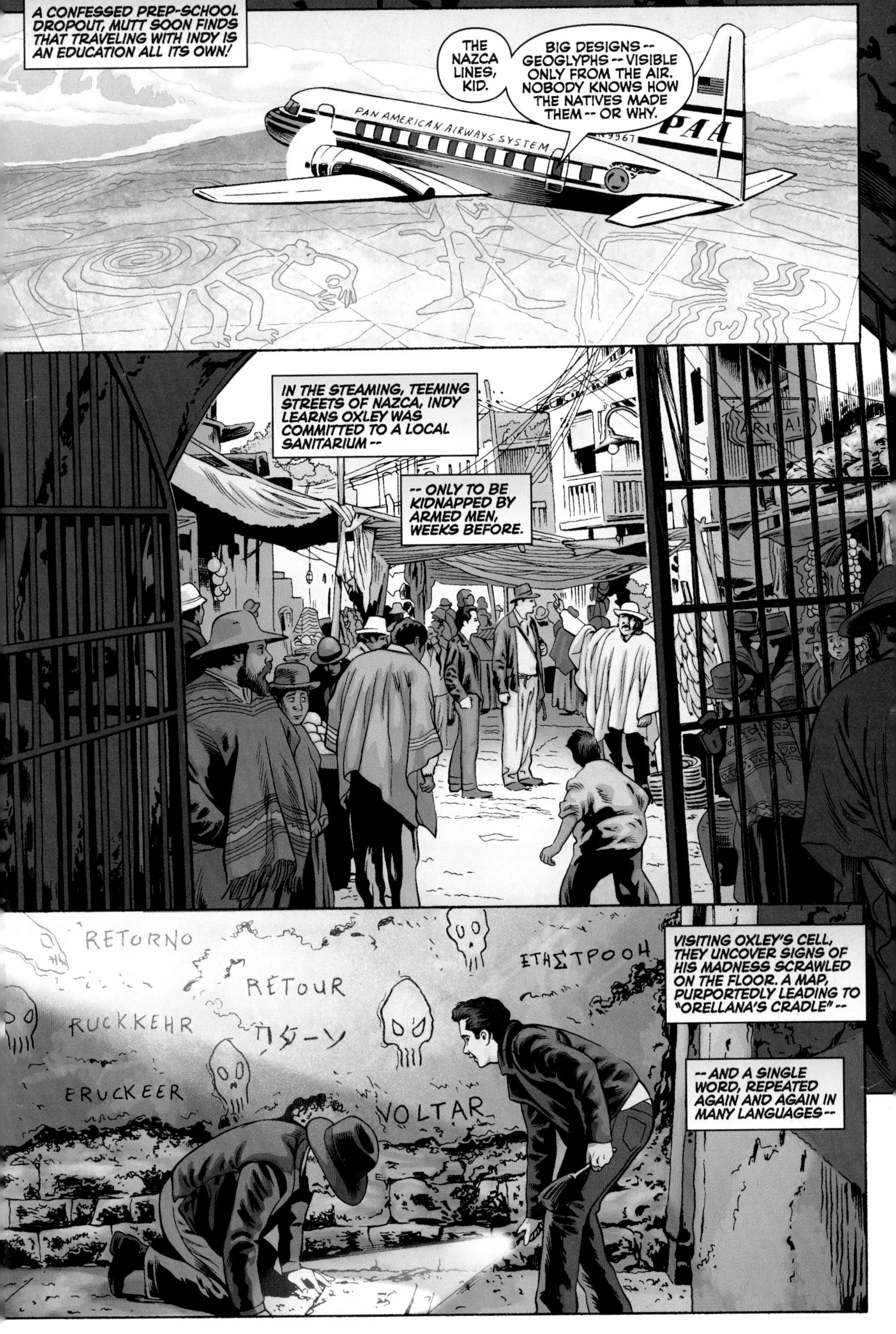
A CONFESSED PREP-SCHOOL DROPOUT, MUTT SOON FINDS THAT TRAVELING WITH INDY IS AN EDUCATION ALL ITS OWN!
THE NAZCA LINES, KID.
BIG DESIGNS -- GEOGLYPHS -- VISIBLE ONLY FROM THE AIR. NOBODY KNOWS HOW THE NATIVES MADE THEM -- OR WHY.
PAN AMERICAN AIRWAYS SYSTEM
PAA
IN THE STEAMING, TEEMING STREETS OF NAZCA, INDY LEARNS OXLEY WAS COMMITTED TO A LOCAL SANITARIUM --
-- ONLY TO BE KIDNAPPED BY ARMED MEN, WEEKS BEFORE.
RETORNO
RETOUR
ΕΤΗΣΤΡΟΟΗ
RUCKKEHR
ካኇーソ
ERUCKEER
VOLTAR
VISITING OXLEY'S CELL, THEY UNCOVER SIGNS OF HIS MADNESS SCRAWLED ON THE FLOOR. A MAP, PURPORTEDLY LEADING TO "ORELLANA'S CRADLE" --
-- AND A SINGLE WORD, REPEATED AGAIN AND AGAIN IN MANY LANGUAGES --

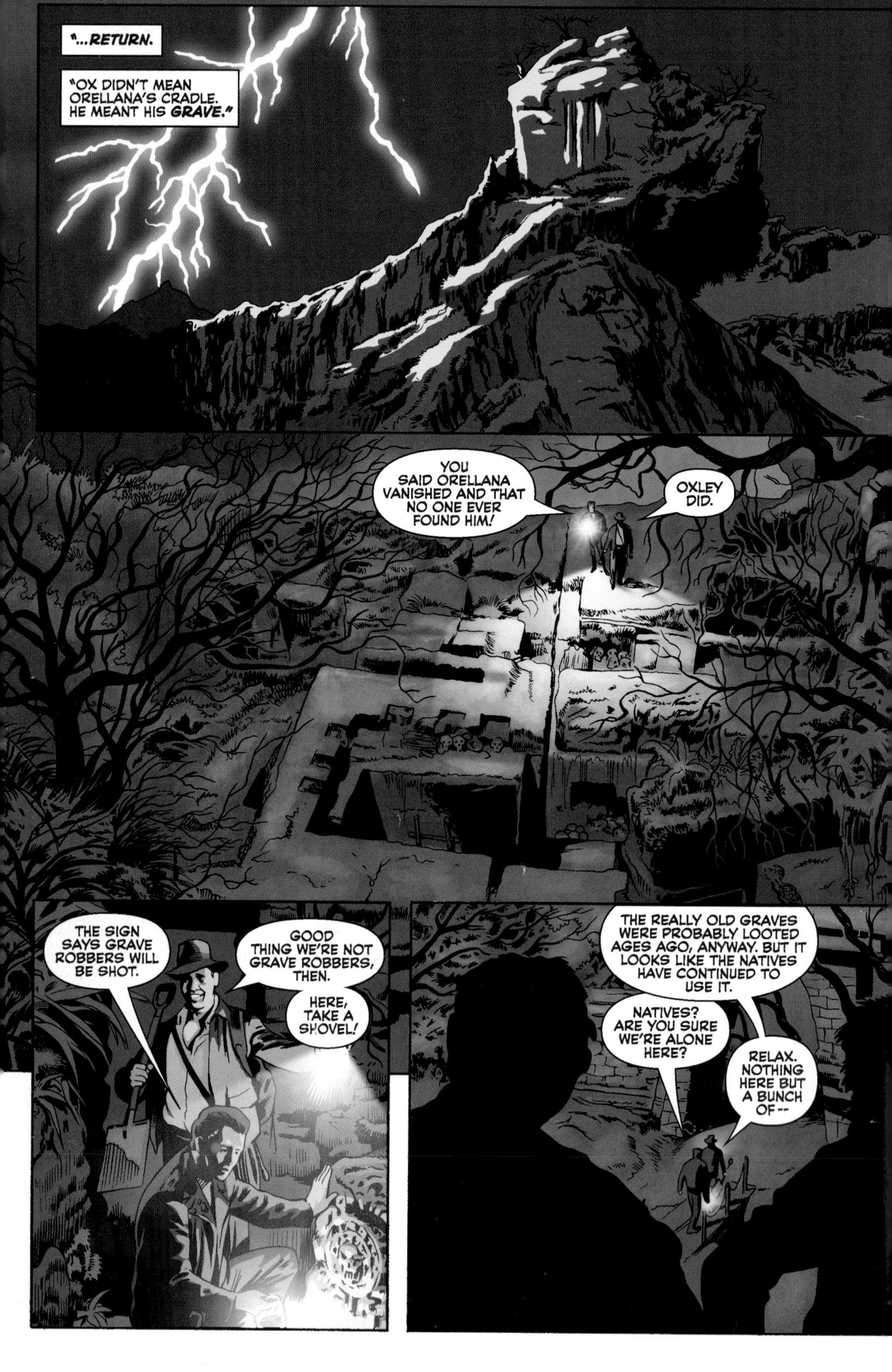
"...RETURN.
"OX DIDN'T MEAN ORELLANA'S CRADLE. HE MEANT HIS GRAVE."
YOU SAID ORELLANA VANISHED AND THAT NO ONE EVER FOUND HIM!
OXLEY DID.
THE SIGN SAYS GRAVE ROBBERS WILL BE SHOT.
GOOD THING WE'RE NOT GRAVE ROBBERS, THEN.
HERE, TAKE A SHOVEL!
THE REALLY OLD GRAVES WERE PROBABLY LOOTED AGES AGO, ANYWAY. BUT IT LOOKS LIKE THE NATIVES HAVE CONTINUED TO USE IT.
NATIVES? ARE YOU SURE WE'RE ALONE HERE?
RELAX. NOTHING HERE BUT A BUNCH OF --

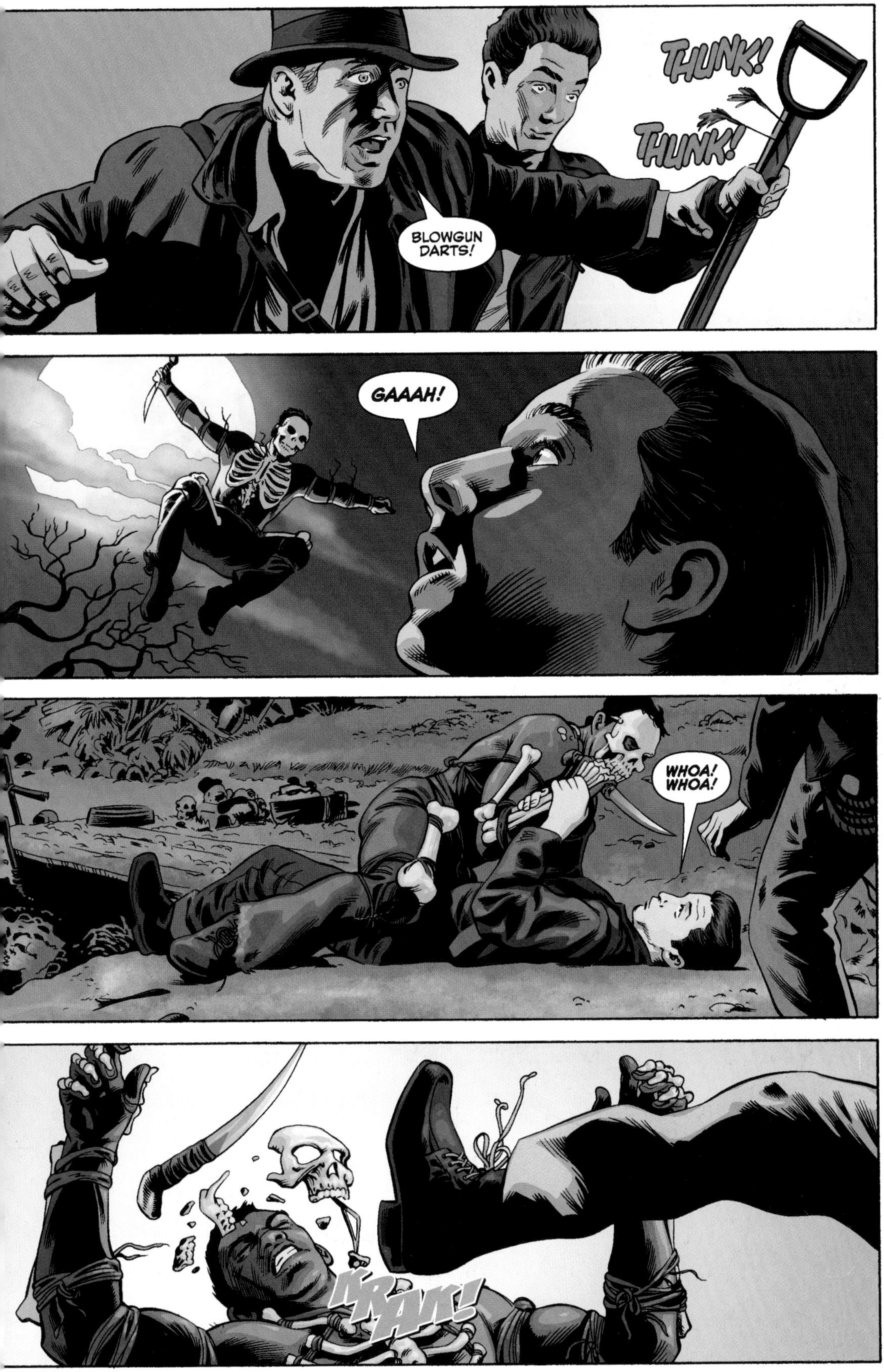
THUNK!
THUNK!
BLOWGUN DARTS!
GAAAH!
WHOA! WHOA!
KRAAK!

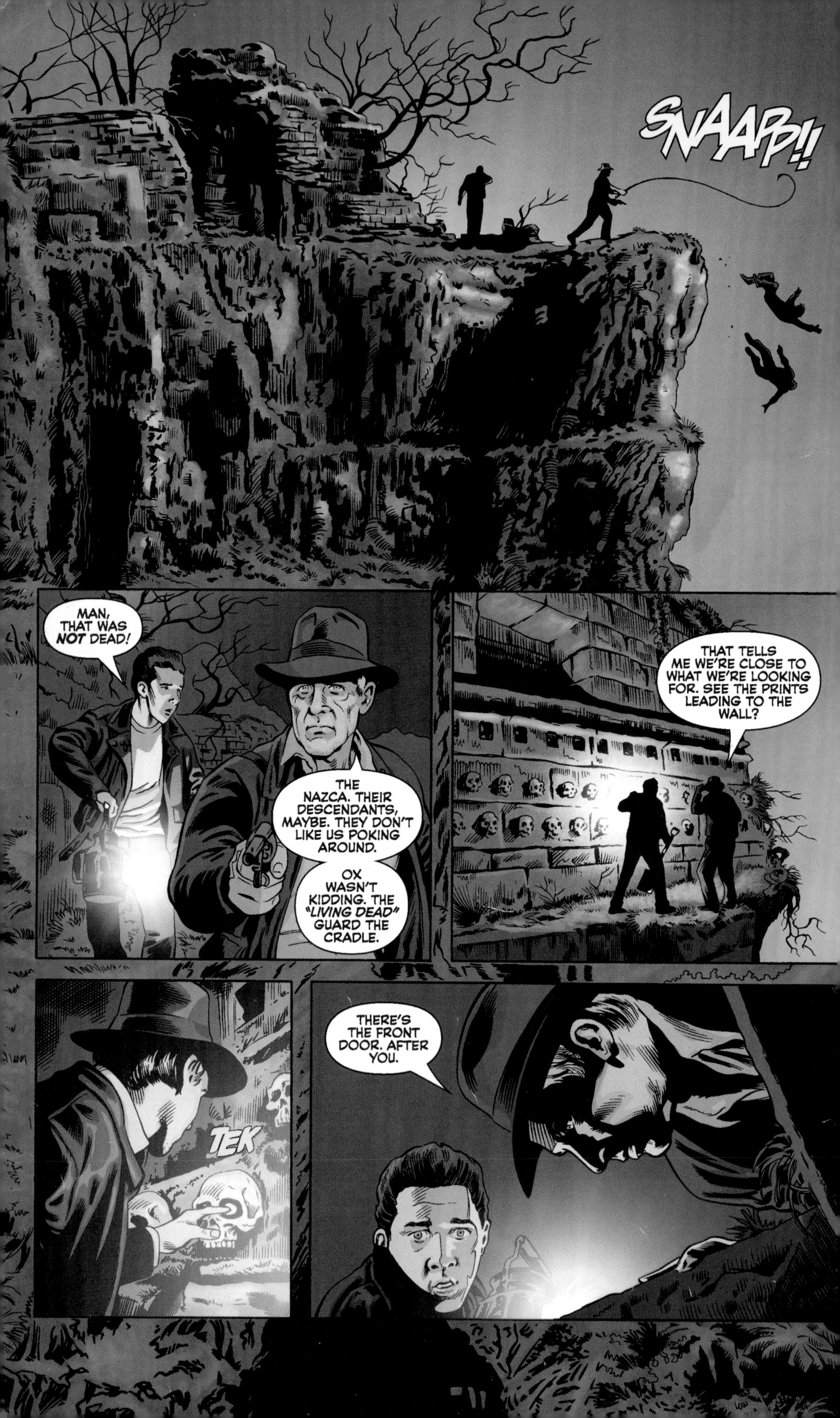
SNAAPP!!
MAN, THAT WAS *NOT* DEAD!
THE NAZCA. THEIR DESCENDANTS, MAYBE. THEY DON'T LIKE US POKING AROUND.
OX WASN'T KIDDING. THE *"LIVING DEAD"* GUARD THE CRADLE.
THAT TELLS ME WE'RE CLOSE TO WHAT WE'RE LOOKING FOR. SEE THE PRINTS LEADING TO THE WALL?
TEK
THERE'S THE FRONT DOOR. AFTER YOU.

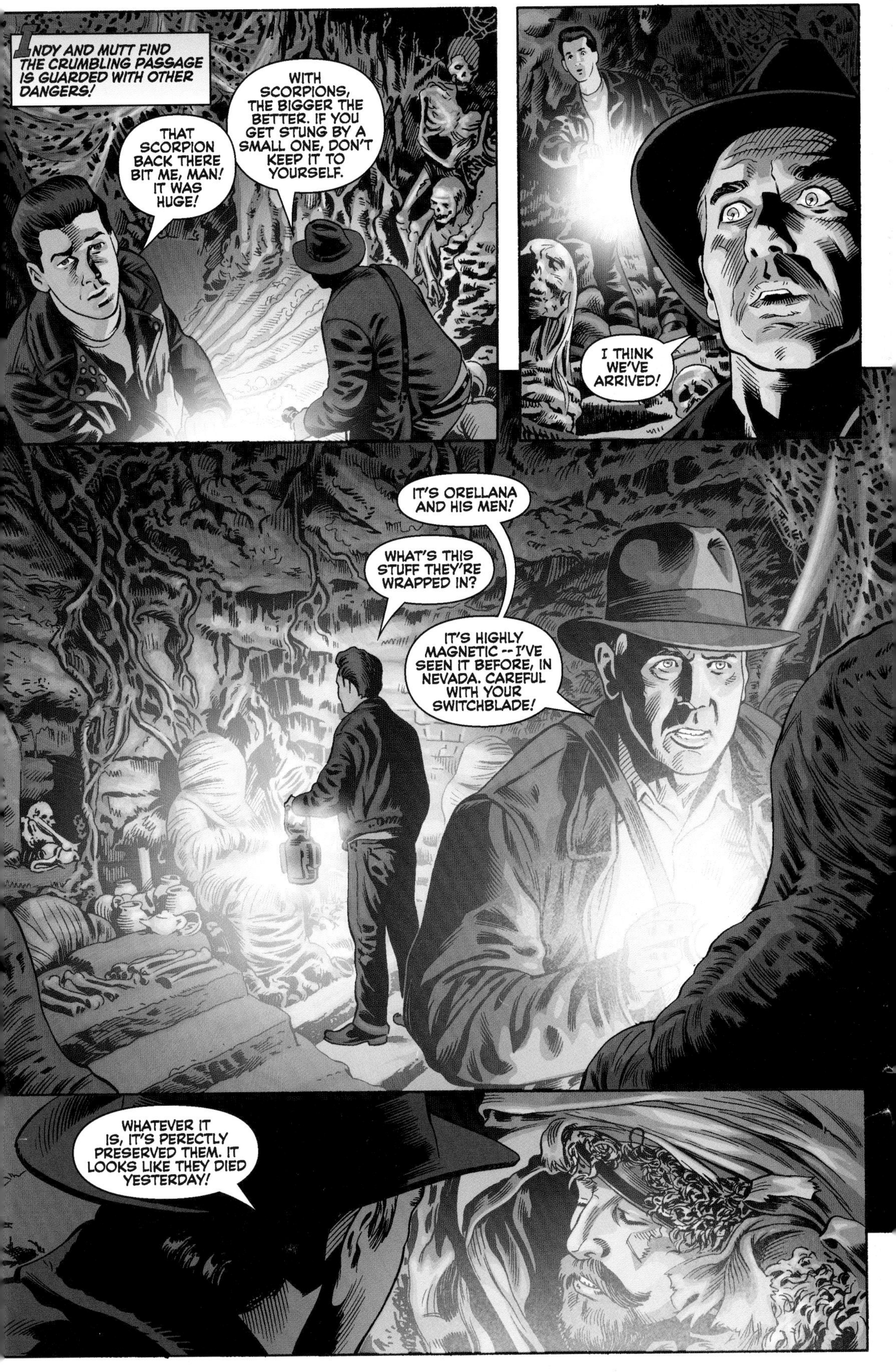
INDY AND MUTT FIND THE CRUMBLING PASSAGE IS GUARDED WITH OTHER DANGERS!
THAT SCORPION BACK THERE BIT ME, MAN! IT WAS HUGE!
WITH SCORPIONS, THE BIGGER THE BETTER. IF YOU GET STUNG BY A SMALL ONE, DON'T KEEP IT TO YOURSELF.
I THINK WE'VE ARRIVED!
IT'S ORELLANA AND HIS MEN!
WHAT'S THIS STUFF THEY'RE WRAPPED IN?
IT'S HIGHLY MAGNETIC -- I'VE SEEN IT BEFORE, IN NEVADA. CAREFUL WITH YOUR SWITCHBLADE!
WHATEVER IT IS, IT'S PERECTLY PRESERVED THEM. IT LOOKS LIKE THEY DIED YESTERDAY!

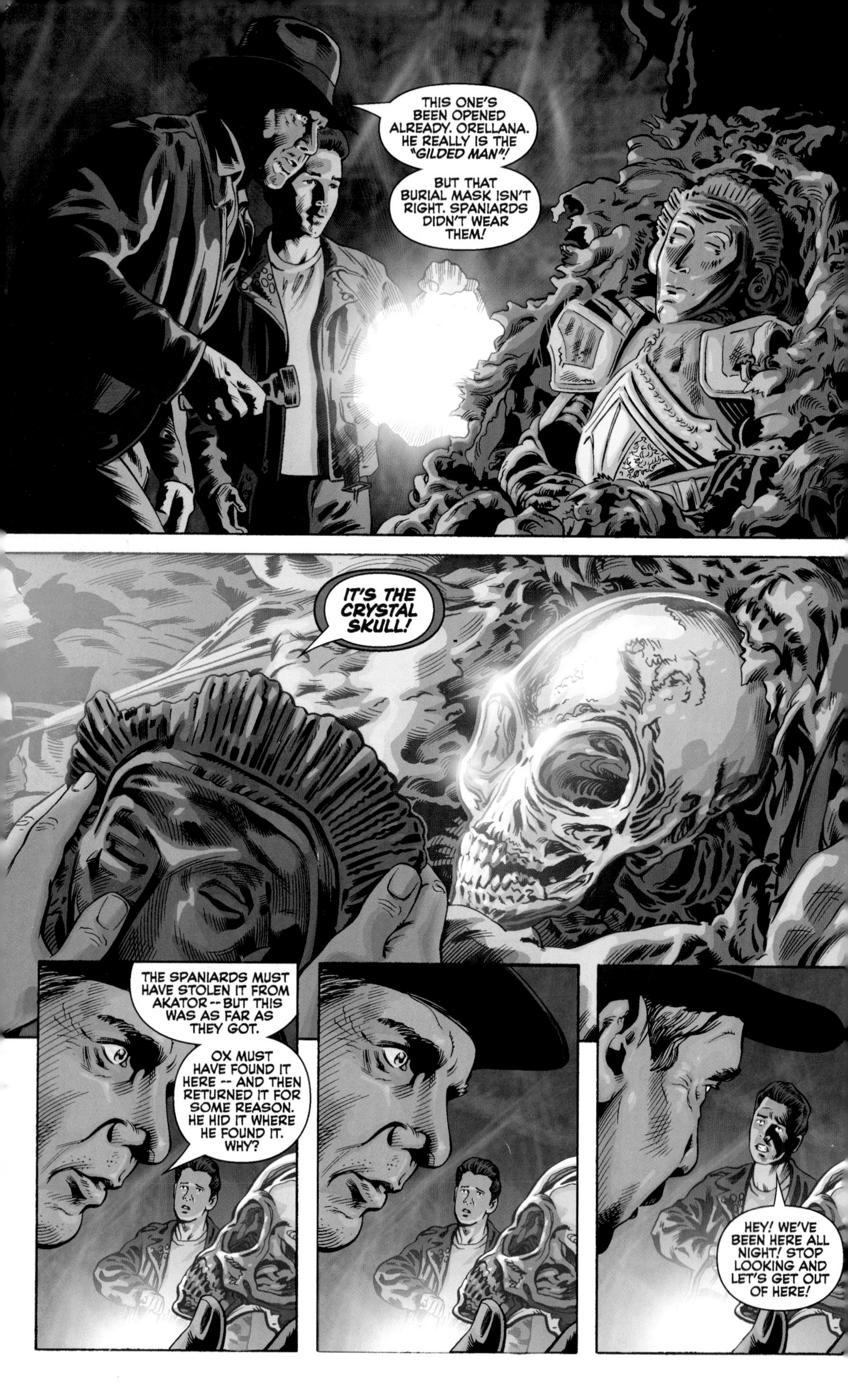
THIS ONE'S BEEN OPENED ALREADY. ORELLANA. HE REALLY IS THE "GILDED MAN"!
BUT THAT BURIAL MASK ISN'T RIGHT. SPANIARDS DIDN'T WEAR THEM!
IT'S THE CRYSTAL SKULL!
THE SPANIARDS MUST HAVE STOLEN IT FROM AKATOR -- BUT THIS WAS AS FAR AS THEY GOT.
OX MUST HAVE FOUND IT HERE -- AND THEN RETURNED IT FOR SOME REASON. HE HID IT WHERE HE FOUND IT. WHY?
HEY! WE'VE BEEN HERE ALL NIGHT! STOP LOOKING AND LET'S GET OUT OF HERE!

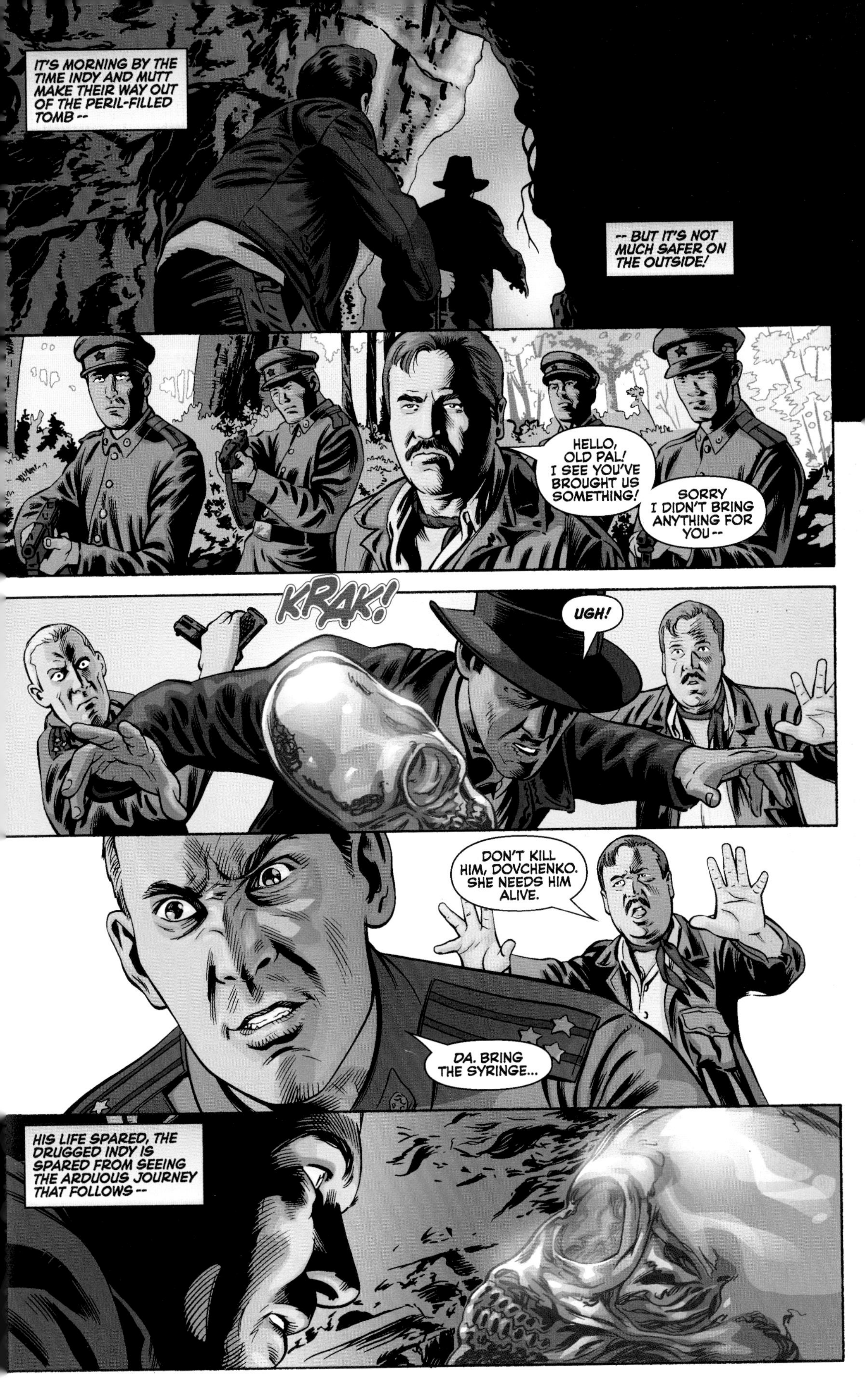
IT'S MORNING BY THE TIME INDY AND MUTT MAKE THEIR WAY OUT OF THE PERIL-FILLED TOMB --
-- BUT IT'S NOT MUCH SAFER ON THE OUTSIDE!
HELLO, OLD PAL! I SEE YOU'VE BROUGHT US SOMETHING!
SORRY I DIDN'T BRING ANYTHING FOR YOU --
KRAK!
UGH!
DON'T KILL HIM, DOVCHENKO. SHE NEEDS HIM ALIVE.
DA. BRING THE SYRINGE...
HIS LIFE SPARED, THE DRUGGED INDY IS SPARED FROM SEEING THE ARDUOUS JOURNEY THAT FOLLOWS --

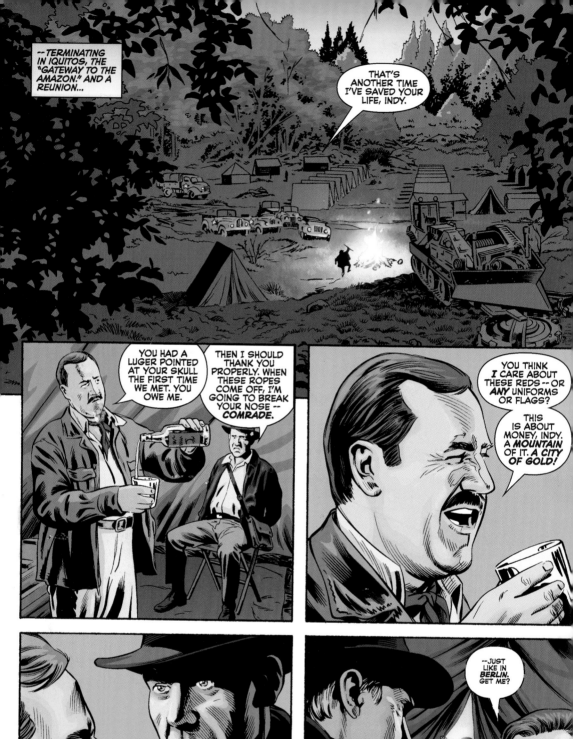

-- TERMINATING IN IQUITOS, THE "GATEWAY TO THE AMAZON." AND A REUNION...

THAT'S ANOTHER TIME I'VE SAVED YOUR LIFE, INDY.

YOU HAD A LUGER POINTED AT YOUR SKULL THE FIRST TIME WE MET. YOU OWE ME.

THEN I SHOULD THANK YOU PROPERLY. WHEN THESE ROPES COME OFF, I'M GOING TO BREAK YOUR NOSE -- COMRADE.

YOU THINK I CARE ABOUT THESE REDS -- OR ANY UNIFORMS OR FLAGS?

THIS IS ABOUT MONEY, INDY. A MOUNTAIN OF IT. A CITY OF GOLD!

I NEED YOU TO SEE THE ANGLE HERE. BE SMART AND PLAY YOUR PART. JUST LIKE --

--JUST LIKE IN BERLIN. GET ME?

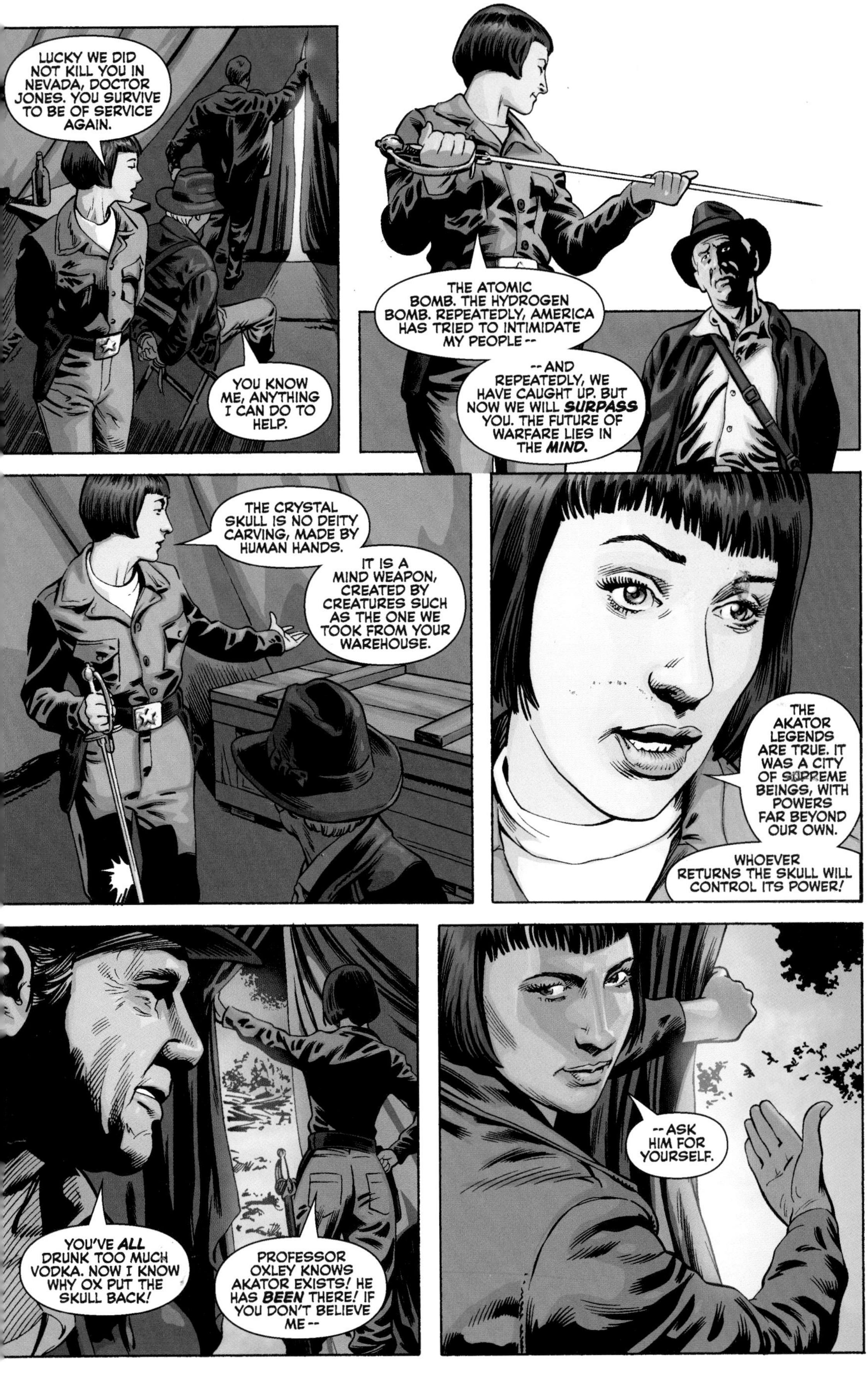
LUCKY WE DID NOT KILL YOU IN NEVADA, DOCTOR JONES. YOU SURVIVE TO BE OF SERVICE AGAIN.
YOU KNOW ME, ANYTHING I CAN DO TO HELP.
THE ATOMIC BOMB. THE HYDROGEN BOMB. REPEATEDLY, AMERICA HAS TRIED TO INTIMIDATE MY PEOPLE --
-- AND REPEATEDLY, WE HAVE CAUGHT UP. BUT NOW WE WILL SURPASS YOU. THE FUTURE OF WARFARE LIES IN THE MIND.
THE CRYSTAL SKULL IS NO DEITY CARVING, MADE BY HUMAN HANDS.
IT IS A MIND WEAPON, CREATED BY CREATURES SUCH AS THE ONE WE TOOK FROM YOUR WAREHOUSE.
THE AKATOR LEGENDS ARE TRUE. IT WAS A CITY OF SUPREME BEINGS, WITH POWERS FAR BEYOND OUR OWN.
WHOEVER RETURNS THE SKULL WILL CONTROL ITS POWER!
YOU'VE ALL DRUNK TOO MUCH VODKA. NOW I KNOW WHY OX PUT THE SKULL BACK!
PROFESSOR OXLEY KNOWS AKATOR EXISTS! HE HAS BEEN THERE! IF YOU DON'T BELIEVE ME --
-- ASK HIM FOR YOURSELF.

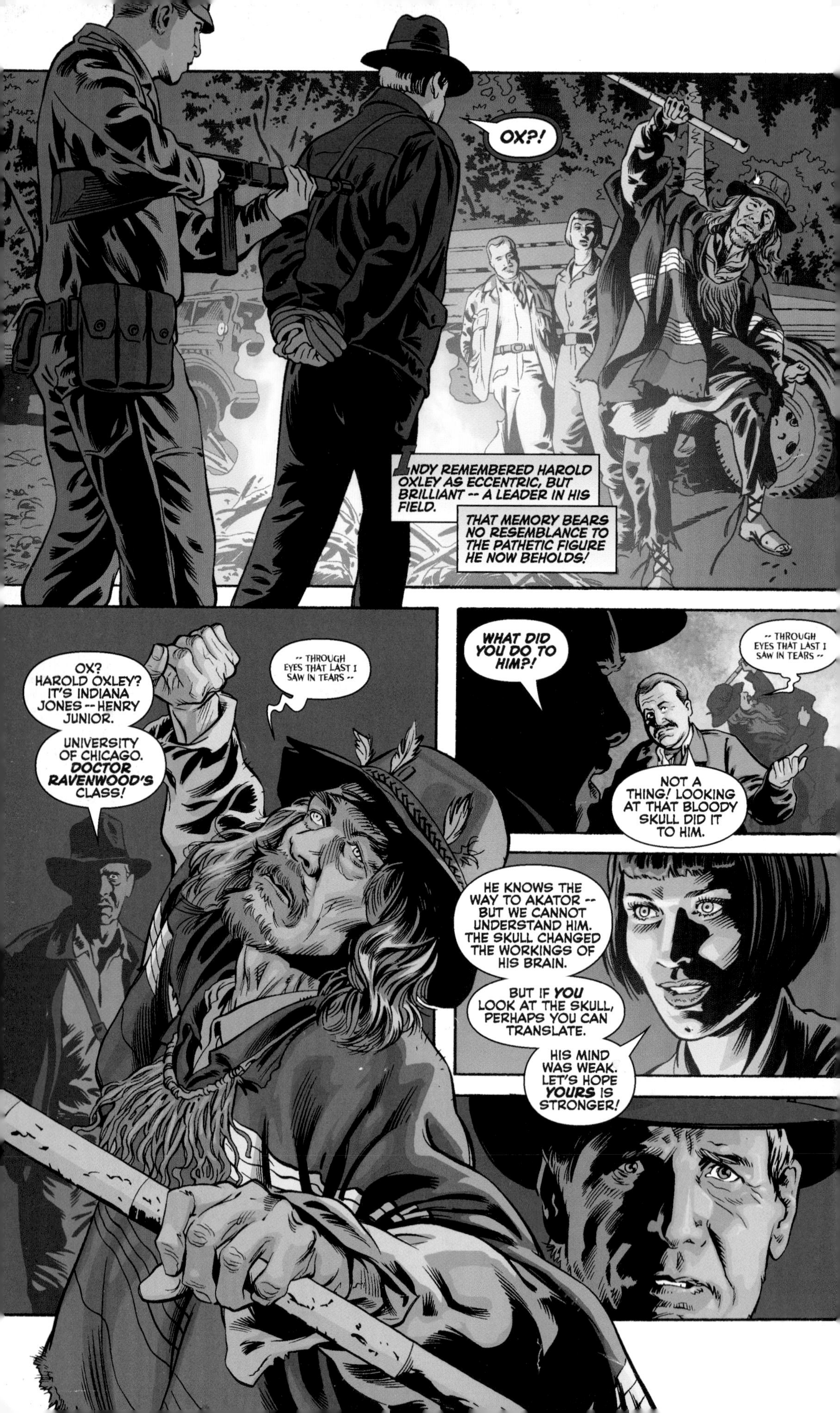
OX?!
INDY REMEMBERED HAROLD OXLEY AS ECCENTRIC, BUT BRILLIANT -- A LEADER IN HIS FIELD.
THAT MEMORY BEARS NO RESEMBLANCE TO THE PATHETIC FIGURE HE NOW BEHOLDS!
OX? HAROLD OXLEY? IT'S INDIANA JONES -- HENRY JUNIOR.
UNIVERSITY OF CHICAGO. DOCTOR RAVENWOOD'S CLASS!
-- THROUGH EYES THAT LAST I SAW IN TEARS --
WHAT DID YOU DO TO HIM?!
-- THROUGH EYES THAT LAST I SAW IN TEARS --
NOT A THING! LOOKING AT THAT BLOODY SKULL DID IT TO HIM.
HE KNOWS THE WAY TO AKATOR -- BUT WE CANNOT UNDERSTAND HIM. THE SKULL CHANGED THE WORKINGS OF HIS BRAIN.
BUT IF YOU LOOK AT THE SKULL, PERHAPS YOU CAN TRANSLATE.
HIS MIND WAS WEAK. LET'S HOPE YOURS IS STRONGER!

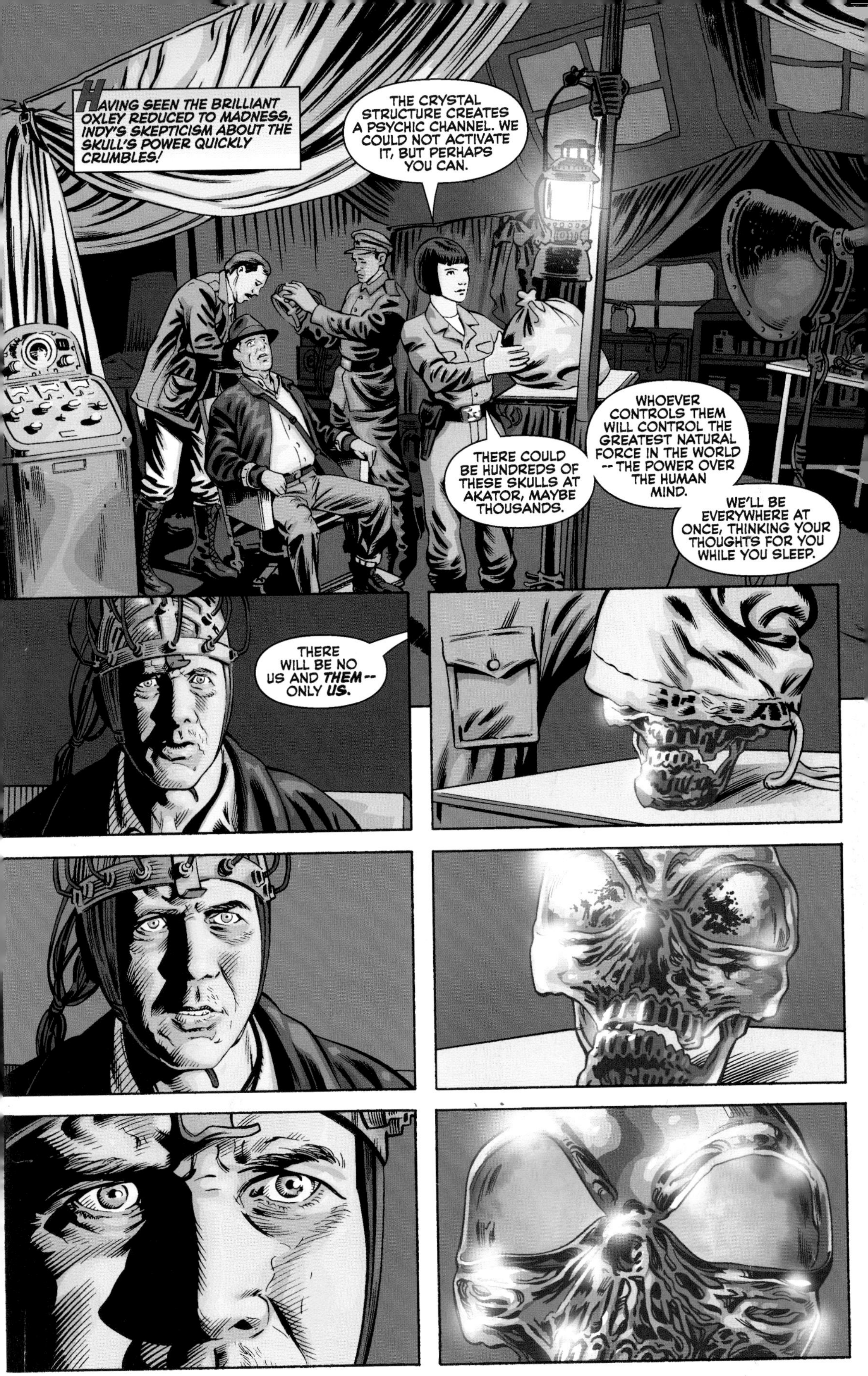
HAVING SEEN THE BRILLIANT OXLEY REDUCED TO MADNESS, INDY'S SKEPTICISM ABOUT THE SKULL'S POWER QUICKLY CRUMBLES!
THE CRYSTAL STRUCTURE CREATES A PSYCHIC CHANNEL. WE COULD NOT ACTIVATE IT, BUT PERHAPS YOU CAN.
THERE COULD BE HUNDREDS OF THESE SKULLS AT AKATOR, MAYBE THOUSANDS.
WHOEVER CONTROLS THEM WILL CONTROL THE GREATEST NATURAL FORCE IN THE WORLD -- THE POWER OVER THE HUMAN MIND.
WE'LL BE EVERYWHERE AT ONCE, THINKING YOUR THOUGHTS FOR YOU WHILE YOU SLEEP.
THERE WILL BE NO US AND THEM -- ONLY US.

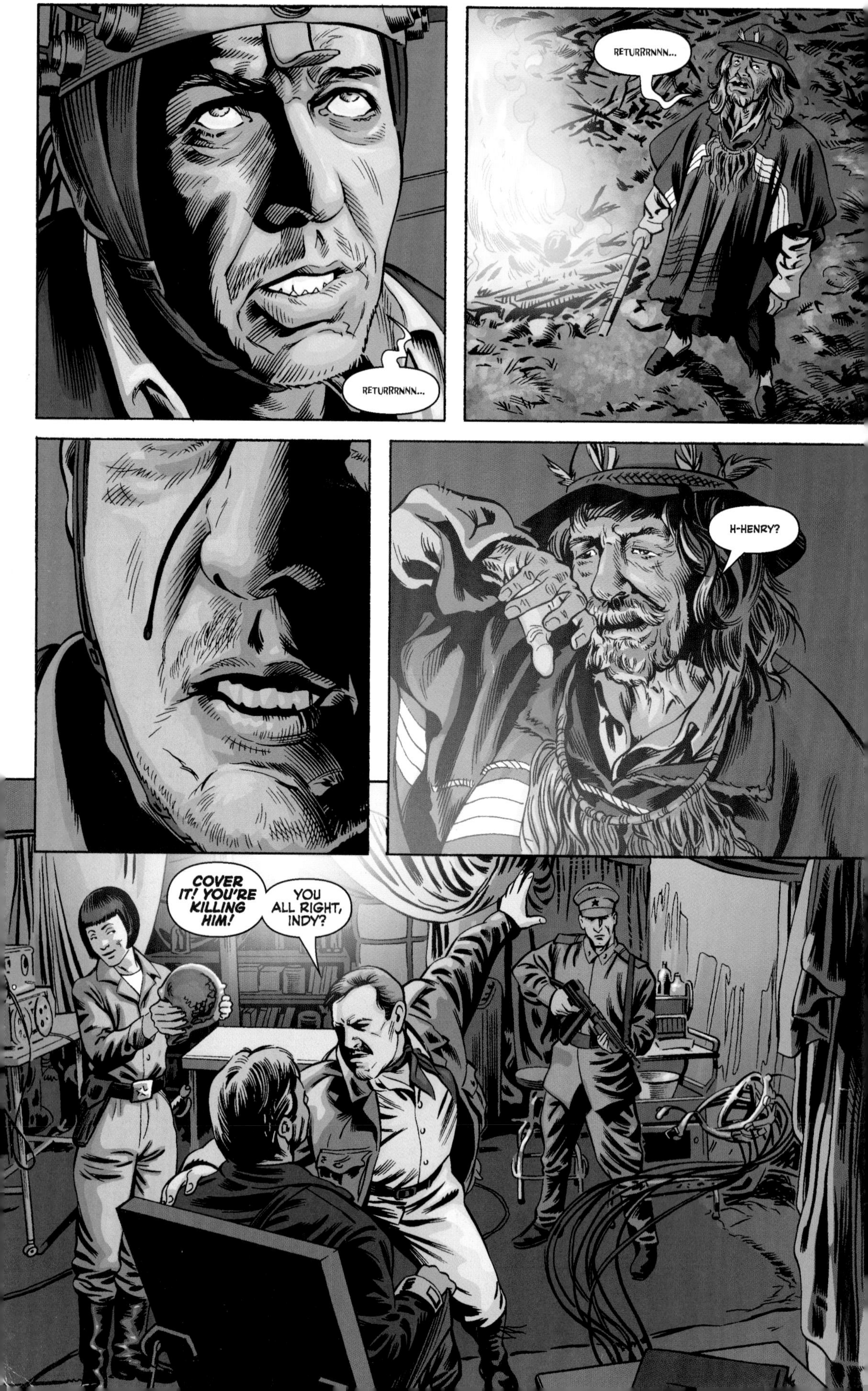
RETURRRNNN...
RETURRRNNN...
H-HENRY?
COVER IT! YOU'RE KILLING HIM!
YOU ALL RIGHT, INDY?

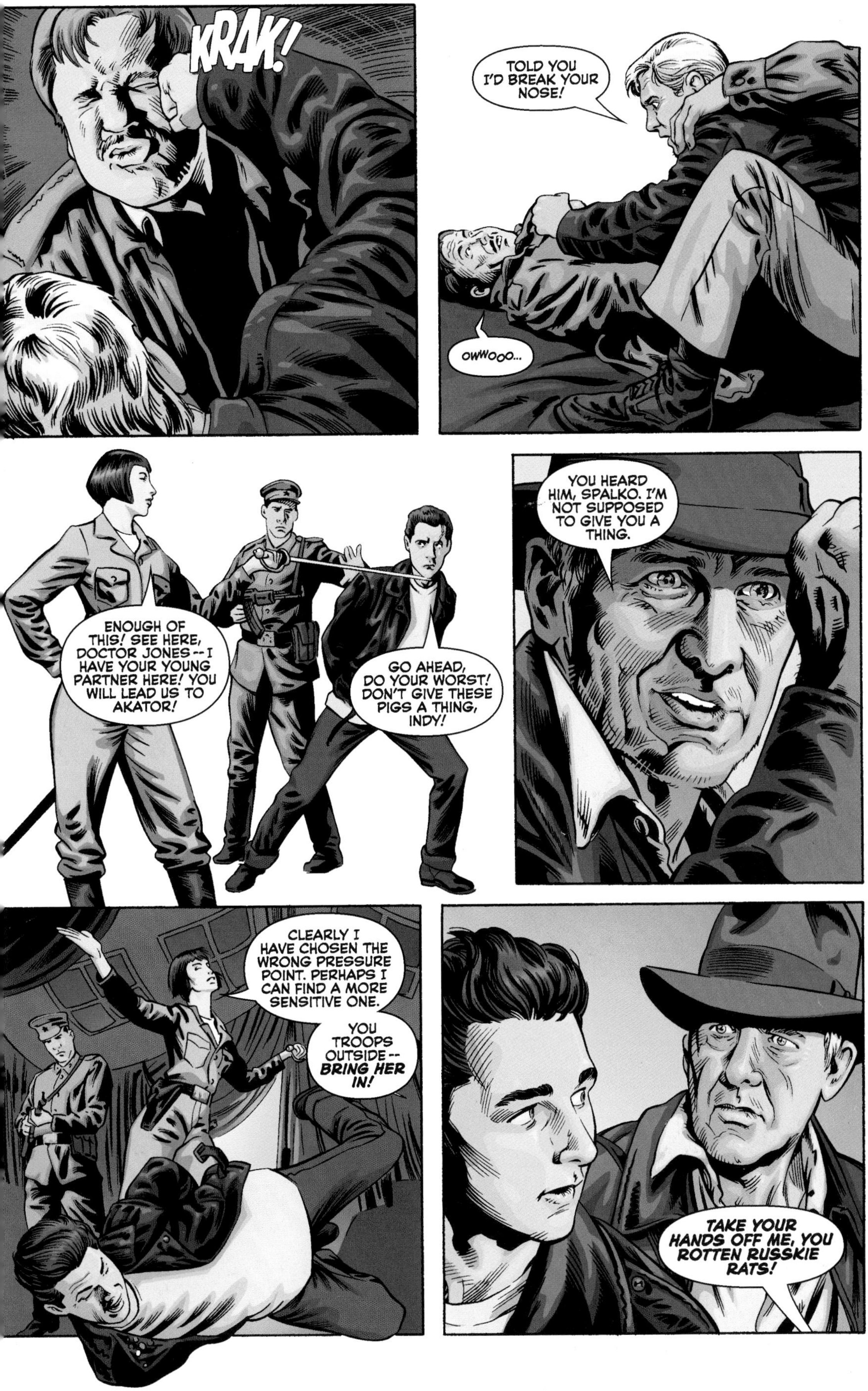
KRAK!
TOLD YOU I'D BREAK YOUR NOSE!
OWWOOO...
ENOUGH OF THIS! SEE HERE, DOCTOR JONES -- I HAVE YOUR YOUNG PARTNER HERE! YOU WILL LEAD US TO AKATOR!
GO AHEAD, DO YOUR WORST! DON'T GIVE THESE PIGS A THING, INDY!
YOU HEARD HIM, SPALKO. I'M NOT SUPPOSED TO GIVE YOU A THING.
CLEARLY I HAVE CHOSEN THE WRONG PRESSURE POINT. PERHAPS I CAN FIND A MORE SENSITIVE ONE.
YOU TROOPS OUTSIDE -- *BRING HER IN!*
TAKE YOUR HANDS OFF ME, YOU ROTTEN RUSSKIE RATS!

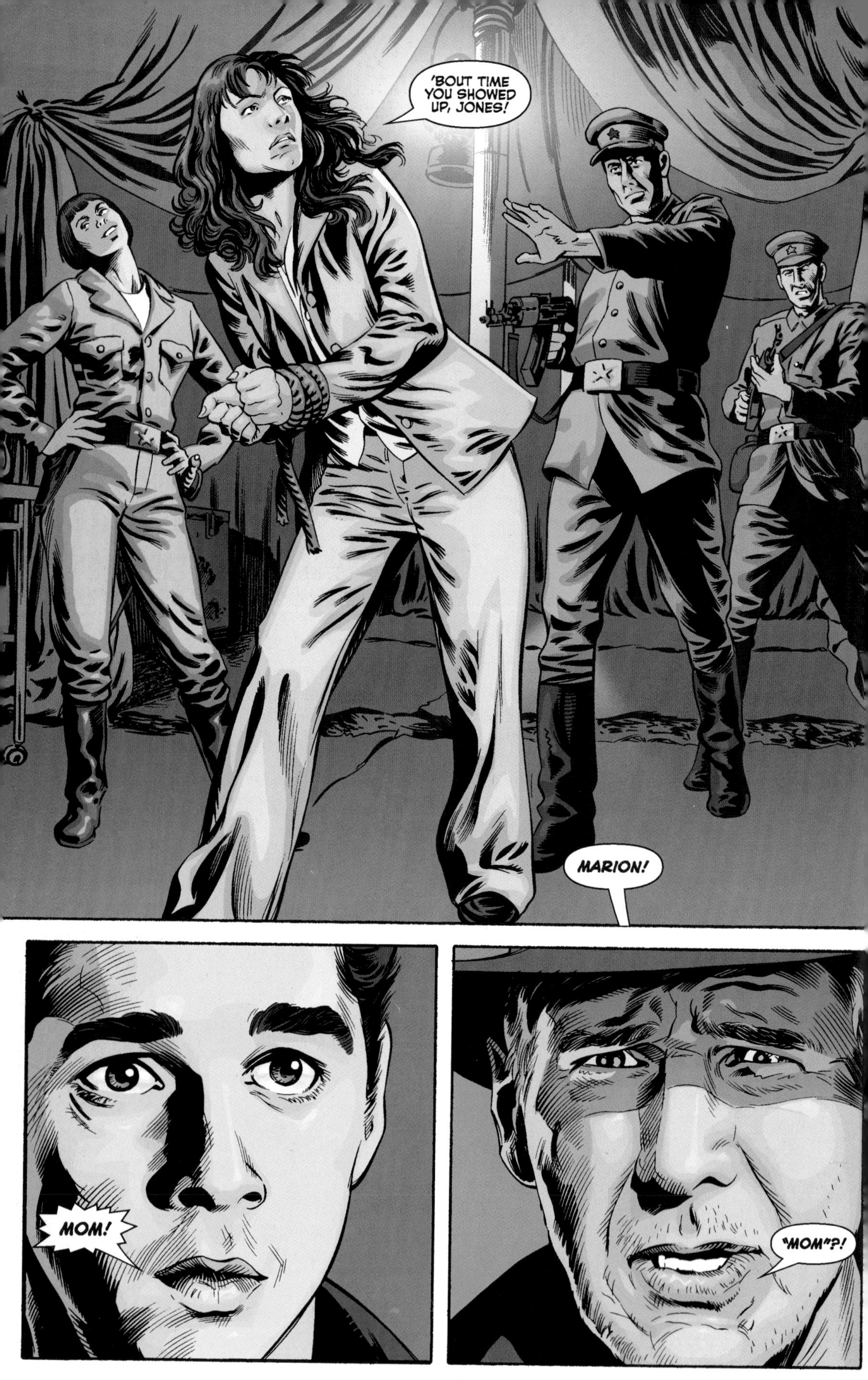
'BOUT TIME YOU SHOWED UP, JONES!
MARION!
MOM!
"MOM"?!

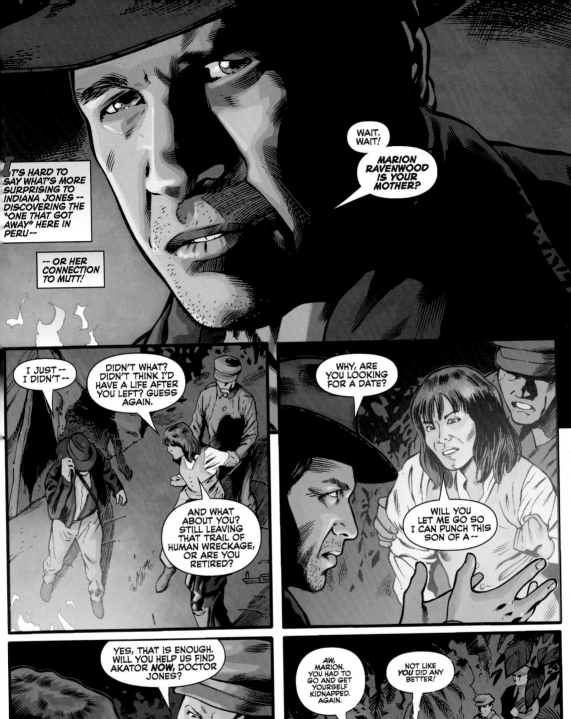

IT'S HARD TO SAY WHAT'S MORE SURPRISING TO INDIANA JONES -- DISCOVERING THE "ONE THAT GOT AWAY" HERE IN PERU --

-- OR HER CONNECTION TO MUTT!

WAIT. WAIT!

MARION RAVENWOOD IS YOUR MOTHER?

I JUST -- I DIDN'T --

DIDN'T WHAT? DIDN'T THINK I'D HAVE A LIFE AFTER YOU LEFT? GUESS AGAIN.

AND WHAT ABOUT YOU? STILL LEAVING THAT TRAIL OF HUMAN WRECKAGE, OR ARE YOU RETIRED?

WHY, ARE YOU LOOKING FOR A DATE?

WILL YOU LET ME GO SO I CAN PUNCH THIS SON OF A --

YES, THAT IS ENOUGH. WILL YOU HELP US FIND AKATOR NOW, DOCTOR JONES?

AW, MARION. YOU HAD TO GO AND GET YOURSELF KIDNAPPED. AGAIN.

NOT LIKE YOU DID ANY BETTER!

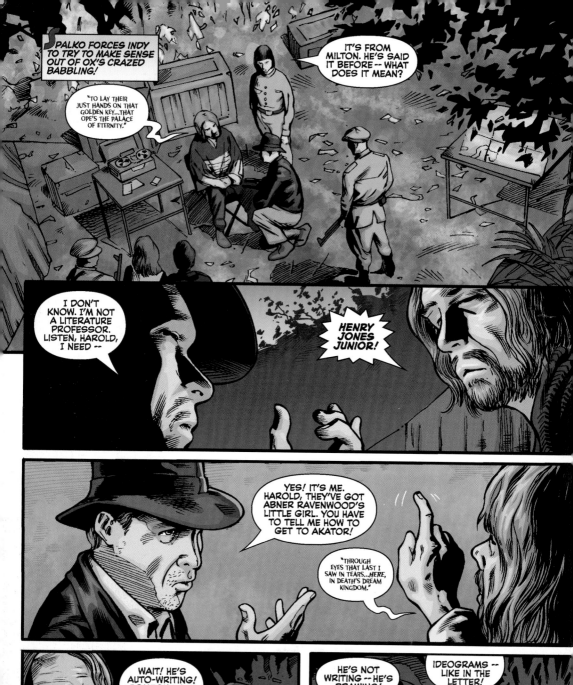

PALKO FORCES INDY TO TRY TO MAKE SENSE OUT OF OX'S CRAZED BABBLING!

IT'S FROM MILTON. HE'S SAID IT BEFORE -- WHAT DOES IT MEAN?

"TO LAY THEIR JUST HANDS ON THAT GOLDEN KEY...THAT OPE'S THE PALACE OF ETERNITY."

I DON'T KNOW. I'M NOT A LITERATURE PROFESSOR. LISTEN, HAROLD, I NEED --

HENRY JONES JUNIOR!

YES! IT'S ME. HAROLD, THEY'VE GOT ABNER RAVENWOOD'S LITTLE GIRL. YOU HAVE TO TELL ME HOW TO GET TO AKATOR!

"THROUGH EYES THAT LAST I SAW IN TEARS...HERE, IN DEATH'S DREAM KINGDOM."

WAIT! HE'S AUTO-WRITING! SOMEONE GET ME SOME PAPER!

HE'S NOT WRITING -- HE'S DRAWING!

IDEOGRAMS -- LIKE IN THE LETTER!

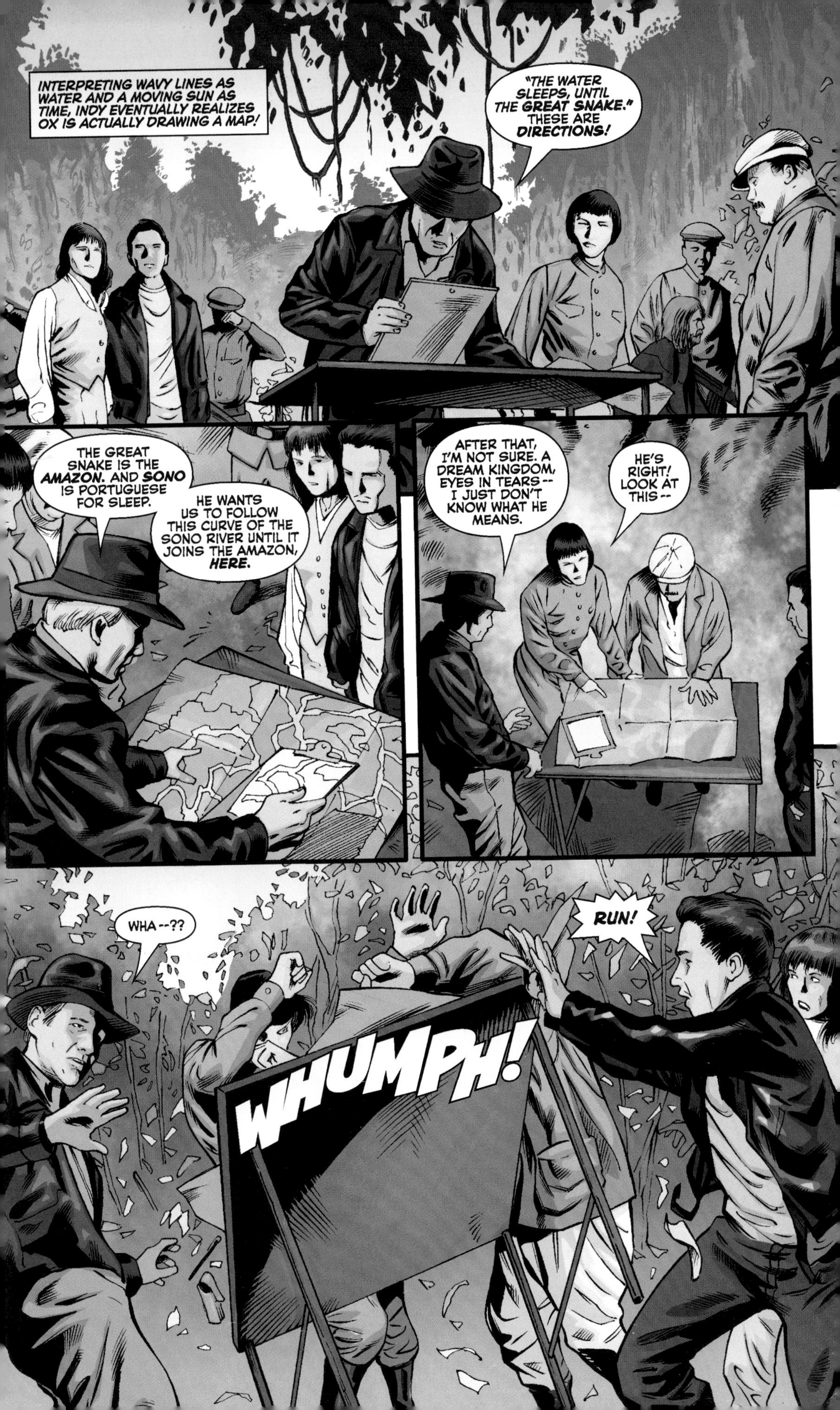
INTERPRETING WAVY LINES AS WATER AND A MOVING SUN AS TIME, INDY EVENTUALLY REALIZES OX IS ACTUALLY DRAWING A MAP!
"THE WATER SLEEPS, UNTIL THE GREAT SNAKE." THESE ARE DIRECTIONS!
THE GREAT SNAKE IS THE AMAZON. AND SONO IS PORTUGUESE FOR SLEEP.
HE WANTS US TO FOLLOW THIS CURVE OF THE SONO RIVER UNTIL IT JOINS THE AMAZON, HERE.
AFTER THAT, I'M NOT SURE. A DREAM KINGDOM, EYES IN TEARS -- I JUST DON'T KNOW WHAT HE MEANS.
HE'S RIGHT! LOOK AT THIS --
WHA --??
RUN!
WHUMPH!

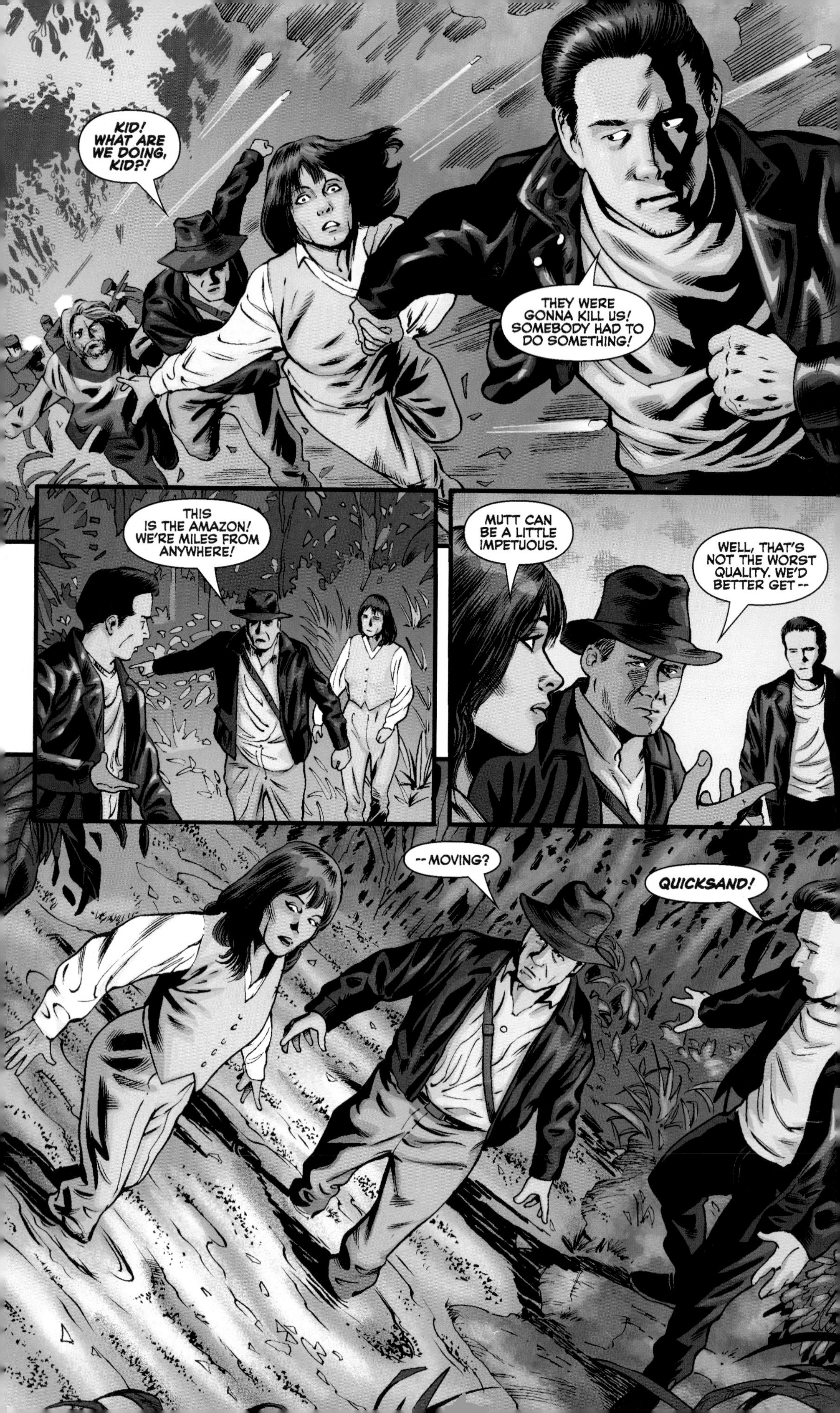
KID! WHAT ARE WE DOING, KID?!
THEY WERE GONNA KILL US! SOMEBODY HAD TO DO SOMETHING!
THIS IS THE AMAZON! WE'RE MILES FROM ANYWHERE!
MUTT CAN BE A LITTLE IMPETUOUS.
WELL, THAT'S NOT THE WORST QUALITY. WE'D BETTER GET --
-- MOVING?
QUICKSAND!

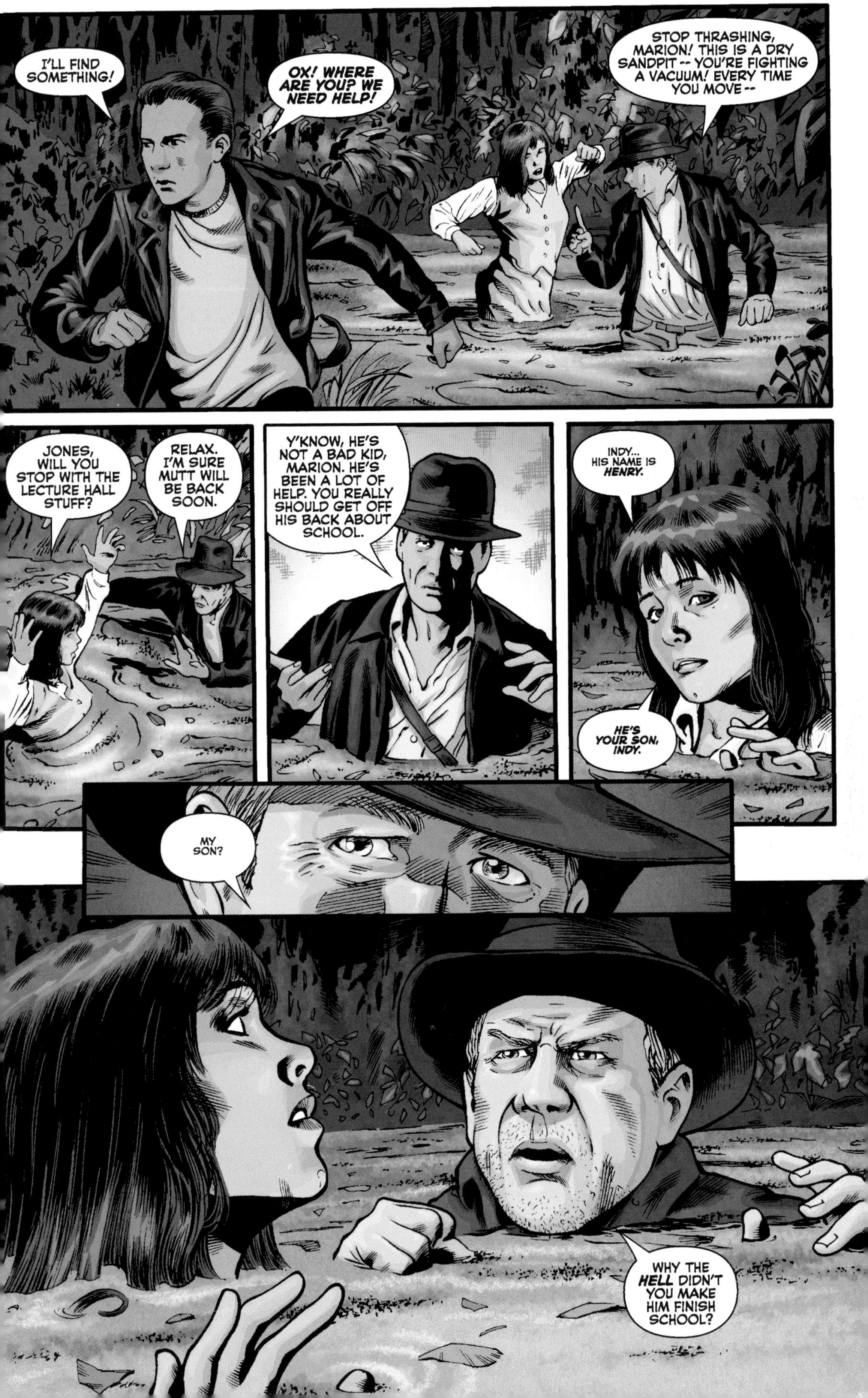
I'LL FIND SOMETHING!
OX! WHERE ARE YOU? WE NEED HELP!
STOP THRASHING, MARION! THIS IS A DRY SANDPIT -- YOU'RE FIGHTING A VACUUM! EVERY TIME YOU MOVE --
JONES, WILL YOU STOP WITH THE LECTURE HALL STUFF?
RELAX. I'M SURE MUTT WILL BE BACK SOON.
Y'KNOW, HE'S NOT A BAD KID, MARION. HE'S BEEN A LOT OF HELP. YOU REALLY SHOULD GET OFF HIS BACK ABOUT SCHOOL.
INDY... HIS NAME IS HENRY.
HE'S YOUR SON, INDY.
MY SON?
WHY THE HELL DIDN'T YOU MAKE HIM FINISH SCHOOL?

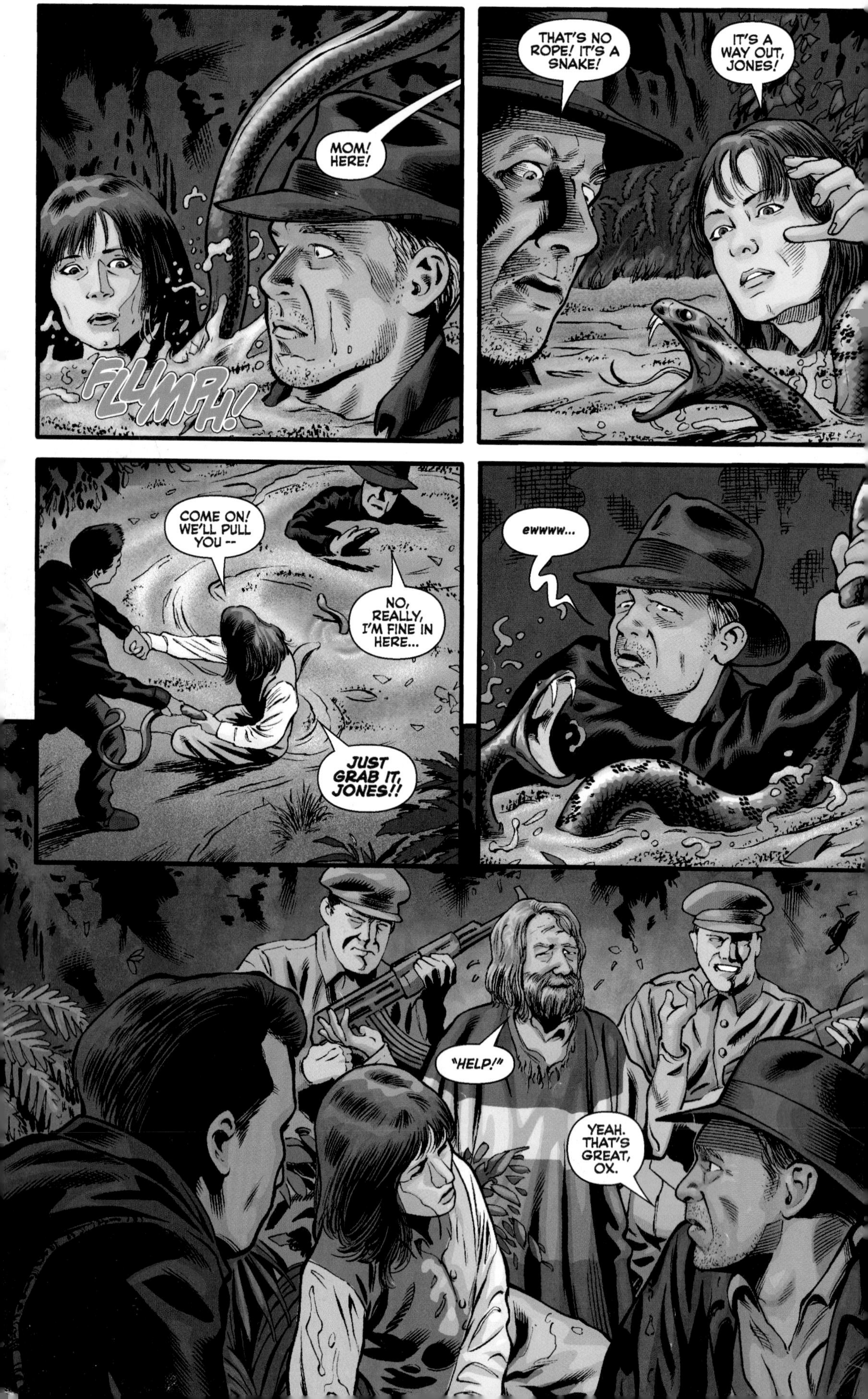
MOM! HERE!
FLUMPH!
THAT'S NO ROPE! IT'S A SNAKE!
IT'S A WAY OUT, JONES!
COME ON! WE'LL PULL YOU --
NO, REALLY, I'M FINE IN HERE...
JUST GRAB IT, JONES!!
ewwww...
"HELP!"
YEAH. THAT'S GREAT, OX.

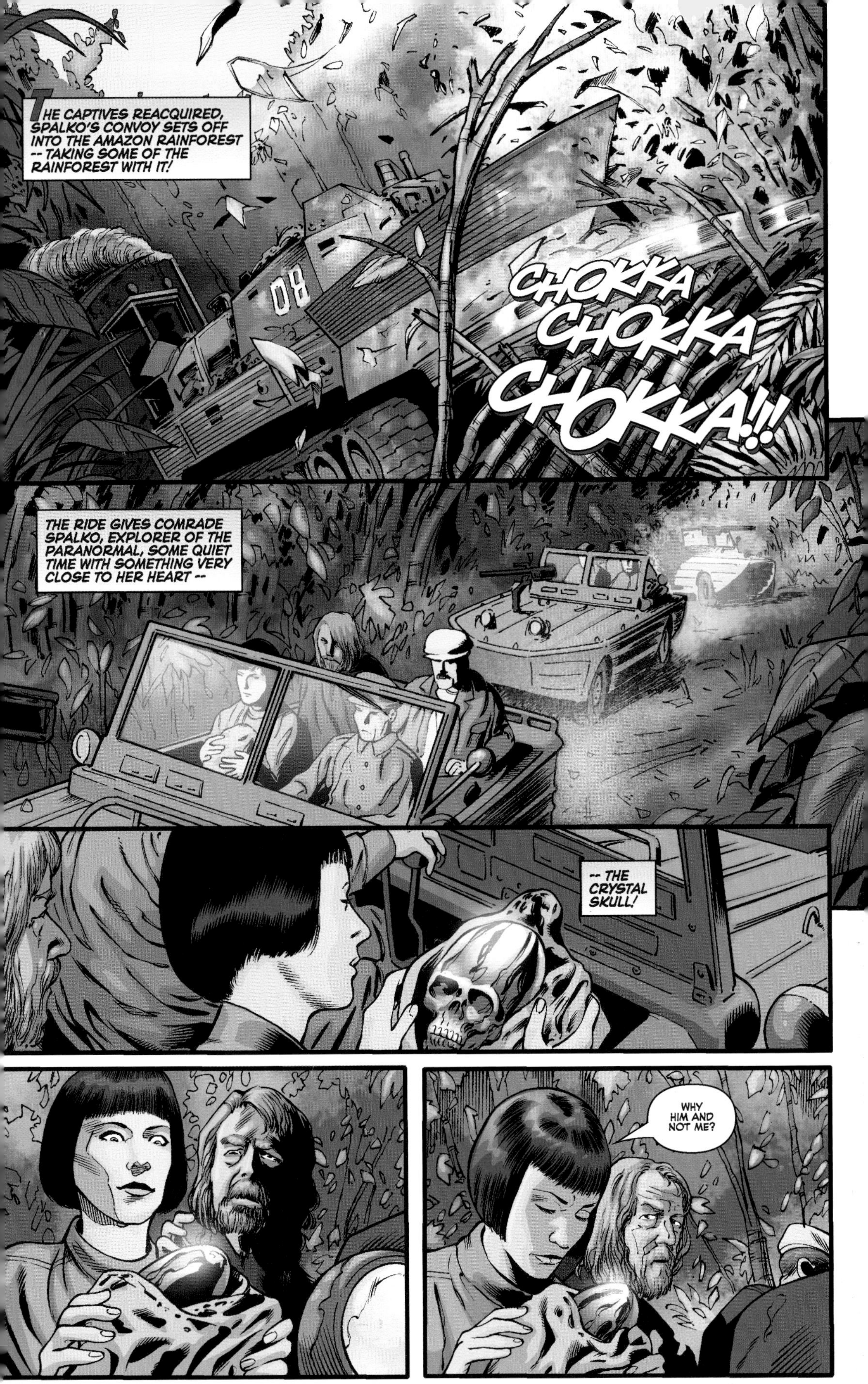
THE CAPTIVES REACQUIRED, SPALKO'S CONVOY SETS OFF INTO THE AMAZON RAINFOREST -- TAKING SOME OF THE RAINFOREST WITH IT!
08
CHOKKA CHOKKA CHOKKA!!!
THE RIDE GIVES COMRADE SPALKO, EXPLORER OF THE PARANORMAL, SOME QUIET TIME WITH SOMETHING VERY CLOSE TO HER HEART --
-- THE CRYSTAL SKULL!
WHY HIM AND NOT ME?

SKULL'S GOT A MIND OF ITS OWN, EH? CHOOSY ABOUT WHO IT TALKS TO.

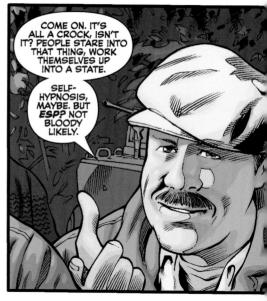

COME ON. IT'S ALL A CROCK, ISN'T IT? PEOPLE STARE INTO THAT THING, WORK THEMSELVES UP INTO A STATE.

SELF-HYPNOSIS, MAYBE. BUT *ESP?* NOT BLOODY LIKELY.

WHY NOT? TELEPATHY ALREADY EXISTS, IN A LESSER DEVELOPED FORM. CONSIDER THE BOND BETWEEN MOTHER AND CHILD.

WE HAVE DONE EXPERIMENTS WITH RABBITS -- WE'VE KILLED THE YOUNG AND SEEN REACTIONS FROM THE MOTHER, MILES AWAY.

LADY, YOU NEED ANOTHER HOBBY!

ALL RIGHT, LET'S SEE IT THEN. I'M THINKING OF A QUESTION. WHAT'S THE ANSWER?

THE ANSWER TO YOUR QUESTION IS --

-- "IF I FEEL THE SLIGHTEST NEED."

MAC RECOILS, REMEMBERING HIS UNSPOKEN QUESTION.

"WOULD SPALKO CUT HIS THROAT WHEN THEY REACHED AKATOR?"

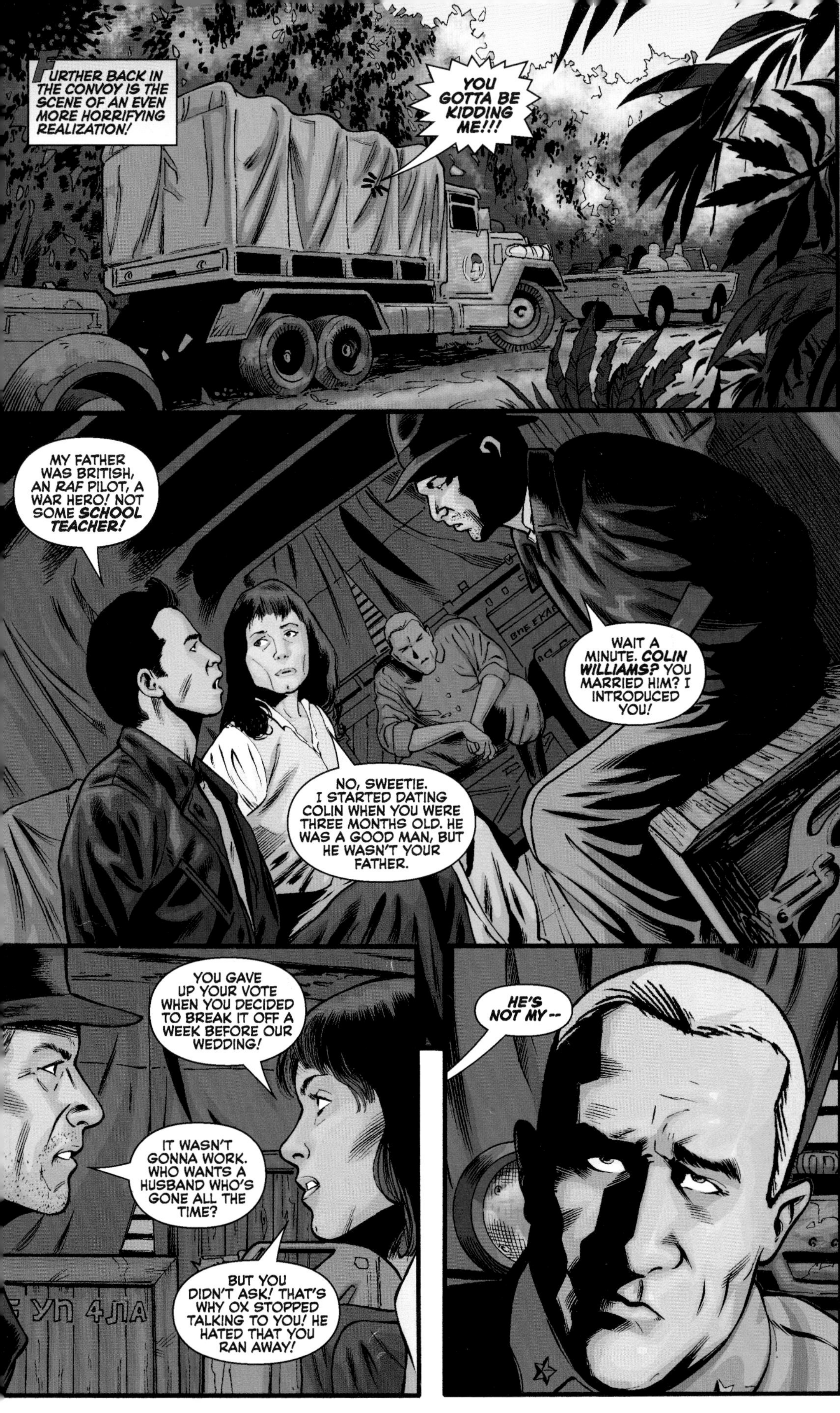
FURTHER BACK IN THE CONVOY IS THE SCENE OF AN EVEN MORE HORRIFYING REALIZATION!
YOU GOTTA BE KIDDING ME!!!
MY FATHER WAS BRITISH, AN RAF PILOT, A WAR HERO! NOT SOME SCHOOL TEACHER!
WAIT A MINUTE. COLIN WILLIAMS? YOU MARRIED HIM? I INTRODUCED YOU!
NO, SWEETIE. I STARTED DATING COLIN WHEN YOU WERE THREE MONTHS OLD. HE WAS A GOOD MAN, BUT HE WASN'T YOUR FATHER.
YOU GAVE UP YOUR VOTE WHEN YOU DECIDED TO BREAK IT OFF A WEEK BEFORE OUR WEDDING!
IT WASN'T GONNA WORK. WHO WANTS A HUSBAND WHO'S GONE ALL THE TIME?
BUT YOU DIDN'T ASK! THAT'S WHY OX STOPPED TALKING TO YOU! HE HATED THAT YOU RAN AWAY!
HE'S NOT MY --

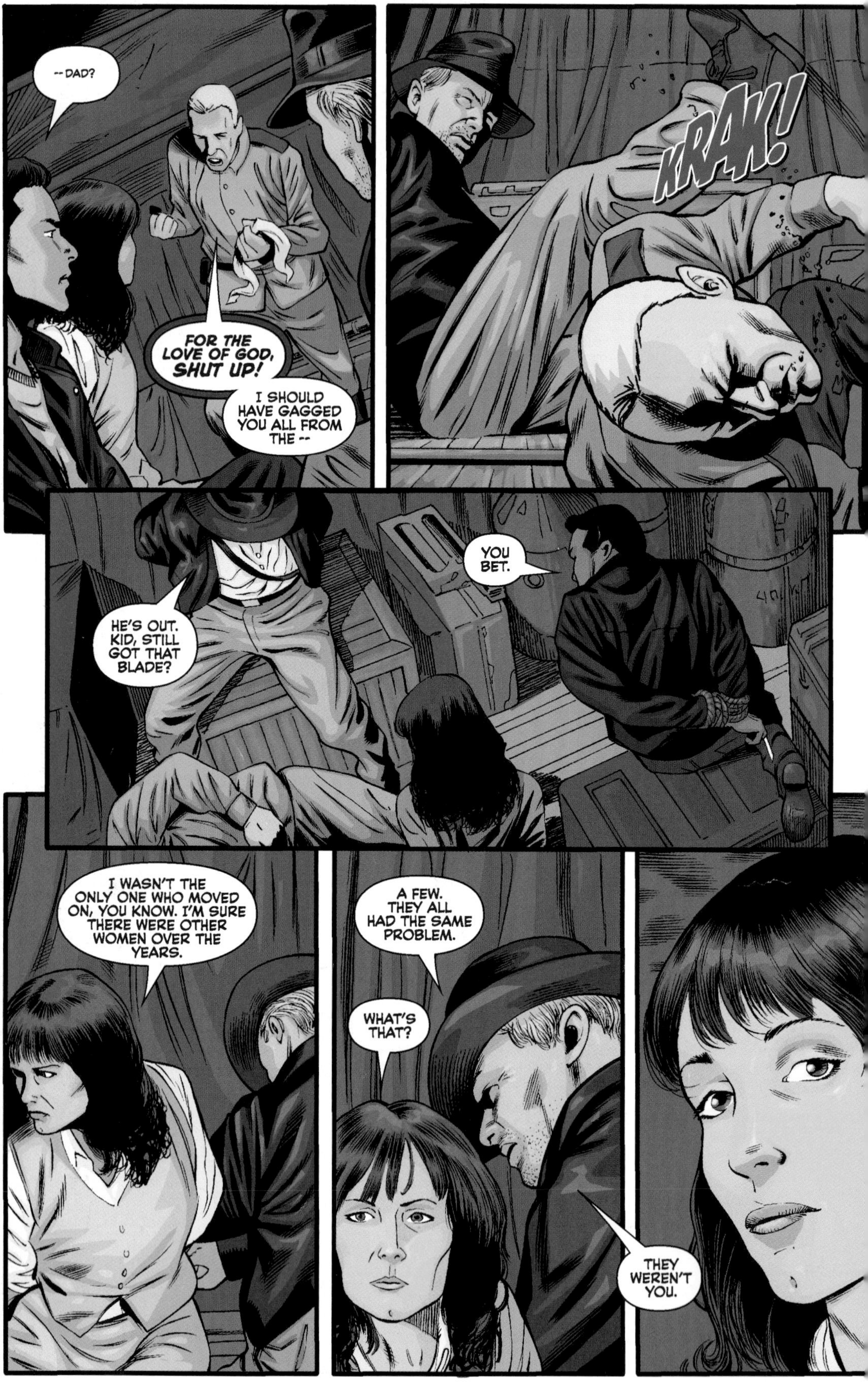
--DAD?
FOR THE LOVE OF GOD, SHUT UP!
I SHOULD HAVE GAGGED YOU ALL FROM THE --
KRAK!
HE'S OUT. KID, STILL GOT THAT BLADE?
YOU BET.
I WASN'T THE ONLY ONE WHO MOVED ON, YOU KNOW. I'M SURE THERE WERE OTHER WOMEN OVER THE YEARS.
A FEW. THEY ALL HAD THE SAME PROBLEM.
WHAT'S THAT?
THEY WEREN'T YOU.

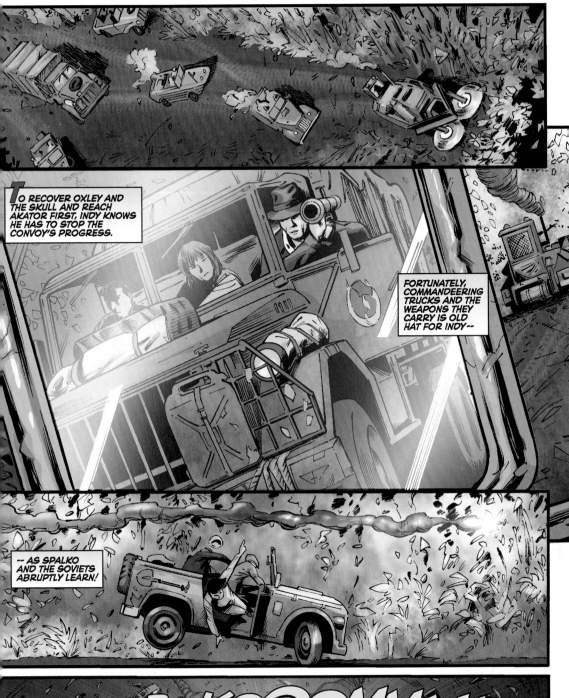

TO RECOVER OXLEY AND THE SKULL AND REACH AKATOR FIRST, INDY KNOWS HE HAS TO STOP THE CONVOY'S PROGRESS.

FORTUNATELY, COMMANDEERING TRUCKS AND THE WEAPONS THEY CARRY IS OLD HAT FOR INDY--

-- AS SPALKO AND THE SOVIETS ABRUPTLY LEARN!

KRA-KOOOMMM!!

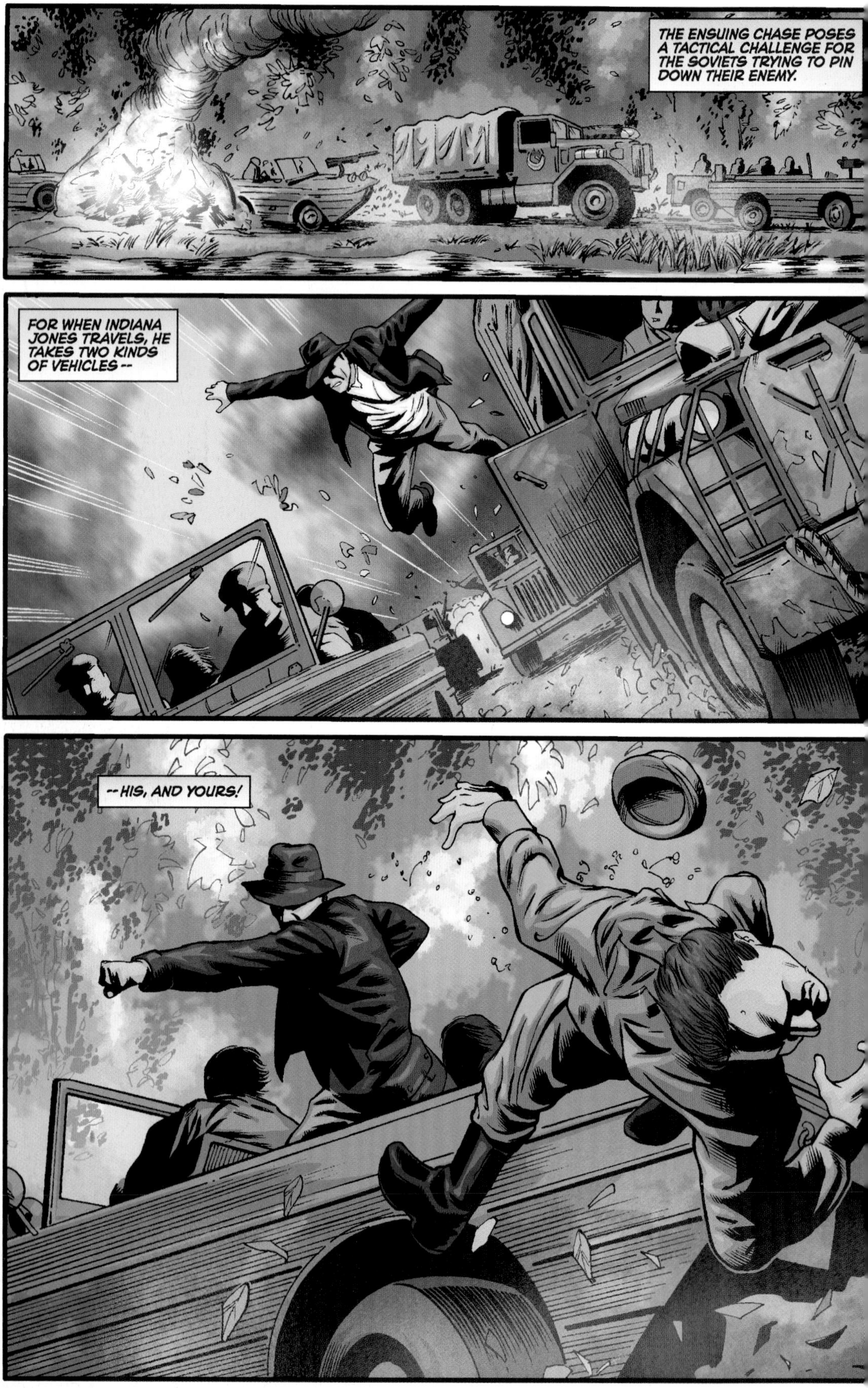
THE ENSUING CHASE POSES A TACTICAL CHALLENGE FOR THE SOVIETS TRYING TO PIN DOWN THEIR ENEMY.
FOR WHEN INDIANA JONES TRAVELS, HE TAKES TWO KINDS OF VEHICLES --
--HIS, AND YOURS!

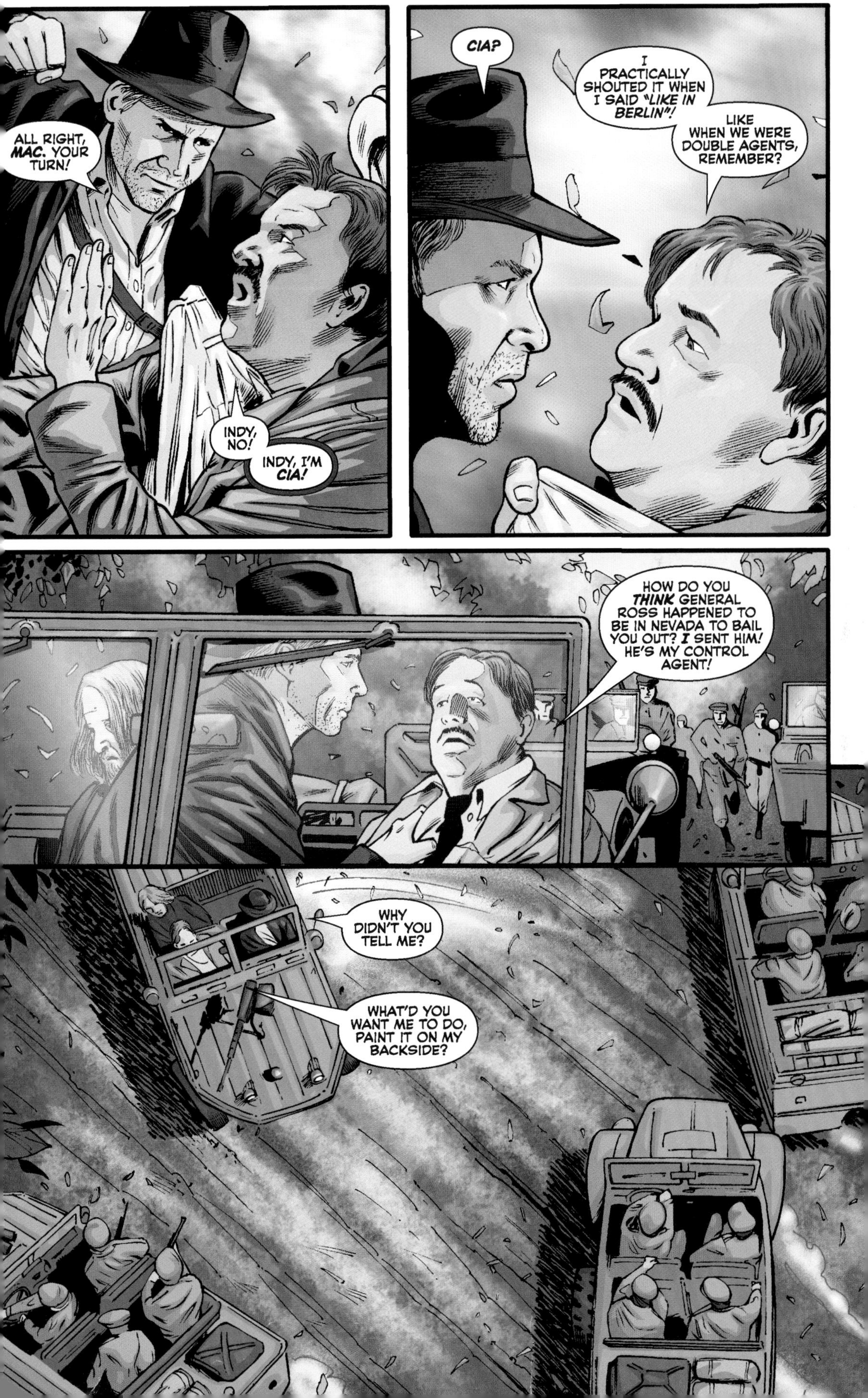
ALL RIGHT, MAC. YOUR TURN!
INDY, NO!
INDY, I'M CIA!
CIA?
I PRACTICALLY SHOUTED IT WHEN I SAID "LIKE IN BERLIN"!
LIKE WHEN WE WERE DOUBLE AGENTS, REMEMBER?
HOW DO YOU THINK GENERAL ROSS HAPPENED TO BE IN NEVADA TO BAIL YOU OUT? I SENT HIM! HE'S MY CONTROL AGENT!
WHY DIDN'T YOU TELL ME?
WHAT'D YOU WANT ME TO DO, PAINT IT ON MY BACKSIDE?

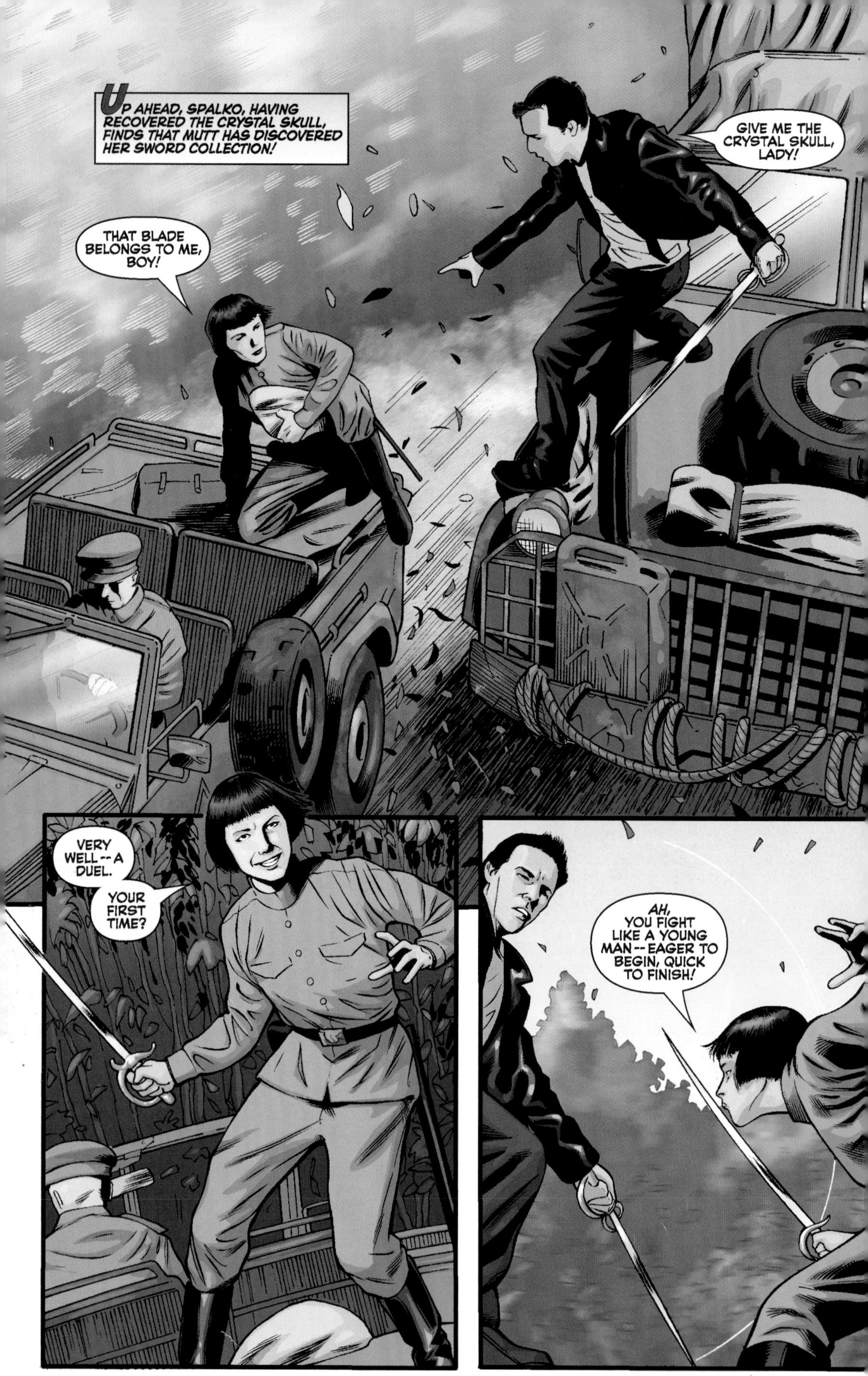
UP AHEAD, SPALKO, HAVING RECOVERED THE CRYSTAL SKULL, FINDS THAT MUTT HAS DISCOVERED HER SWORD COLLECTION!
GIVE ME THE CRYSTAL SKULL, LADY!
THAT BLADE BELONGS TO ME, BOY!
VERY WELL -- A DUEL.
YOUR FIRST TIME?
AH, YOU FIGHT LIKE A YOUNG MAN -- EAGER TO BEGIN, QUICK TO FINISH!

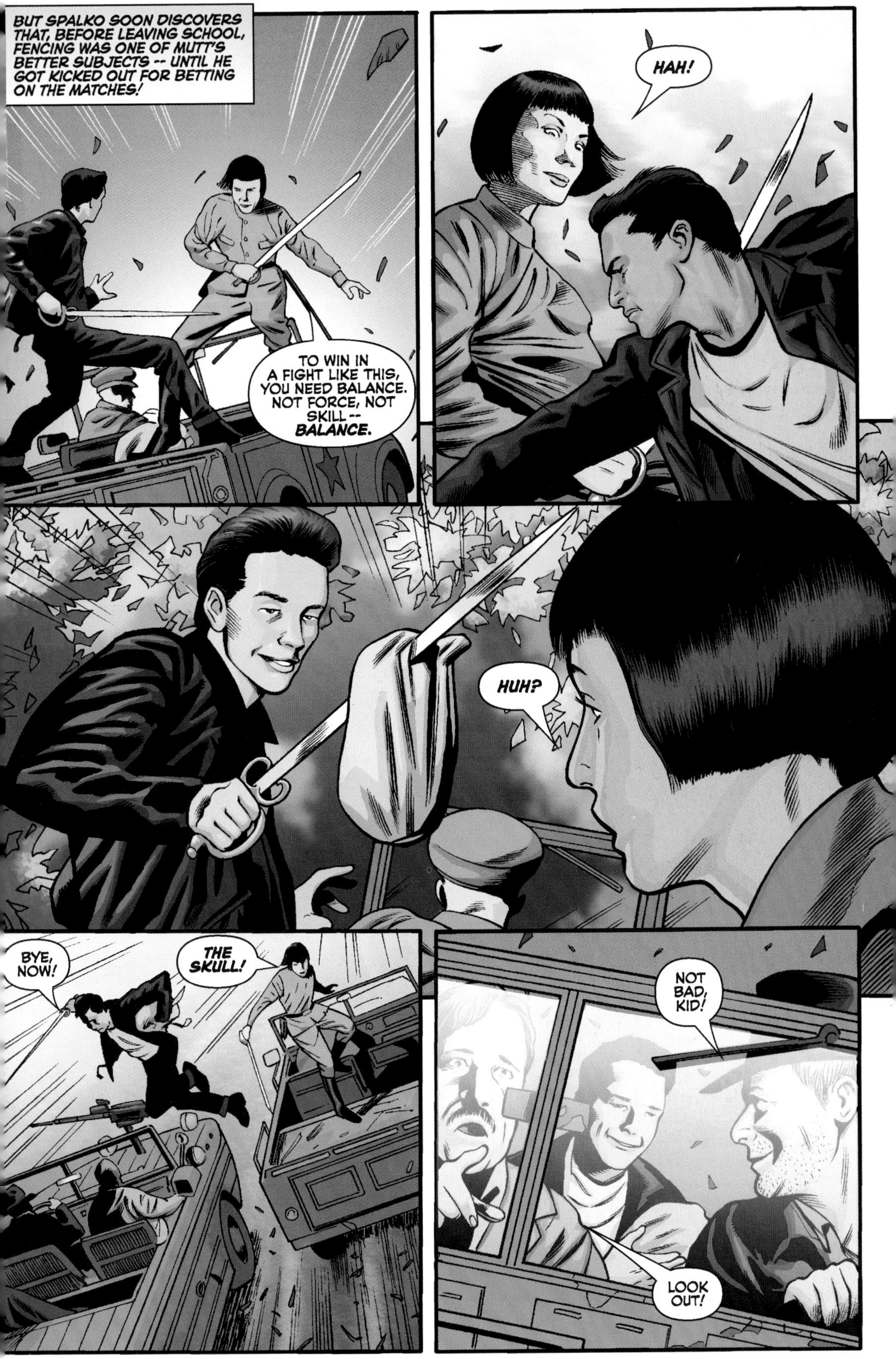
BUT SPALKO SOON DISCOVERS THAT, BEFORE LEAVING SCHOOL, FENCING WAS ONE OF MUTT'S BETTER SUBJECTS -- UNTIL HE GOT KICKED OUT FOR BETTING ON THE MATCHES!
TO WIN IN A FIGHT LIKE THIS, YOU NEED BALANCE. NOT FORCE, NOT SKILL -- BALANCE.
HAH!
HUH?
BYE, NOW!
THE SKULL!
NOT BAD, KID!
LOOK OUT!

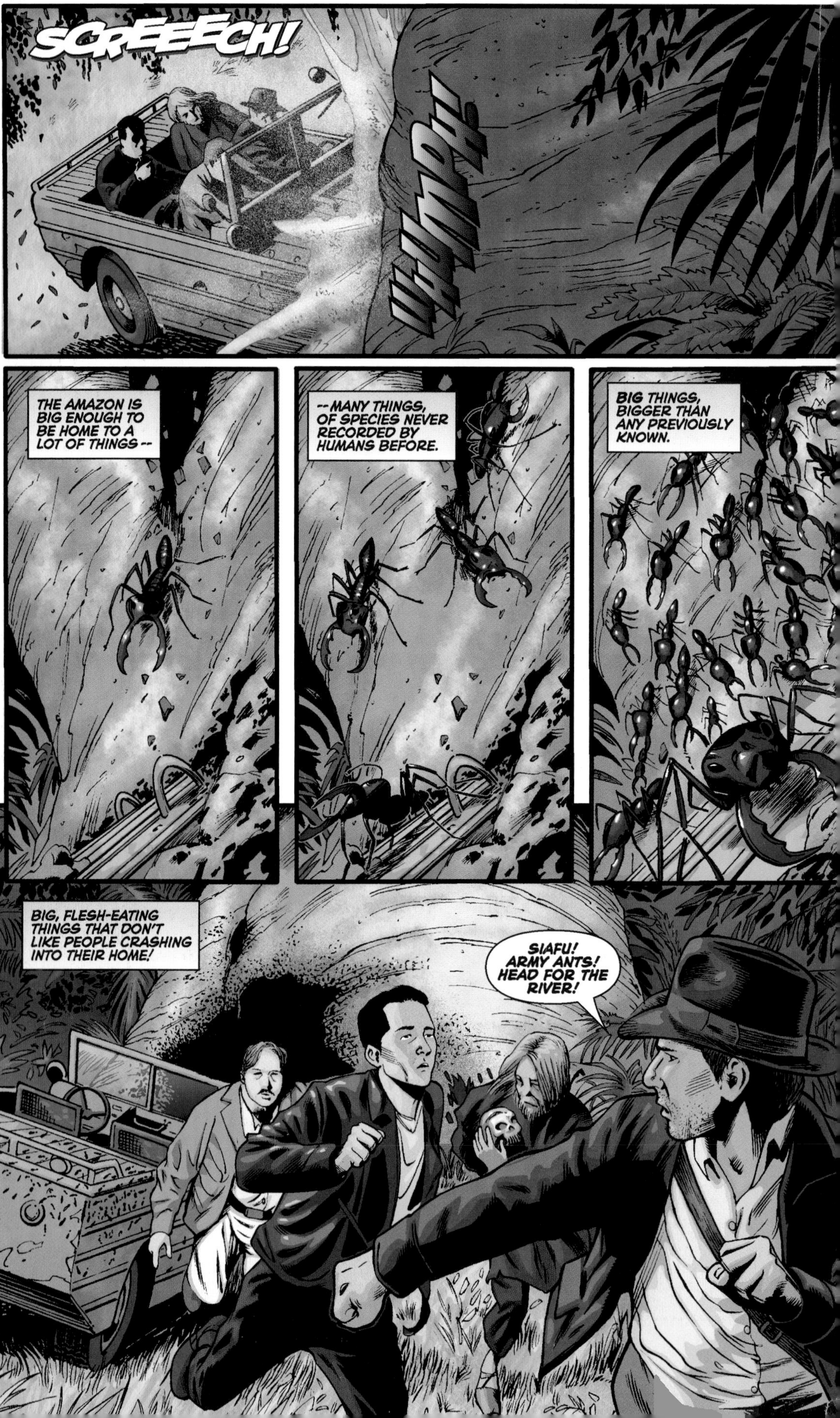
SCREEEECH!
WHUMP!
THE AMAZON IS BIG ENOUGH TO BE HOME TO A LOT OF THINGS --
-- MANY THINGS, OF SPECIES NEVER RECORDED BY HUMANS BEFORE.
BIG THINGS, BIGGER THAN ANY PREVIOUSLY KNOWN.
BIG, FLESH-EATING THINGS THAT DON'T LIKE PEOPLE CRASHING INTO THEIR HOME!
SIAFU! ARMY ANTS! HEAD FOR THE RIVER!

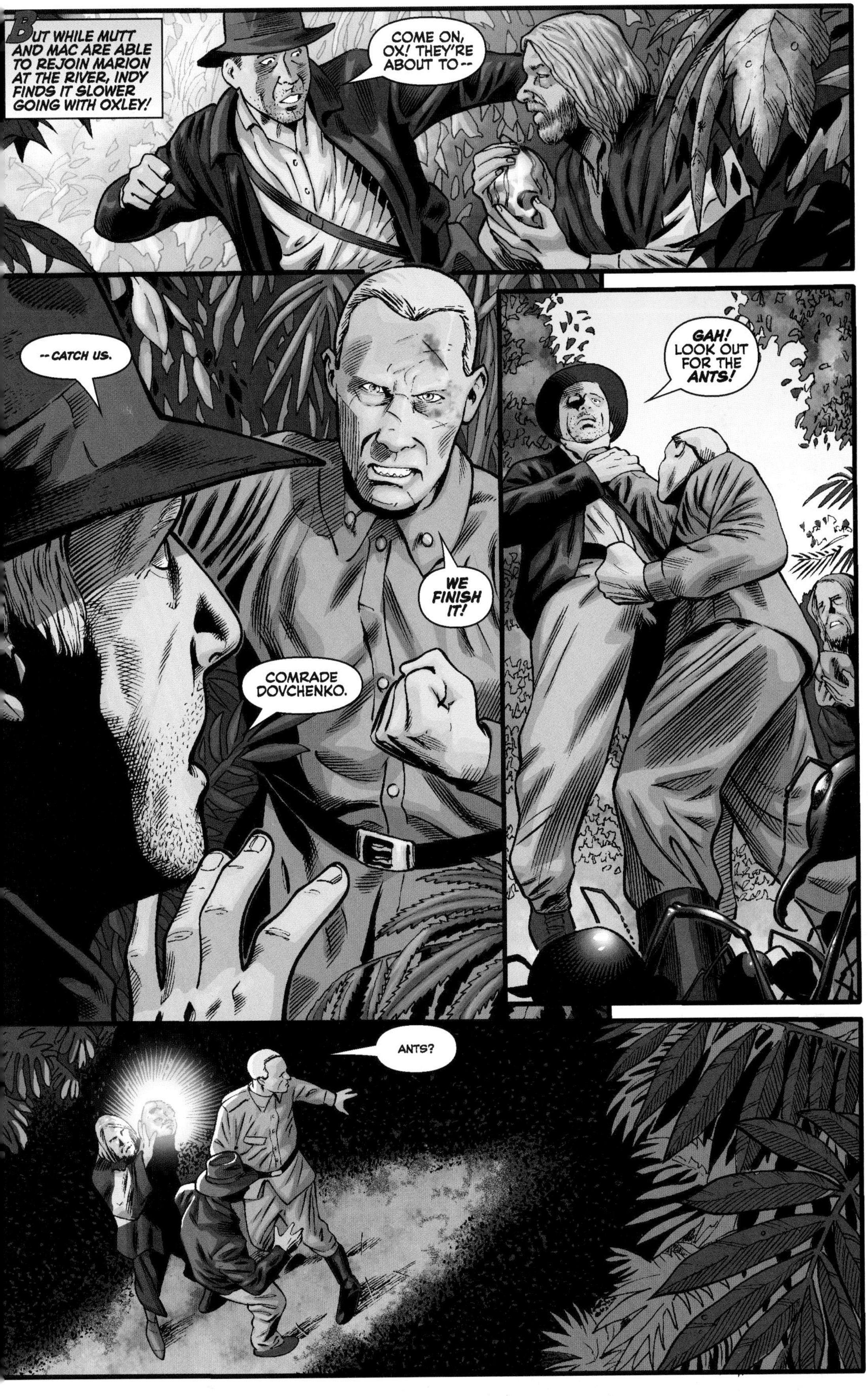
BUT WHILE MUTT AND MAC ARE ABLE TO REJOIN MARION AT THE RIVER, INDY FINDS IT SLOWER GOING WITH OXLEY!
COME ON, OX! THEY'RE ABOUT TO --
-- CATCH US.
WE FINISH IT!
COMRADE DOVCHENKO.
GAH! LOOK OUT FOR THE ANTS!
ANTS?

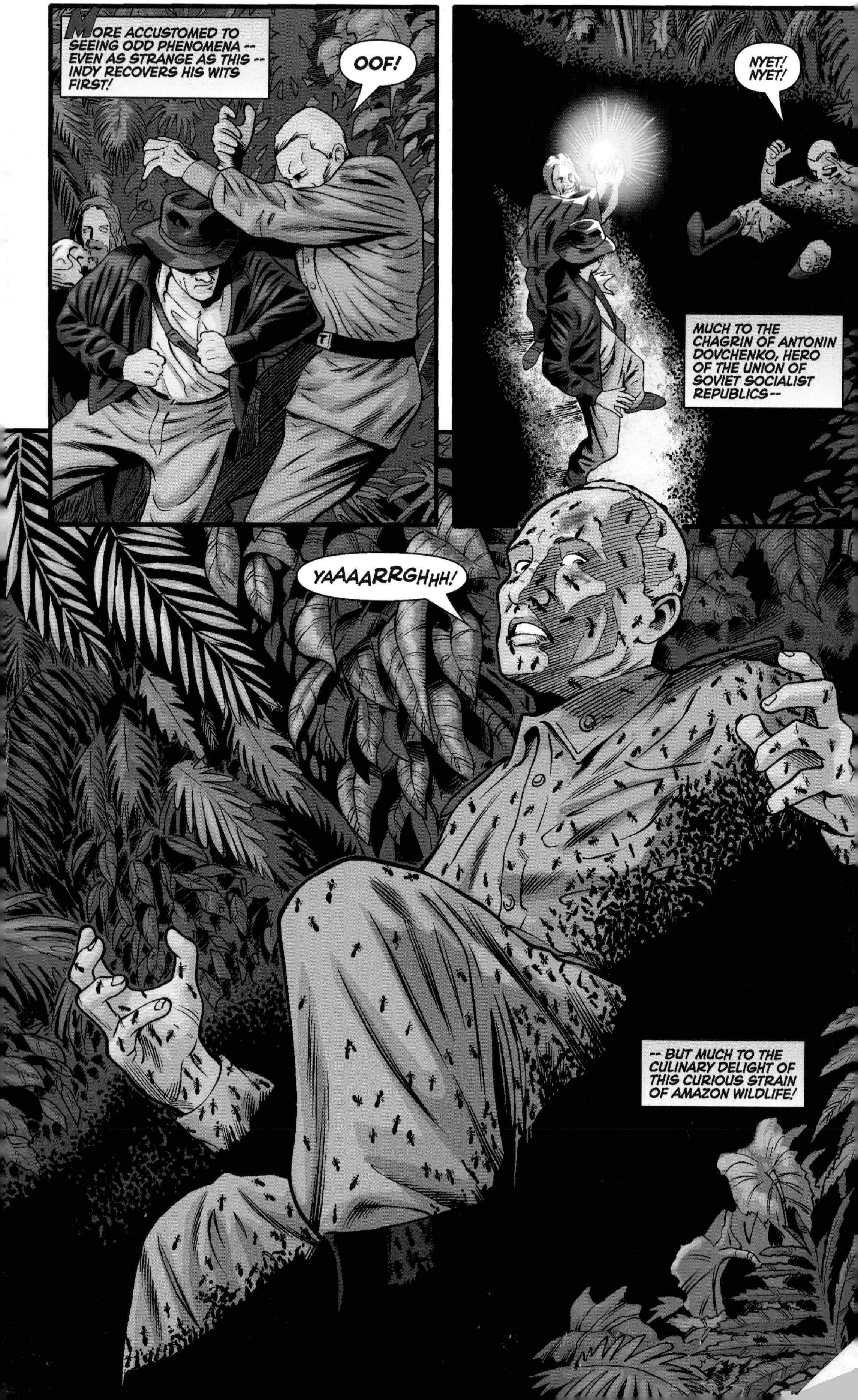
MORE ACCUSTOMED TO SEEING ODD PHENOMENA -- EVEN AS STRANGE AS THIS -- INDY RECOVERS HIS WITS FIRST!
OOF!
NYET! NYET!
MUCH TO THE CHAGRIN OF ANTONIN DOVCHENKO, HERO OF THE UNION OF SOVIET SOCIALIST REPUBLICS --
YAAAARRGHHH!
-- BUT MUCH TO THE CULINARY DELIGHT OF THIS CURIOUS STRAIN OF AMAZON WILDLIFE!

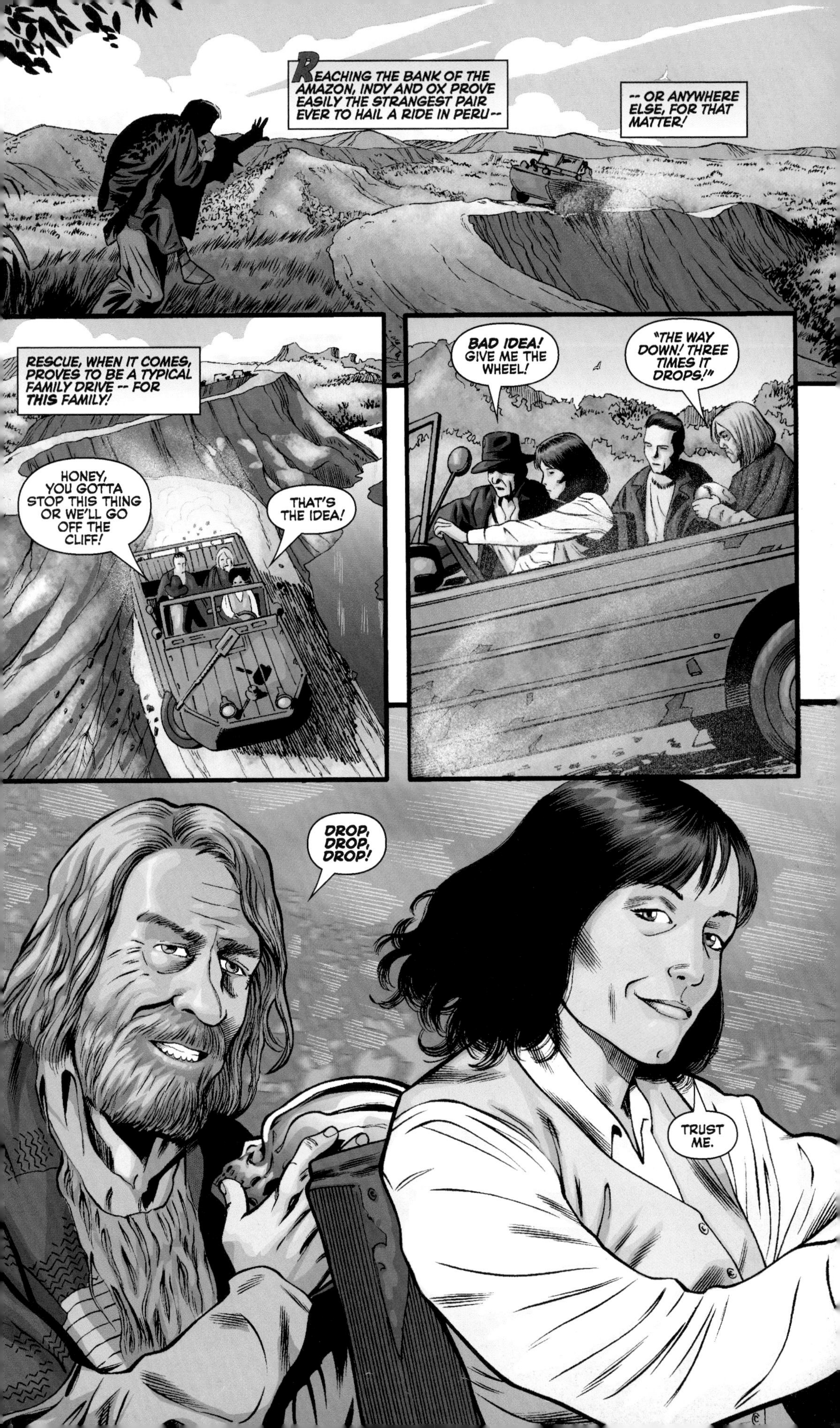
REACHING THE BANK OF THE AMAZON, INDY AND OX PROVE EASILY THE STRANGEST PAIR EVER TO HAIL A RIDE IN PERU--
-- OR ANYWHERE ELSE, FOR THAT MATTER!
RESCUE, WHEN IT COMES, PROVES TO BE A TYPICAL FAMILY DRIVE -- FOR THIS FAMILY!
HONEY, YOU GOTTA STOP THIS THING OR WE'LL GO OFF THE CLIFF!
THAT'S THE IDEA!
BAD IDEA! GIVE ME THE WHEEL!
"THE WAY DOWN! THREE TIMES IT DROPS!"
DROP, DROP, DROP!
TRUST ME.

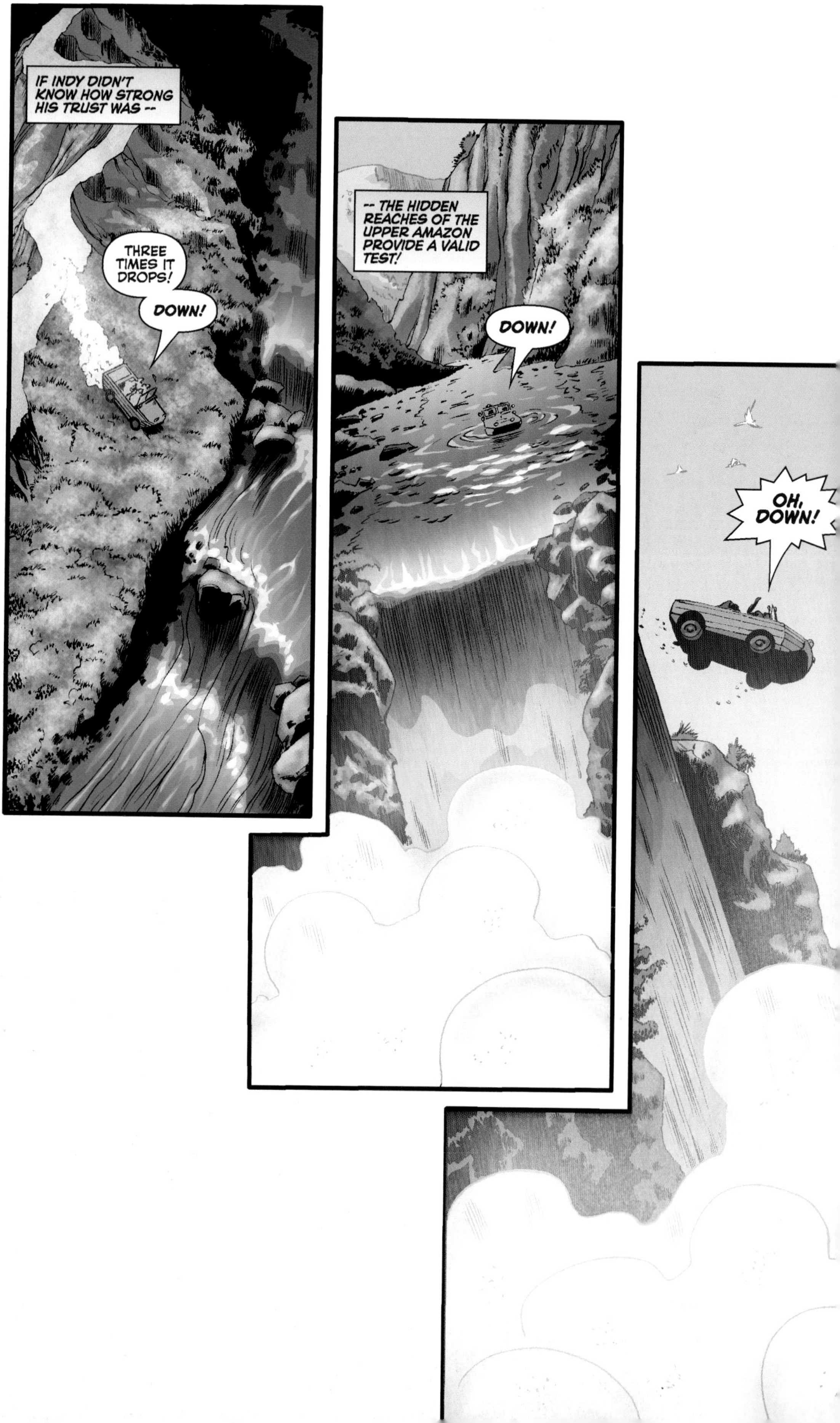
IF INDY DIDN'T KNOW HOW STRONG HIS TRUST WAS --
THREE TIMES IT DROPS!
DOWN!
-- THE HIDDEN REACHES OF THE UPPER AMAZON PROVIDE A VALID TEST!
DOWN!
OH, DOWN!

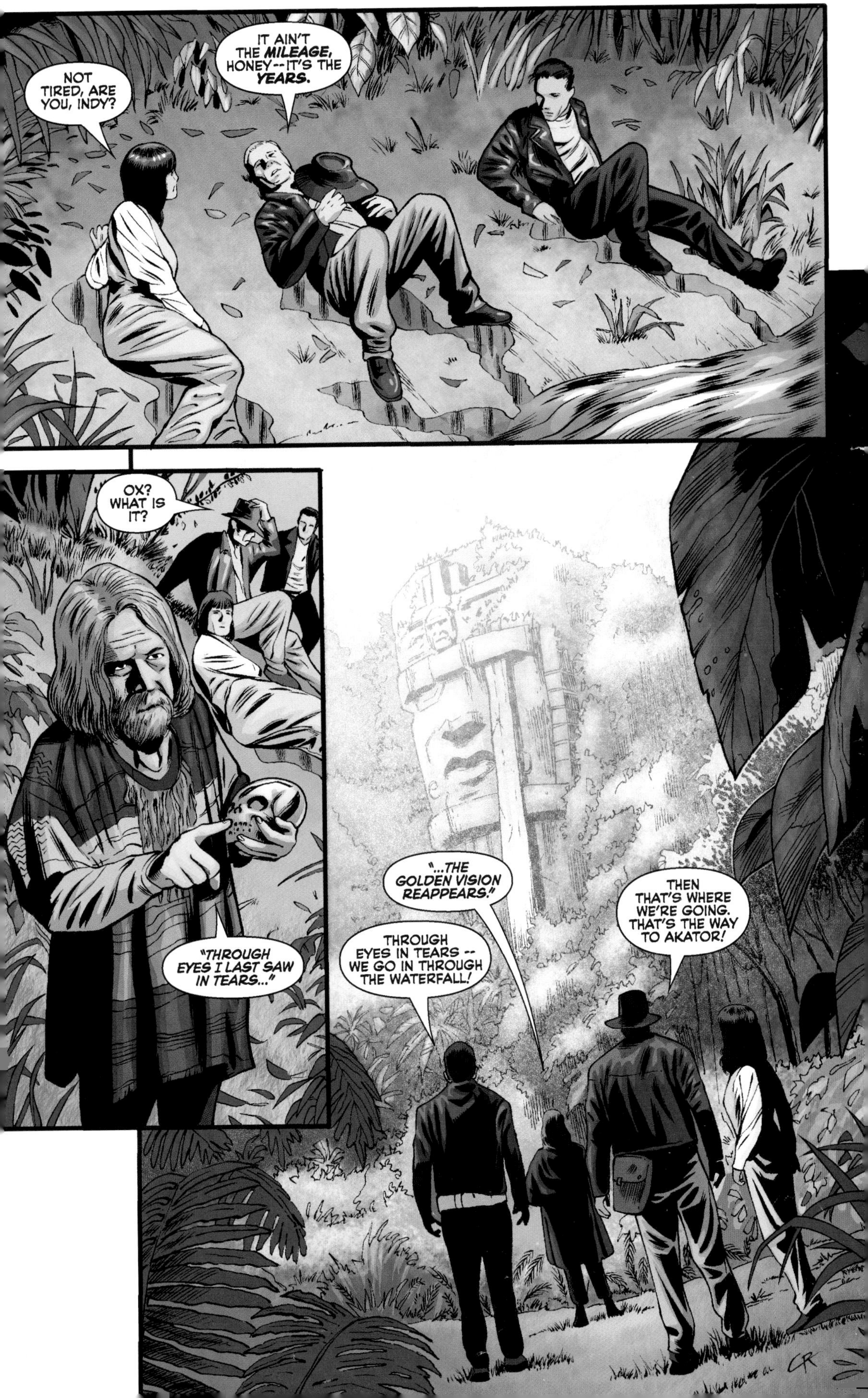
NOT TIRED, ARE YOU, INDY?
IT AIN'T THE *MILEAGE,* HONEY--IT'S THE *YEARS.*
OX? WHAT IS IT?
"THROUGH EYES I LAST SAW IN TEARS..."
"...THE GOLDEN VISION REAPPEARS."
THROUGH EYES IN TEARS -- WE GO IN THROUGH THE WATERFALL!
THEN THAT'S WHERE WE'RE GOING. THAT'S THE WAY TO AKATOR!

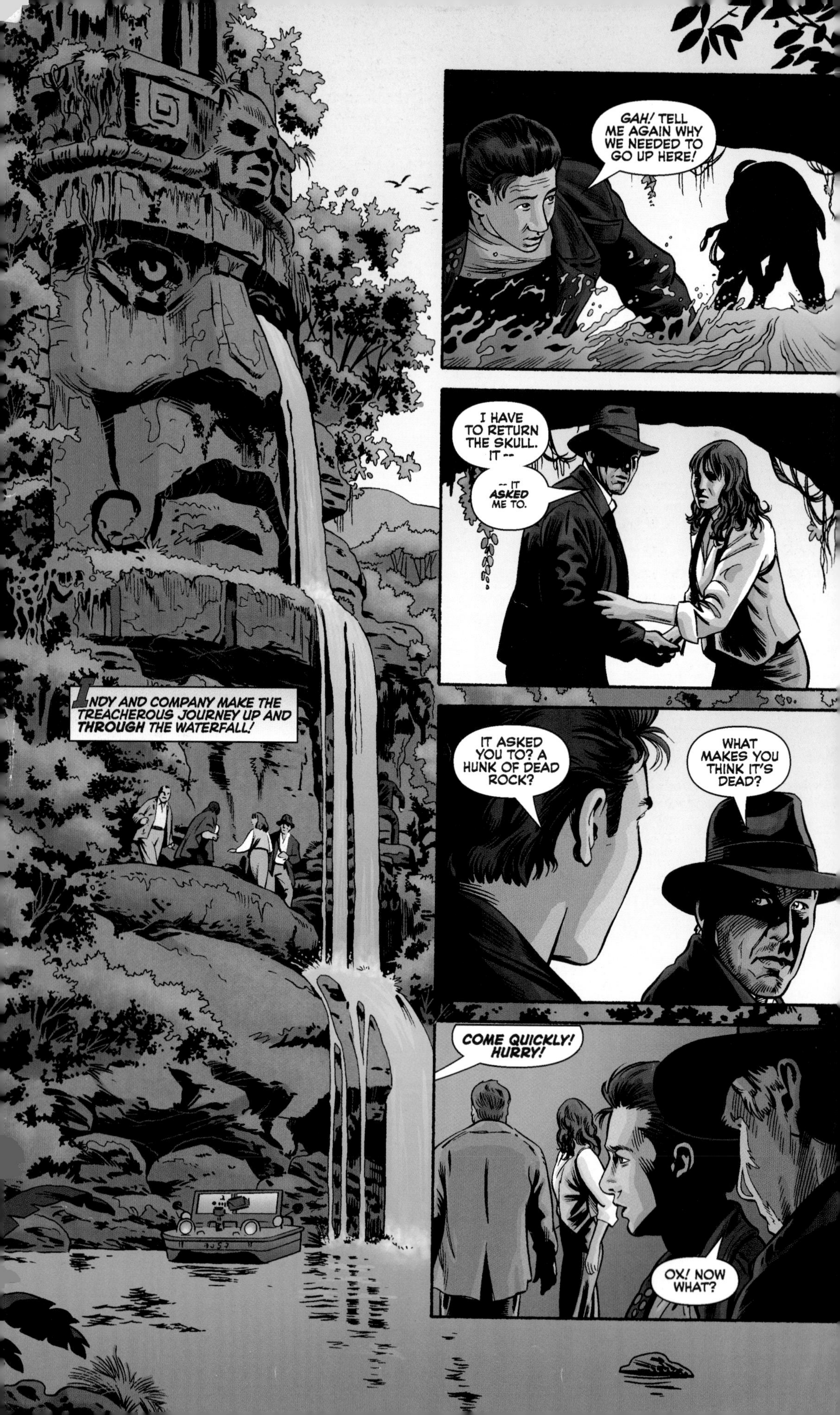
INDY AND COMPANY MAKE THE TREACHEROUS JOURNEY UP AND THROUGH THE WATERFALL!
GAH! TELL ME AGAIN WHY WE NEEDED TO GO UP HERE!
I HAVE TO RETURN THE SKULL. IT --
-- IT ASKED ME TO.
IT ASKED YOU TO? A HUNK OF DEAD ROCK?
WHAT MAKES YOU THINK IT'S DEAD?
COME QUICKLY! HURRY!
OX! NOW WHAT?

OXLEY SHOWS INDY WHAT HE FOUND HERE ON HIS FIRST VISIT -- AN ARCHAEOLOGIST'S DREAM. A GRAPHIC RECORD --

OH...

-- OF A HISTORY BEFORE HISTORY!

HOW OLD ARE THESE PAINTINGS?

MESOLITHIC. POSSIBLY SIX, EIGHT THOUSAND YEARS?

THESE DEPICT THE UGHA -- OLDEST OF THE CULTURES HERE.

BUT SOMEBODY NEW CAME. *FROM ABOVE.*

THIRTEEN OF THEM. THEY TAUGHT THE UGHA -- DOMESTICATED ANIMALS, IRRIGATION.

ALWAYS A GROUP, ALWAYS STANDING IN A CIRCLE. AND ALL WITH SKULLS LIKE THE ONE WE FOUND.

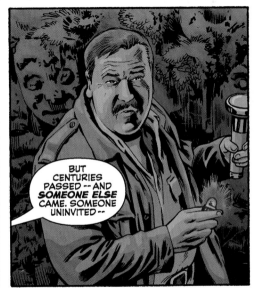

BUT CENTURIES PASSED -- AND *SOMEONE ELSE* CAME. SOMEONE UNINVITED --

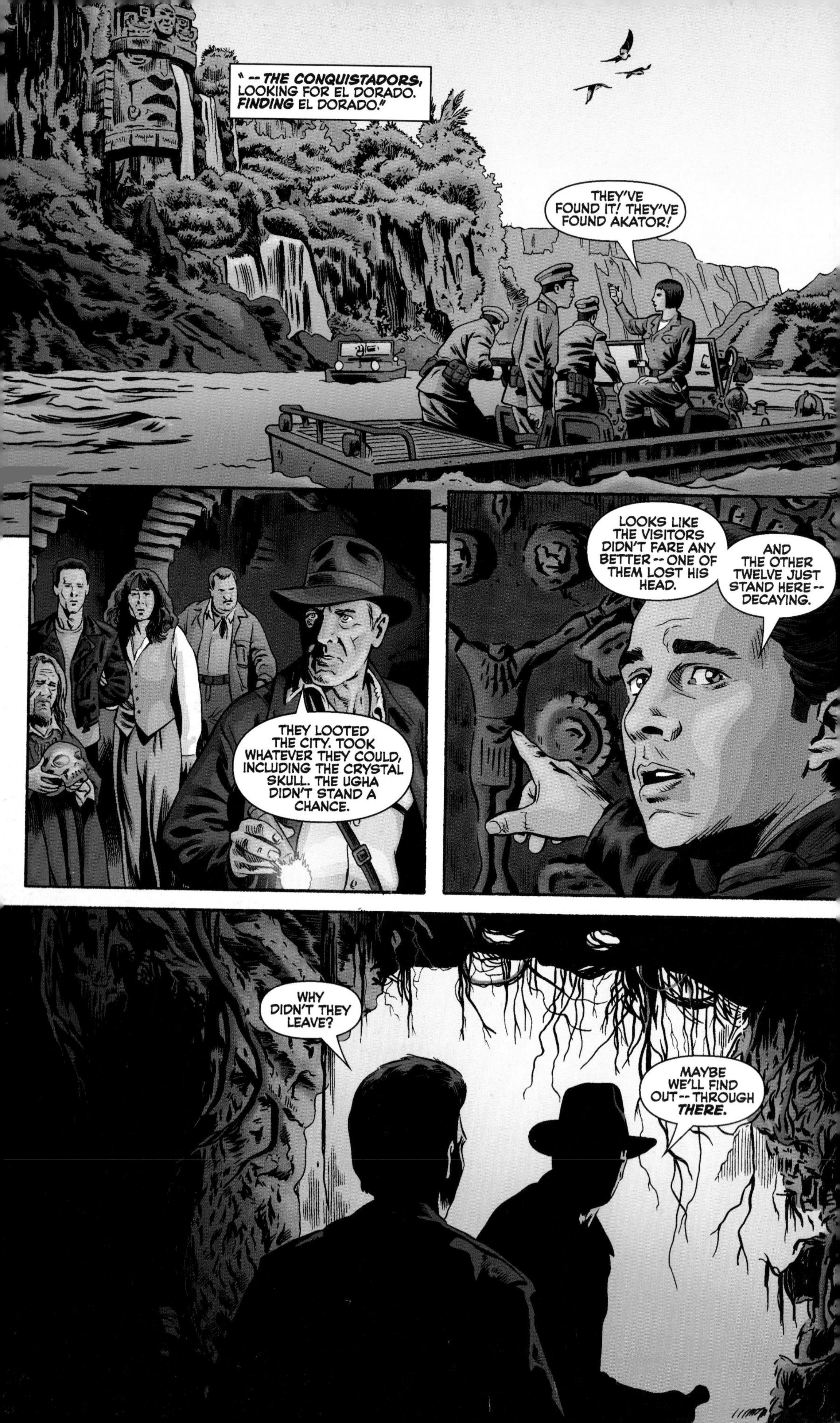
"--THE CONQUISTADORS, LOOKING FOR EL DORADO. FINDING EL DORADO."
THEY'VE FOUND IT! THEY'VE FOUND AKATOR!
THEY LOOTED THE CITY. TOOK WHATEVER THEY COULD, INCLUDING THE CRYSTAL SKULL. THE UGHA DIDN'T STAND A CHANCE.
LOOKS LIKE THE VISITORS DIDN'T FARE ANY BETTER--ONE OF THEM LOST HIS HEAD.
AND THE OTHER TWELVE JUST STAND HERE--DECAYING.
WHY DIDN'T THEY LEAVE?
MAYBE WE'LL FIND OUT--THROUGH THERE.

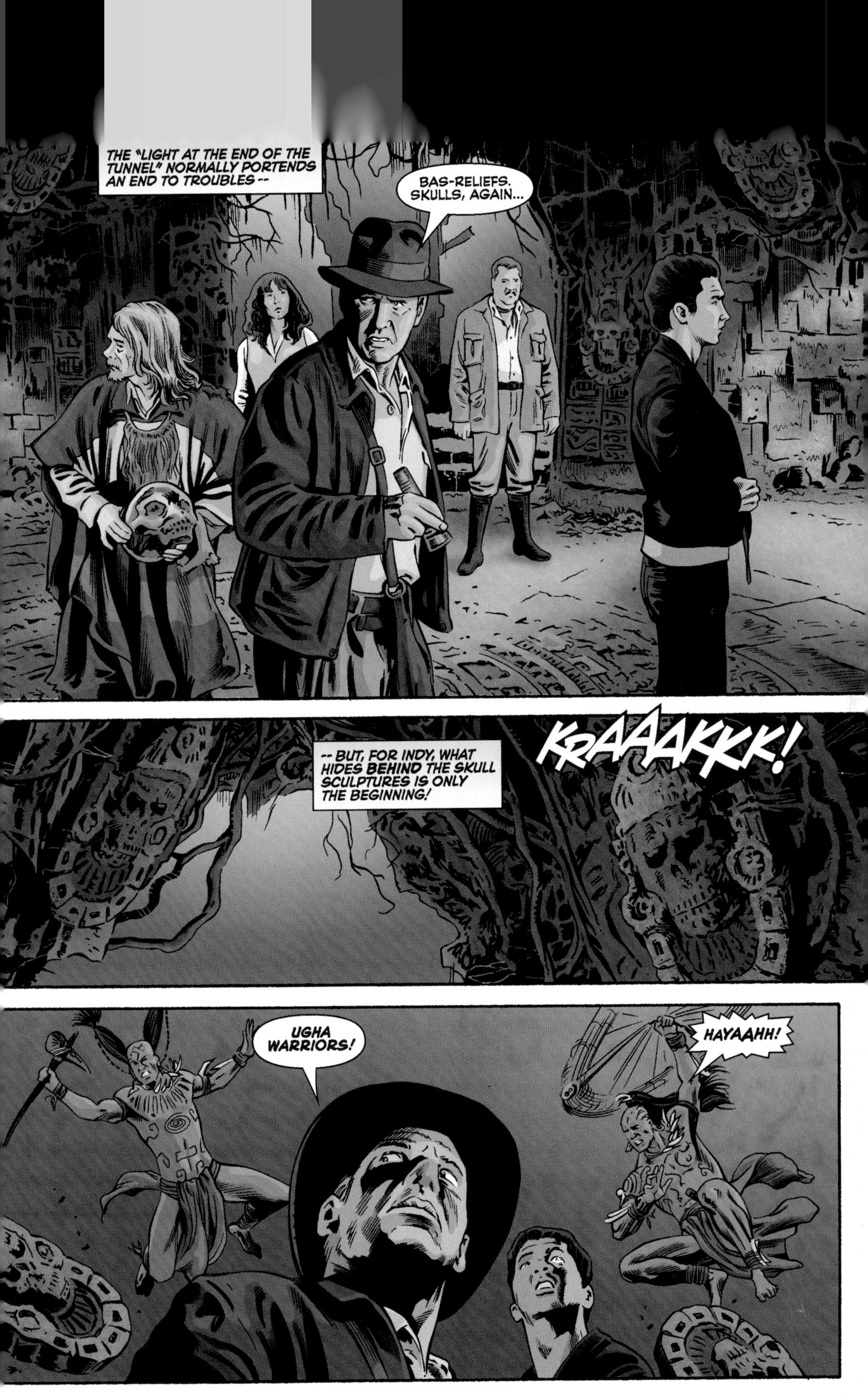
THE "LIGHT AT THE END OF THE TUNNEL" NORMALLY PORTENDS AN END TO TROUBLES --
BAS-RELIEFS. SKULLS, AGAIN...
-- BUT, FOR INDY, WHAT HIDES BEHIND THE SKULL SCULPTURES IS ONLY THE BEGINNING!
KRAAAKKK!
UGHA WARRIORS!
HAYAAHH!

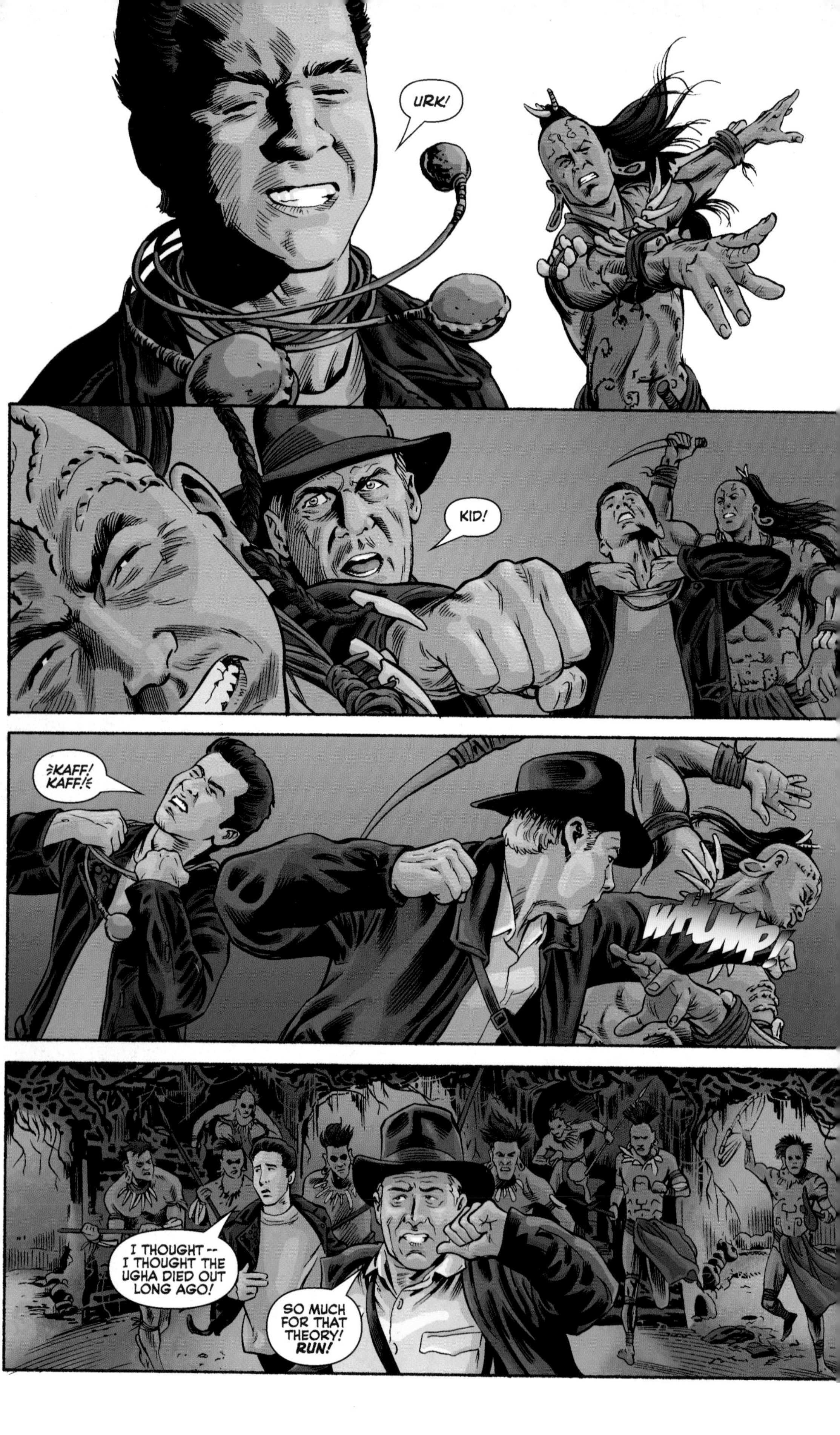
URK!
KID!
KAFF! KAFF!
WHUMP!
I THOUGHT -- I THOUGHT THE UGHA DIED OUT LONG AGO!
SO MUCH FOR THAT THEORY! RUN!

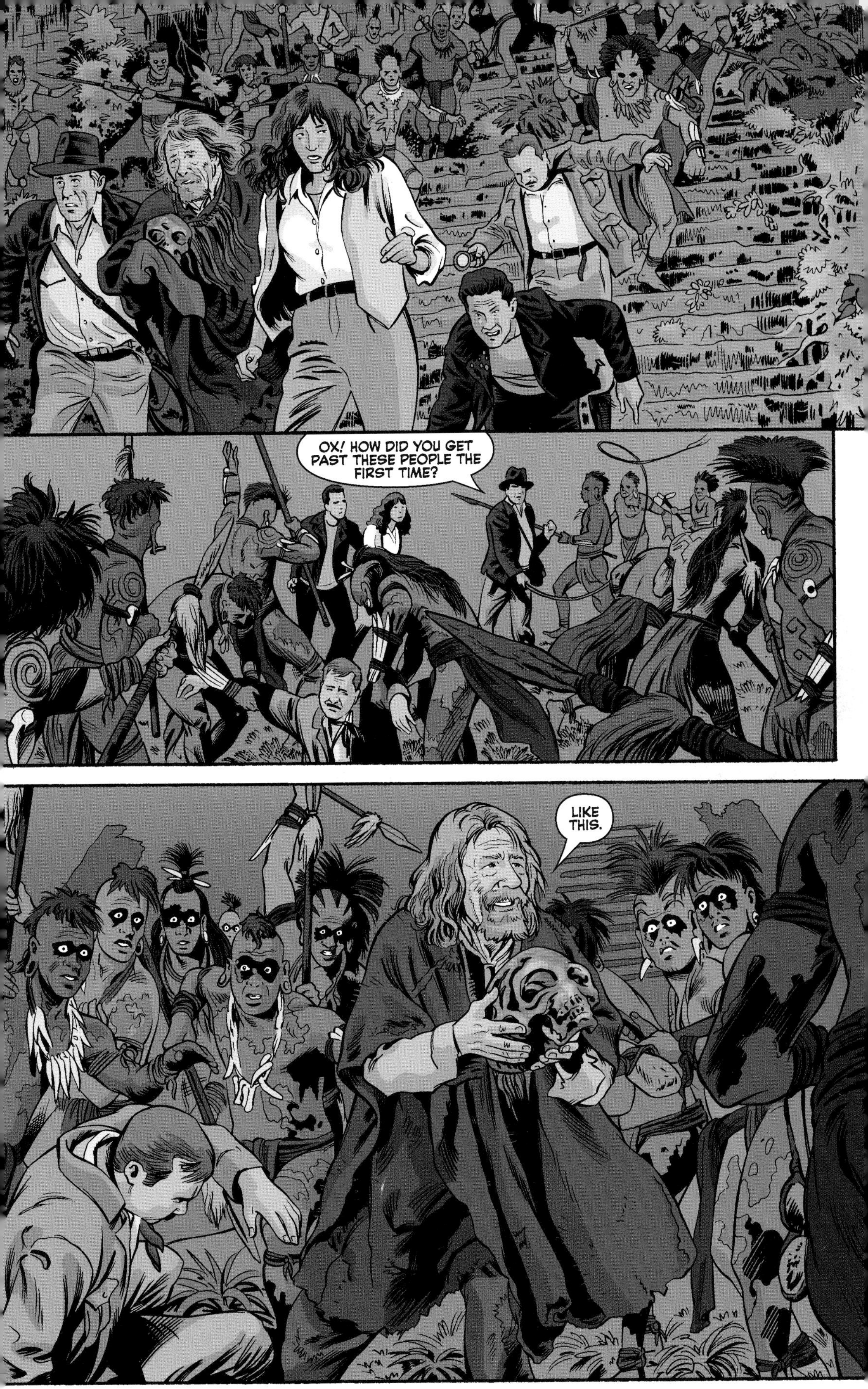
OX! HOW DID YOU GET PAST THESE PEOPLE THE FIRST TIME?
LIKE THIS.

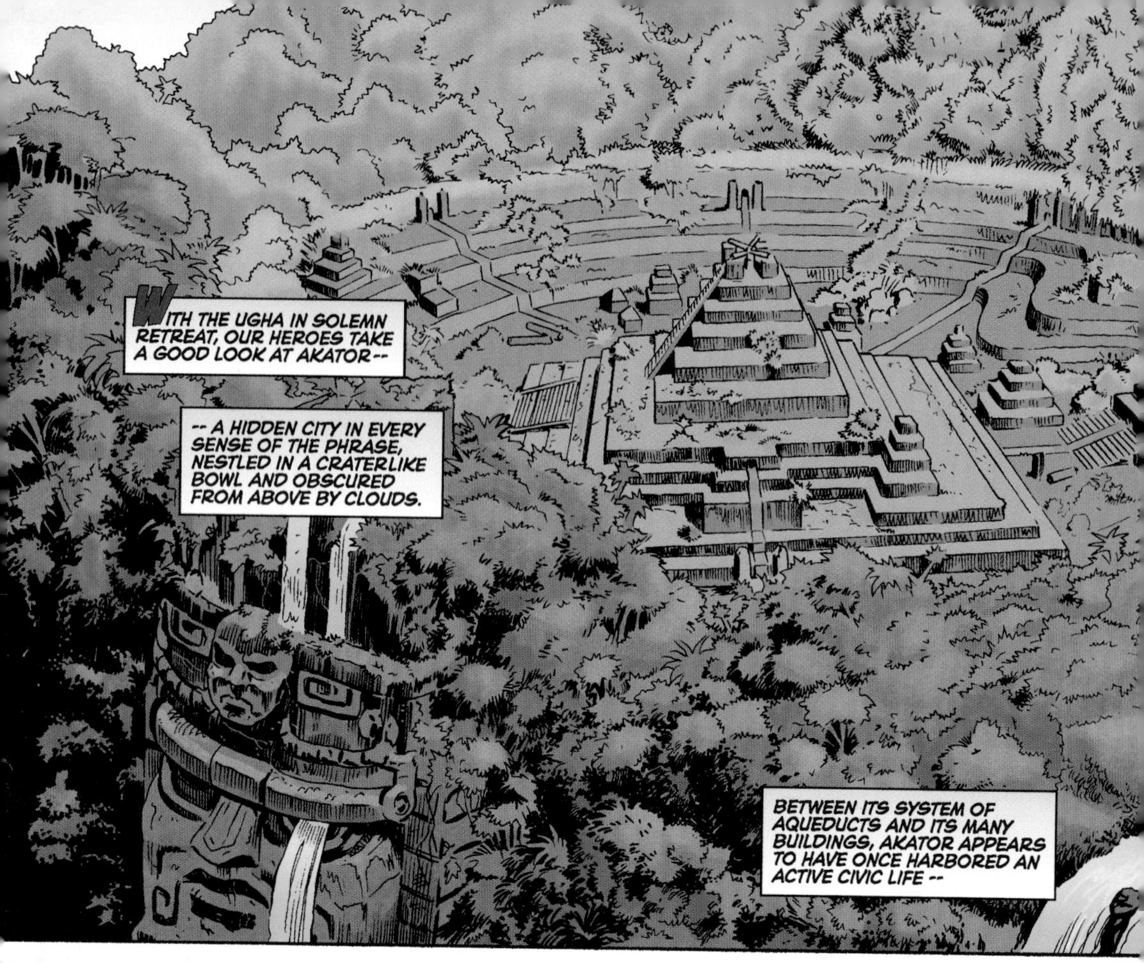
WITH THE UGHA IN SOLEMN RETREAT, OUR HEROES TAKE A GOOD LOOK AT AKATOR --
-- A HIDDEN CITY IN EVERY SENSE OF THE PHRASE, NESTLED IN A CRATERLIKE BOWL AND OBSCURED FROM ABOVE BY CLOUDS.
BETWEEN ITS SYSTEM OF AQUEDUCTS AND ITS MANY BUILDINGS, AKATOR APPEARS TO HAVE ONCE HARBORED AN ACTIVE CIVIC LIFE --

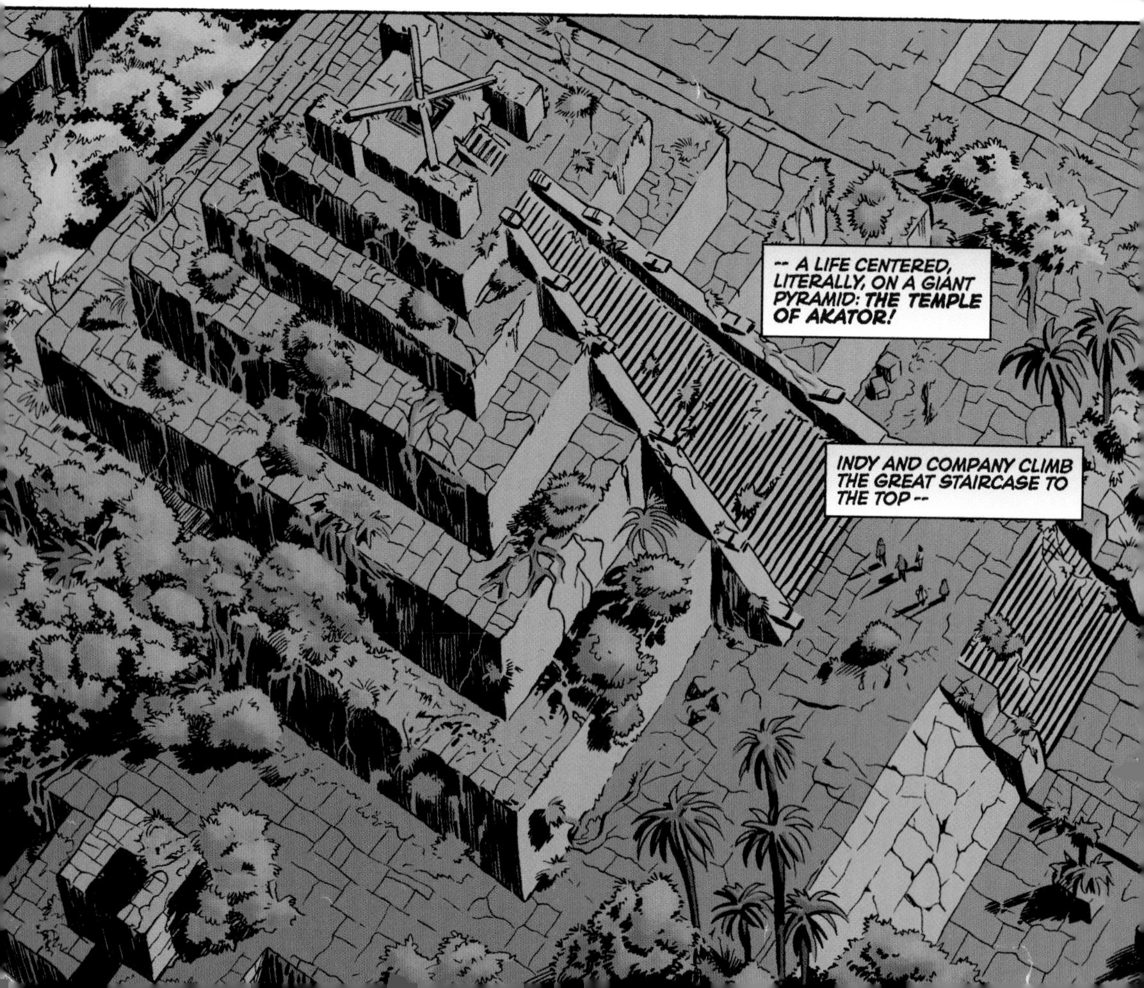
-- A LIFE CENTERED, LITERALLY, ON A GIANT PYRAMID: THE TEMPLE OF AKATOR!
INDY AND COMPANY CLIMB THE GREAT STAIRCASE TO THE TOP --

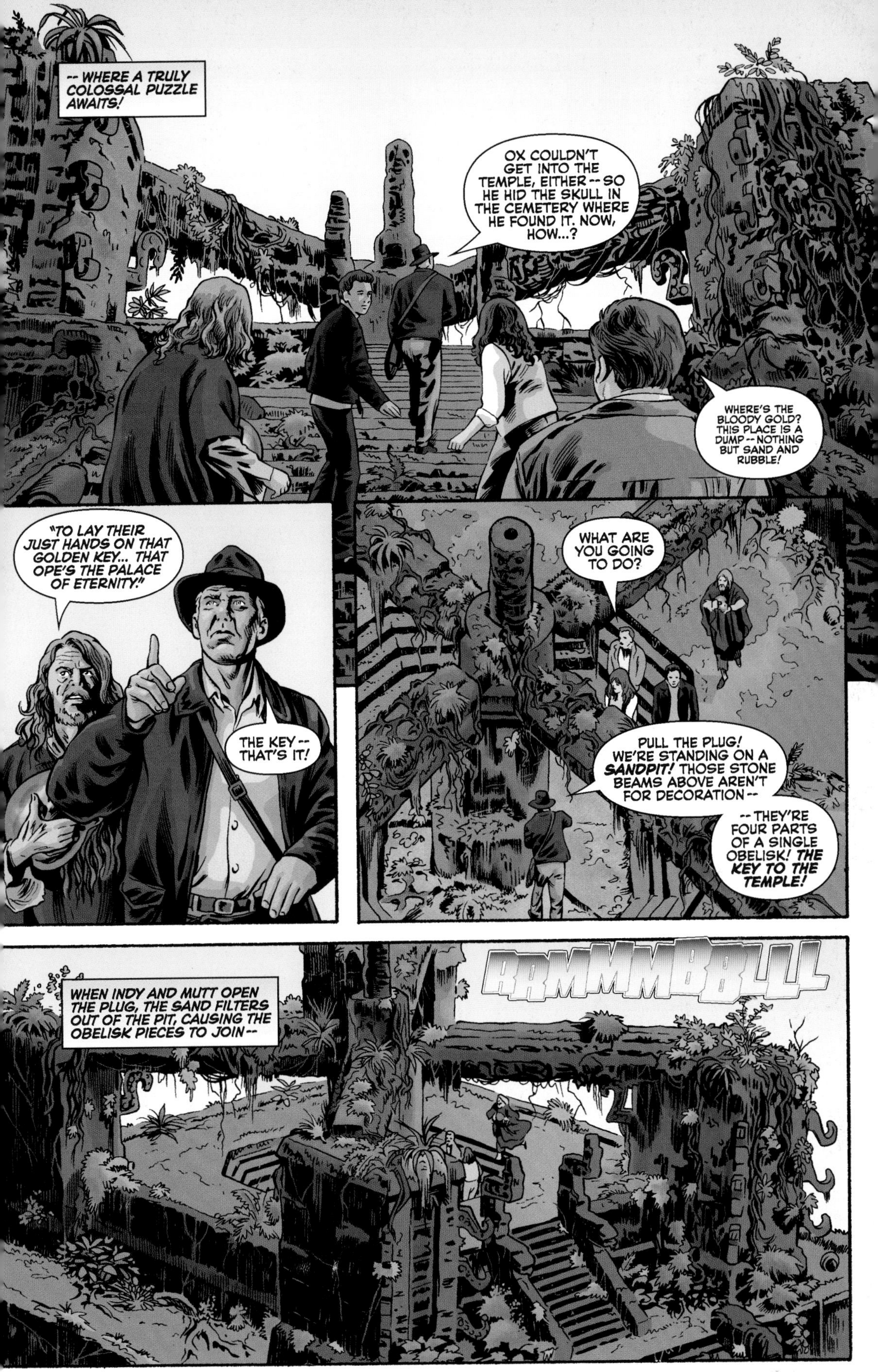
-- WHERE A TRULY COLOSSAL PUZZLE AWAITS!
OX COULDN'T GET INTO THE TEMPLE, EITHER -- SO HE HID THE SKULL IN THE CEMETERY WHERE HE FOUND IT. NOW, HOW...?
WHERE'S THE BLOODY GOLD? THIS PLACE IS A DUMP -- NOTHING BUT SAND AND RUBBLE!
"TO LAY THEIR JUST HANDS ON THAT GOLDEN KEY... THAT OPE'S THE PALACE OF ETERNITY."
THE KEY -- THAT'S IT!
WHAT ARE YOU GOING TO DO?
PULL THE PLUG! WE'RE STANDING ON A SANDPIT! THOSE STONE BEAMS ABOVE AREN'T FOR DECORATION --
-- THEY'RE FOUR PARTS OF A SINGLE OBELISK! THE KEY TO THE TEMPLE!
RRMMMBBLLL
WHEN INDY AND MUTT OPEN THE PLUG, THE SAND FILTERS OUT OF THE PIT, CAUSING THE OBELISK PIECES TO JOIN --

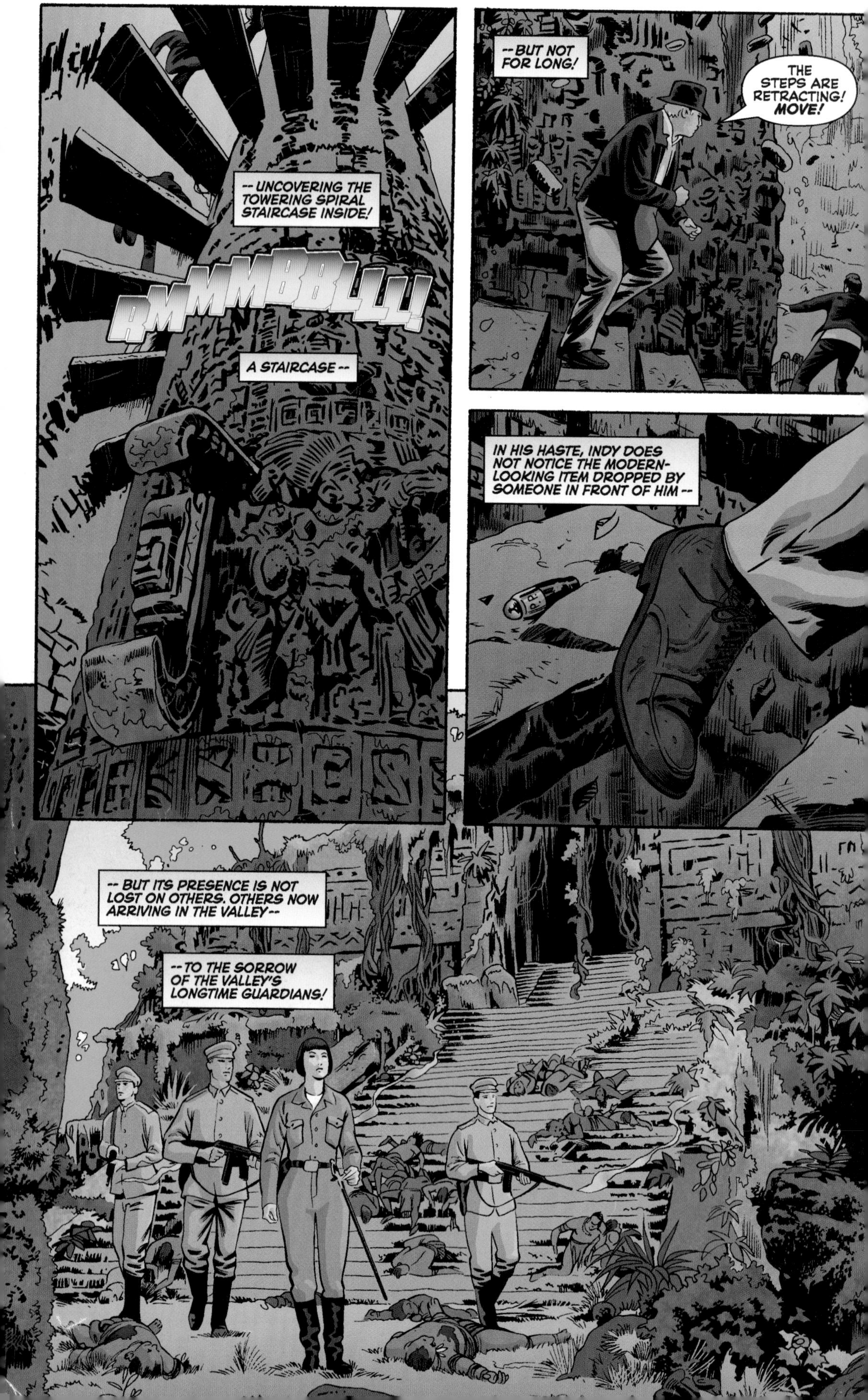
-- UNCOVERING THE TOWERING SPIRAL STAIRCASE INSIDE!
RMMMBBLLL!
A STAIRCASE --
-- BUT NOT FOR LONG!
THE STEPS ARE RETRACTING! MOVE!
IN HIS HASTE, INDY DOES NOT NOTICE THE MODERN-LOOKING ITEM DROPPED BY SOMEONE IN FRONT OF HIM --
-- BUT ITS PRESENCE IS NOT LOST ON OTHERS. OTHERS NOW ARRIVING IN THE VALLEY--
-- TO THE SORROW OF THE VALLEY'S LONGTIME GUARDIANS!

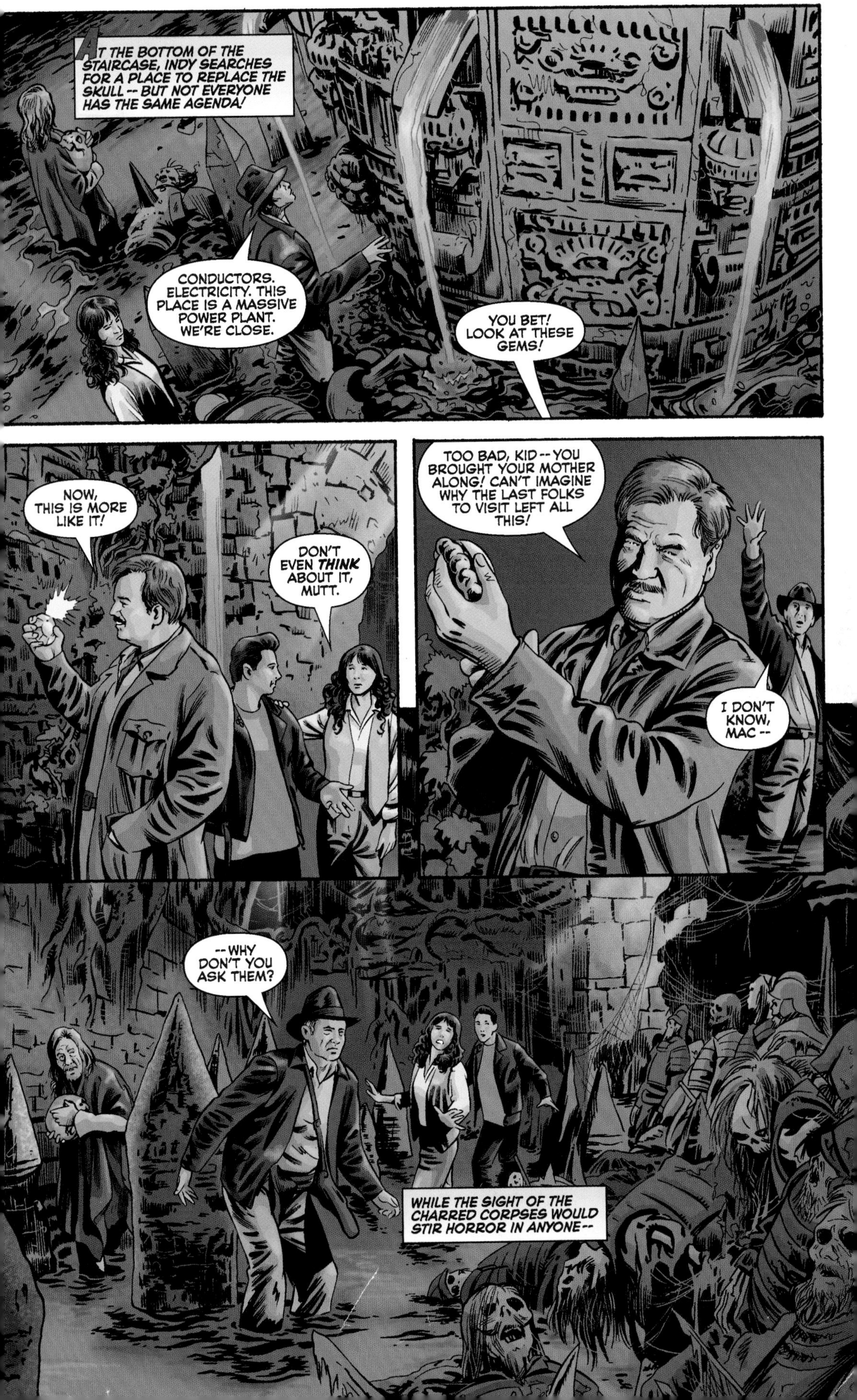
AT THE BOTTOM OF THE STAIRCASE, INDY SEARCHES FOR A PLACE TO REPLACE THE SKULL -- BUT NOT EVERYONE HAS THE SAME AGENDA!
CONDUCTORS. ELECTRICITY. THIS PLACE IS A MASSIVE POWER PLANT. WE'RE CLOSE.
YOU BET! LOOK AT THESE GEMS!
NOW, THIS IS MORE LIKE IT!
DON'T EVEN THINK ABOUT IT, MUTT.
TOO BAD, KID -- YOU BROUGHT YOUR MOTHER ALONG! CAN'T IMAGINE WHY THE LAST FOLKS TO VISIT LEFT ALL THIS!
I DON'T KNOW, MAC --
-- WHY DON'T YOU ASK THEM?
WHILE THE SIGHT OF THE CHARRED CORPSES WOULD STIR HORROR IN ANYONE --

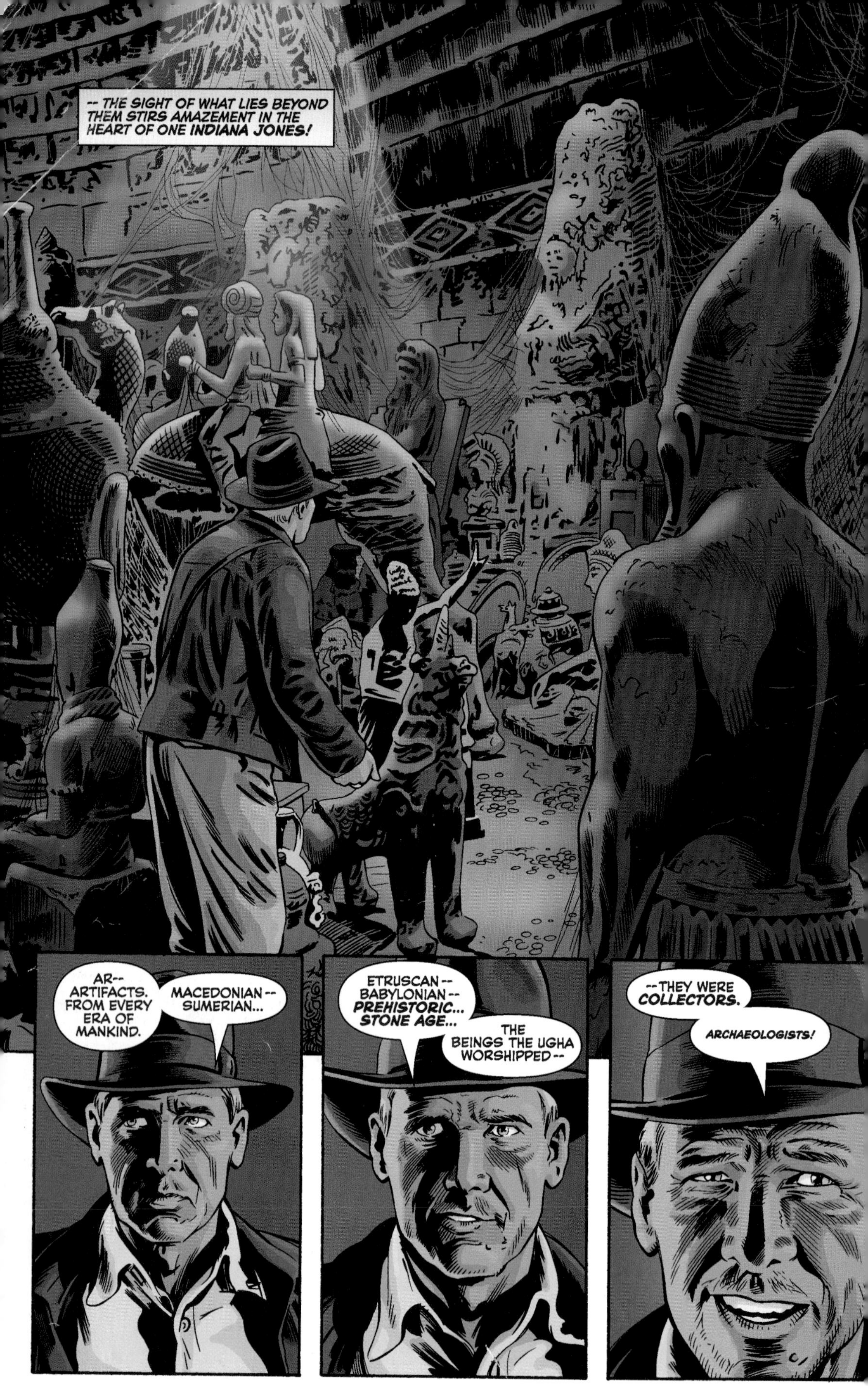
-- THE SIGHT OF WHAT LIES BEYOND THEM STIRS AMAZEMENT IN THE HEART OF ONE INDIANA JONES!
AR-- ARTIFACTS. FROM EVERY ERA OF MANKIND.
MACEDONIAN -- SUMERIAN...
ETRUSCAN -- BABYLONIAN -- PREHISTORIC... STONE AGE...
THE BEINGS THE UGHA WORSHIPPED --
-- THEY WERE COLLECTORS.
ARCHAEOLOGISTS!

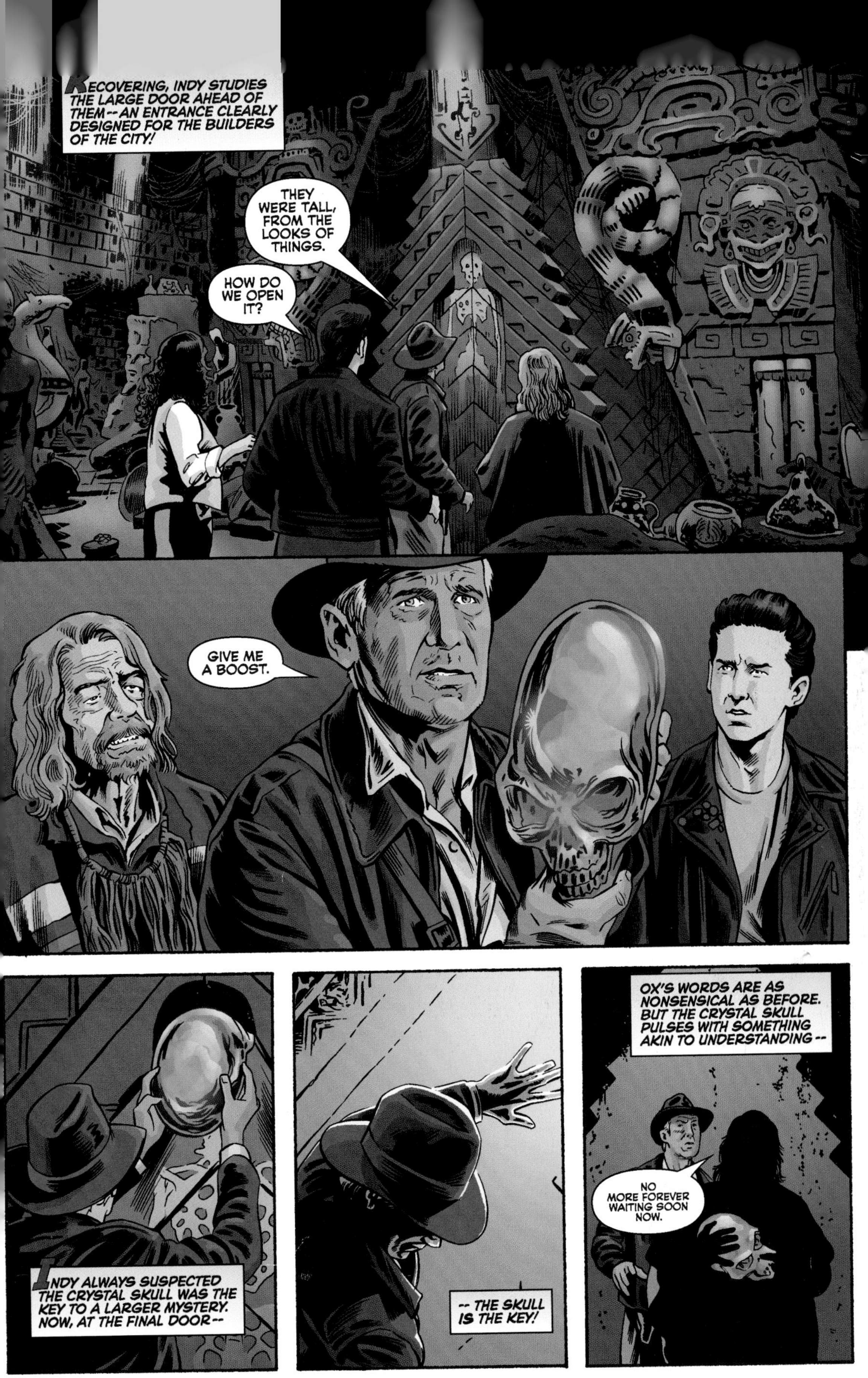
RECOVERING, INDY STUDIES THE LARGE DOOR AHEAD OF THEM--AN ENTRANCE CLEARLY DESIGNED FOR THE BUILDERS OF THE CITY!
THEY WERE TALL, FROM THE LOOKS OF THINGS.
HOW DO WE OPEN IT?
GIVE ME A BOOST.
INDY ALWAYS SUSPECTED THE CRYSTAL SKULL WAS THE KEY TO A LARGER MYSTERY. NOW, AT THE FINAL DOOR--
-- THE SKULL IS THE KEY!
OX'S WORDS ARE AS NONSENSICAL AS BEFORE. BUT THE CRYSTAL SKULL PULSES WITH SOMETHING AKIN TO UNDERSTANDING--
NO MORE FOREVER WAITING SOON NOW.

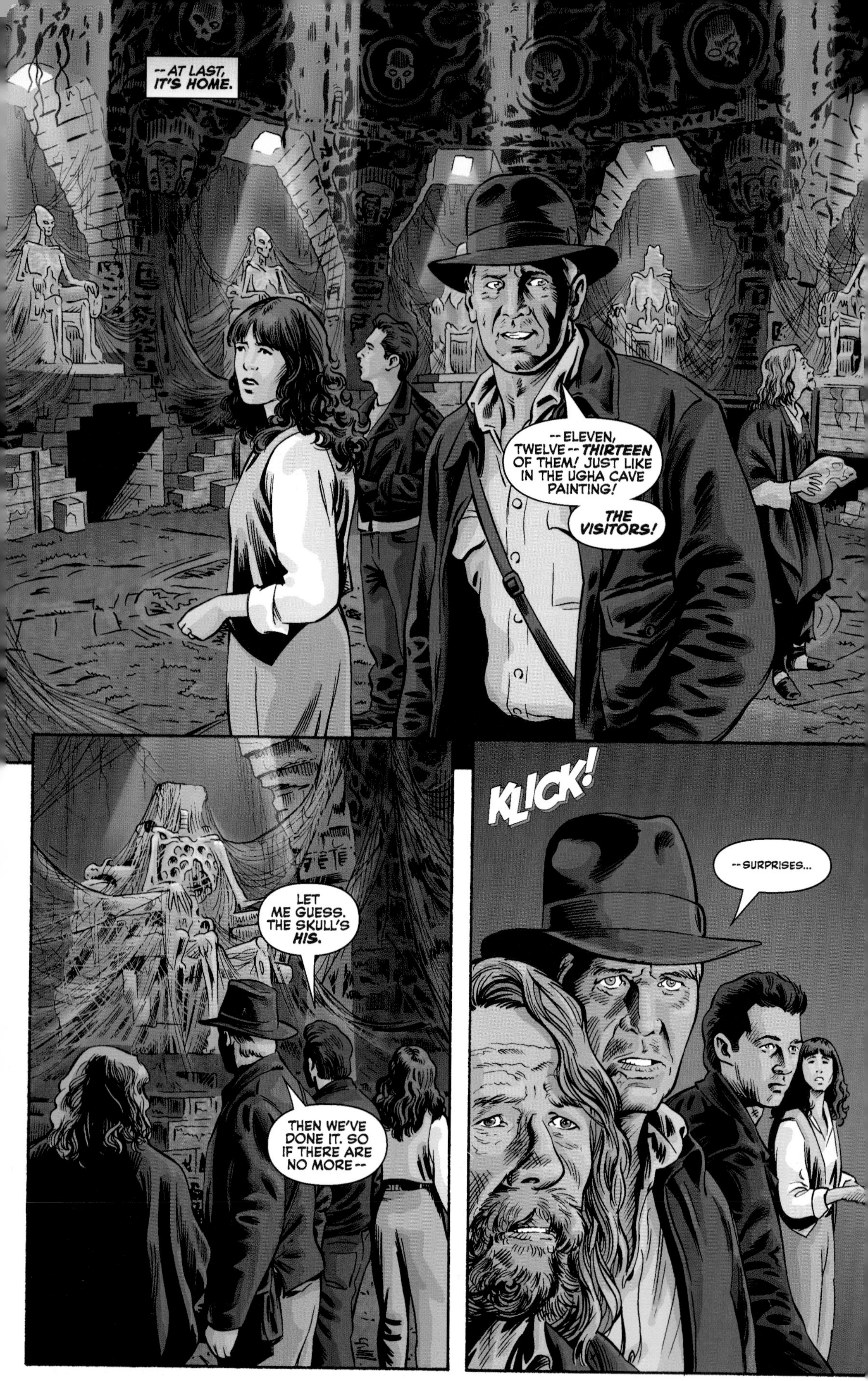
--AT LAST, IT'S HOME.
--ELEVEN, TWELVE--THIRTEEN OF THEM! JUST LIKE IN THE UGHA CAVE PAINTING!
THE VISITORS!
LET ME GUESS. THE SKULL'S HIS.
THEN WE'VE DONE IT. SO IF THERE ARE NO MORE--
KLICK!
--SURPRISES...

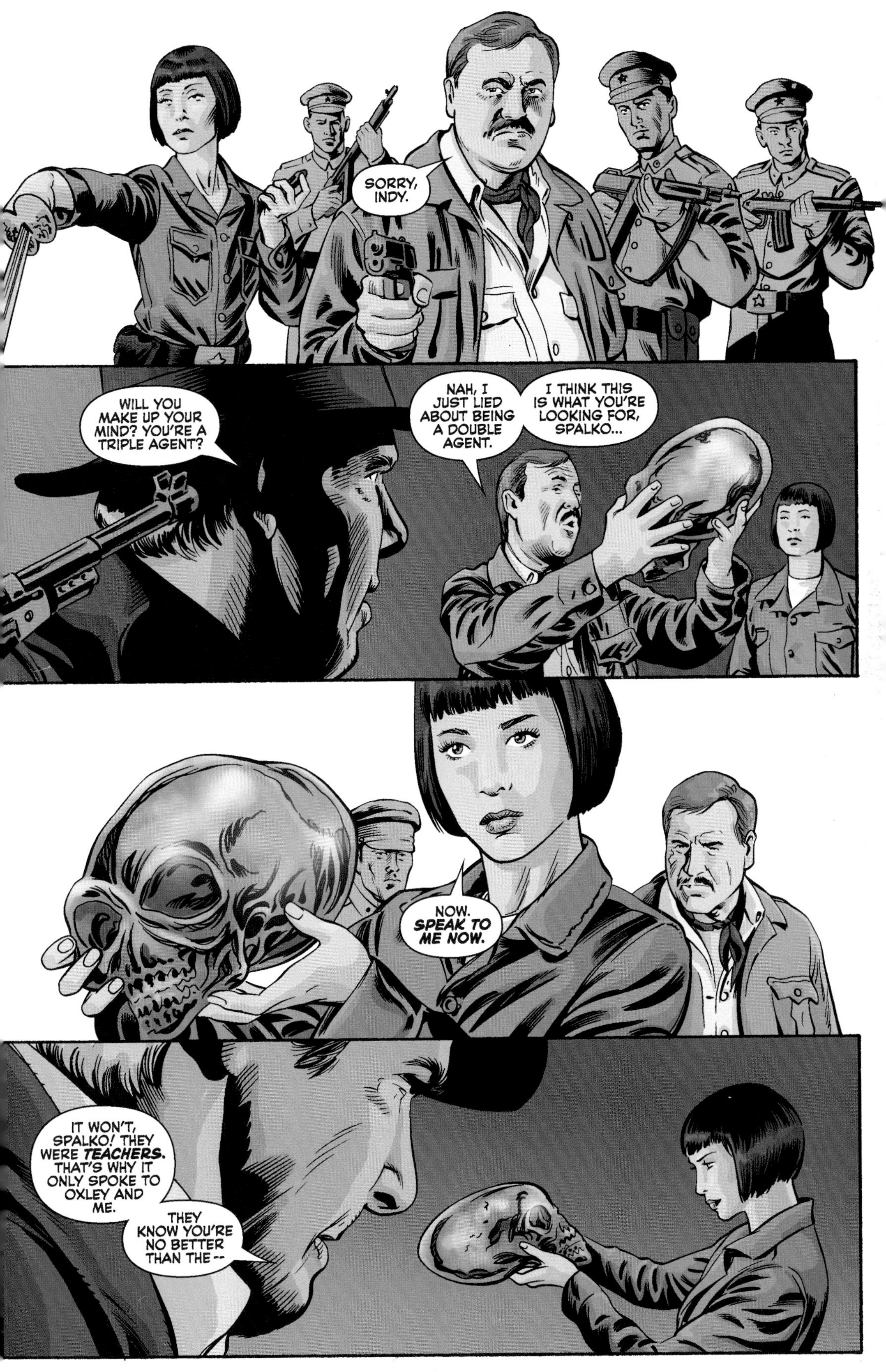
SORRY, INDY.
WILL YOU MAKE UP YOUR MIND? YOU'RE A TRIPLE AGENT?
NAH, I JUST LIED ABOUT BEING A DOUBLE AGENT.
I THINK THIS IS WHAT YOU'RE LOOKING FOR, SPALKO...
NOW. SPEAK TO ME NOW.
IT WON'T, SPALKO! THEY WERE TEACHERS. THAT'S WHY IT ONLY SPOKE TO OXLEY AND ME.
THEY KNOW YOU'RE NO BETTER THAN THE --

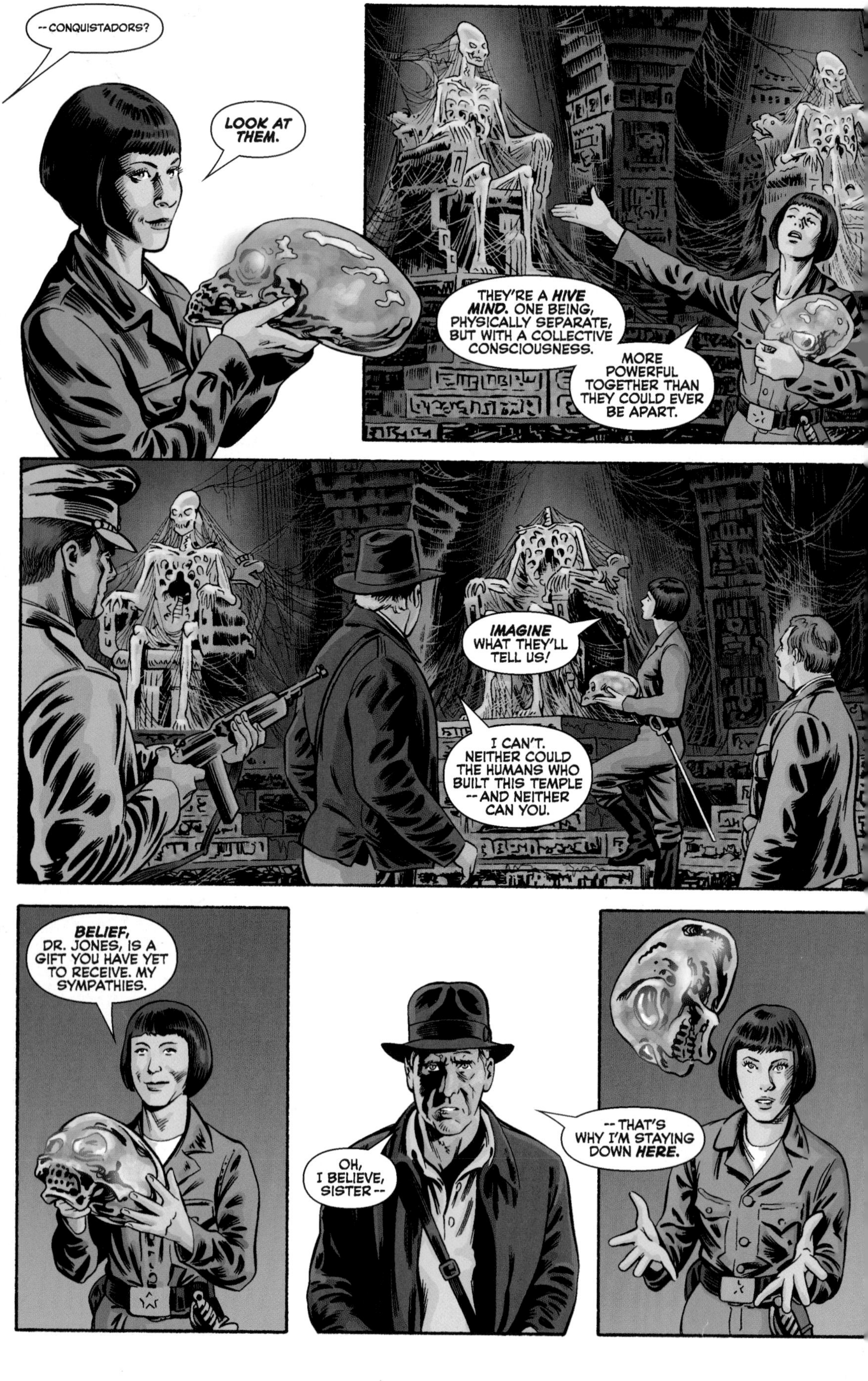
--CONQUISTADORS?
LOOK AT THEM.
THEY'RE A HIVE MIND. ONE BEING, PHYSICALLY SEPARATE, BUT WITH A COLLECTIVE CONSCIOUSNESS.
MORE POWERFUL TOGETHER THAN THEY COULD EVER BE APART.
IMAGINE WHAT THEY'LL TELL US!
I CAN'T. NEITHER COULD THE HUMANS WHO BUILT THIS TEMPLE --AND NEITHER CAN YOU.
BELIEF, DR. JONES, IS A GIFT YOU HAVE YET TO RECEIVE. MY SYMPATHIES.
OH, I BELIEVE, SISTER--
--THAT'S WHY I'M STAYING DOWN HERE.

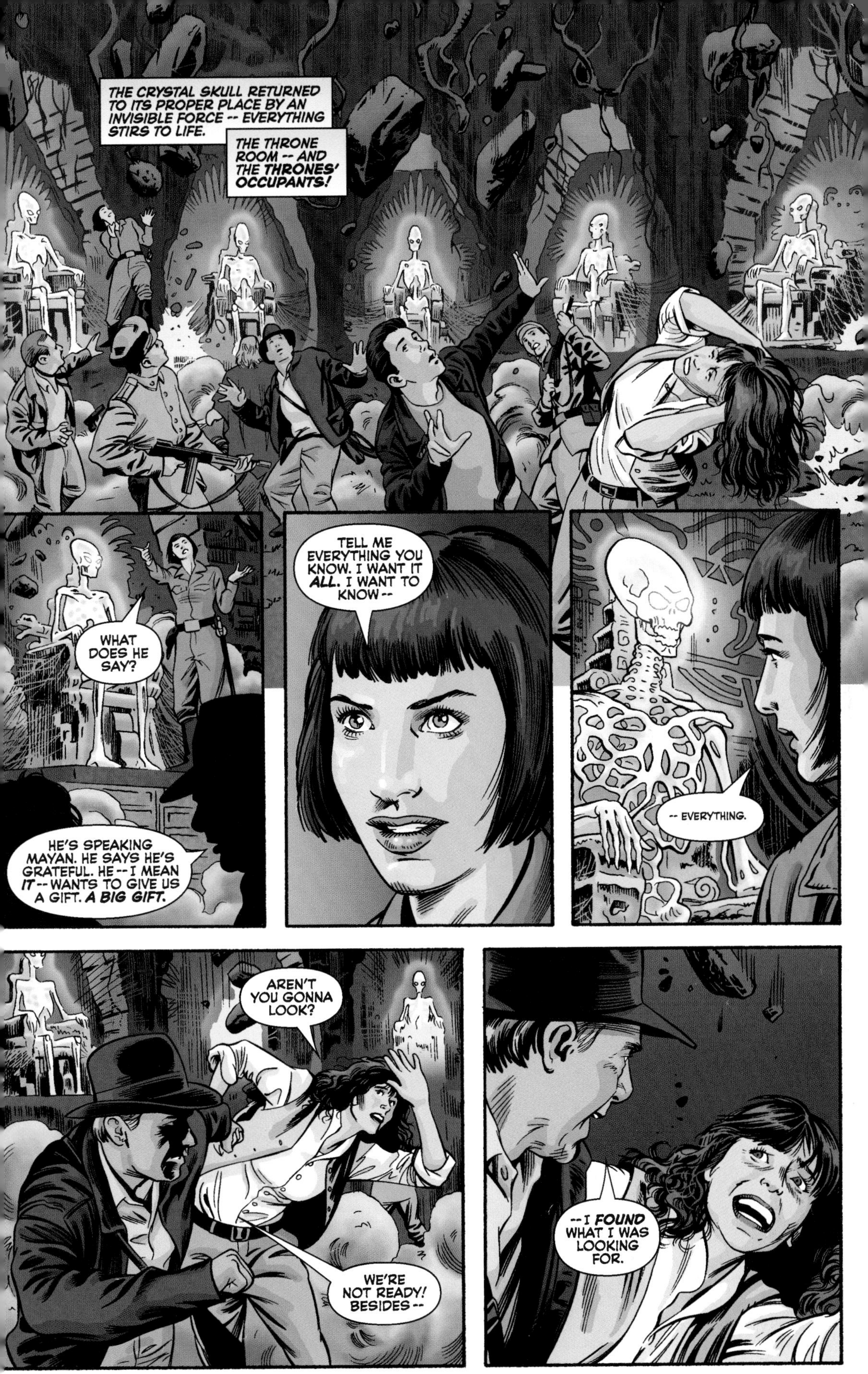
THE CRYSTAL SKULL RETURNED TO ITS PROPER PLACE BY AN INVISIBLE FORCE -- EVERYTHING STIRS TO LIFE.
THE THRONE ROOM -- AND THE THRONES' OCCUPANTS!
WHAT DOES HE SAY?
HE'S SPEAKING MAYAN. HE SAYS HE'S GRATEFUL. HE -- I MEAN IT -- WANTS TO GIVE US A GIFT. A BIG GIFT.
TELL ME EVERYTHING YOU KNOW. I WANT IT ALL. I WANT TO KNOW --
-- EVERYTHING.
AREN'T YOU GONNA LOOK?
WE'RE NOT READY! BESIDES --
-- I FOUND WHAT I WAS LOOKING FOR.

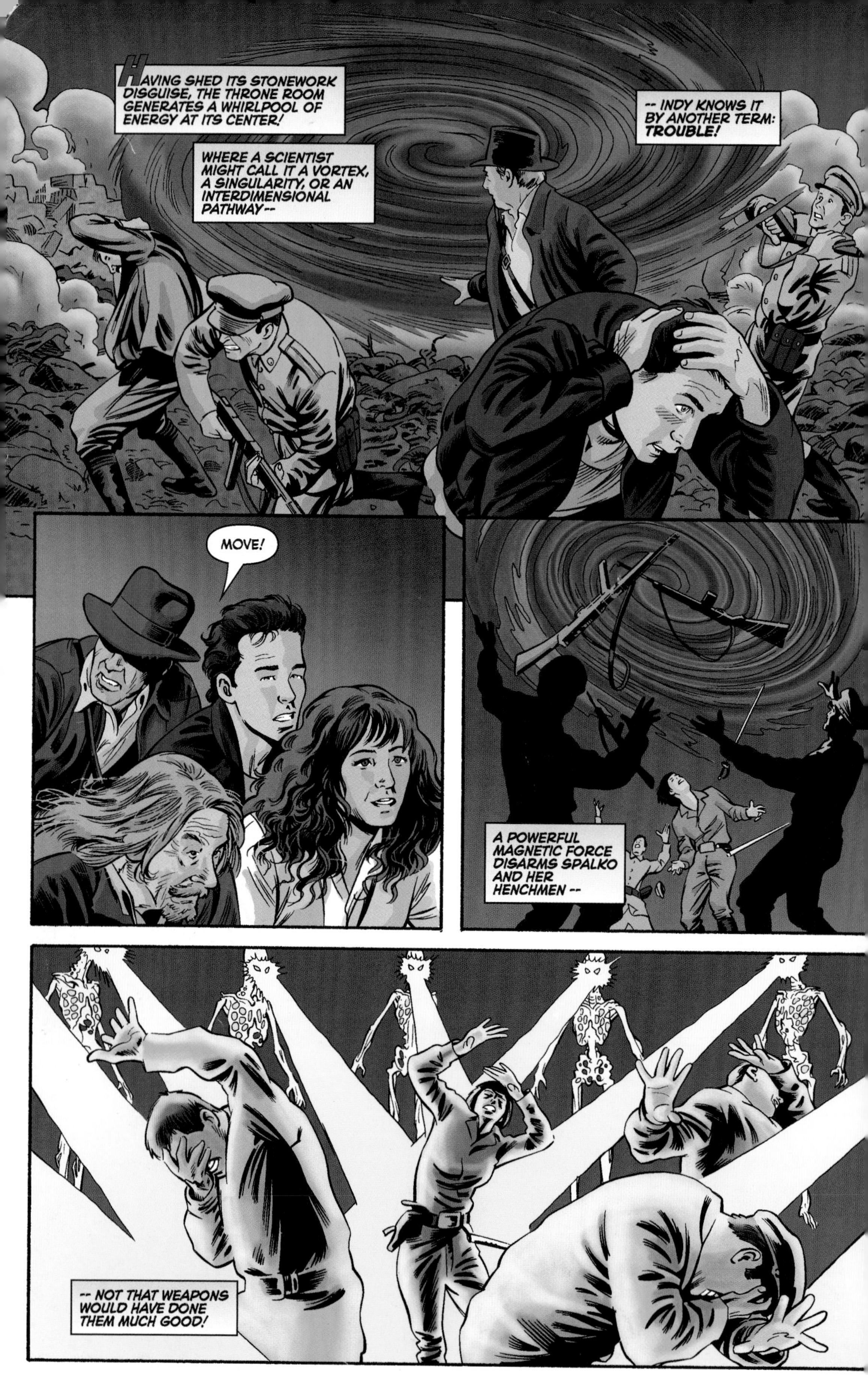
HAVING SHED ITS STONEWORK DISGUISE, THE THRONE ROOM GENERATES A WHIRLPOOL OF ENERGY AT ITS CENTER!
WHERE A SCIENTIST MIGHT CALL IT A VORTEX, A SINGULARITY, OR AN INTERDIMENSIONAL PATHWAY--
-- INDY KNOWS IT BY ANOTHER TERM: TROUBLE!
MOVE!
A POWERFUL MAGNETIC FORCE DISARMS SPALKO AND HER HENCHMEN --
-- NOT THAT WEAPONS WOULD HAVE DONE THEM MUCH GOOD!

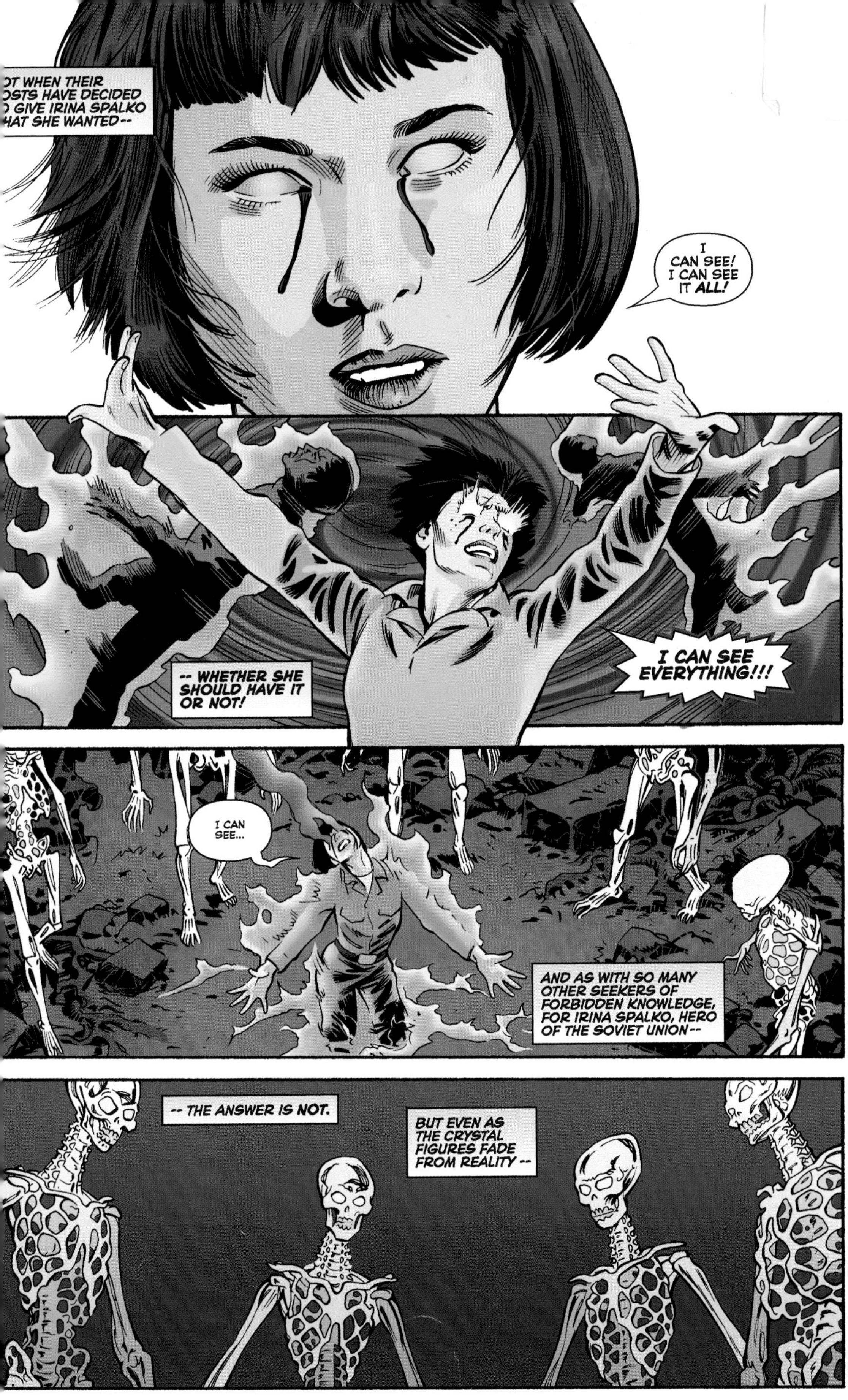

OT WHEN THEIR OSTS HAVE DECIDED O GIVE IRINA SPALKO HAT SHE WANTED --
I CAN SEE! I CAN SEE IT ALL!
-- WHETHER SHE SHOULD HAVE IT OR NOT!
I CAN SEE EVERYTHING!!!
I CAN SEE...
AND AS WITH SO MANY OTHER SEEKERS OF FORBIDDEN KNOWLEDGE, FOR IRINA SPALKO, HERO OF THE SOVIET UNION --
-- THE ANSWER IS NOT.
BUT EVEN AS THE CRYSTAL FIGURES FADE FROM REALITY --

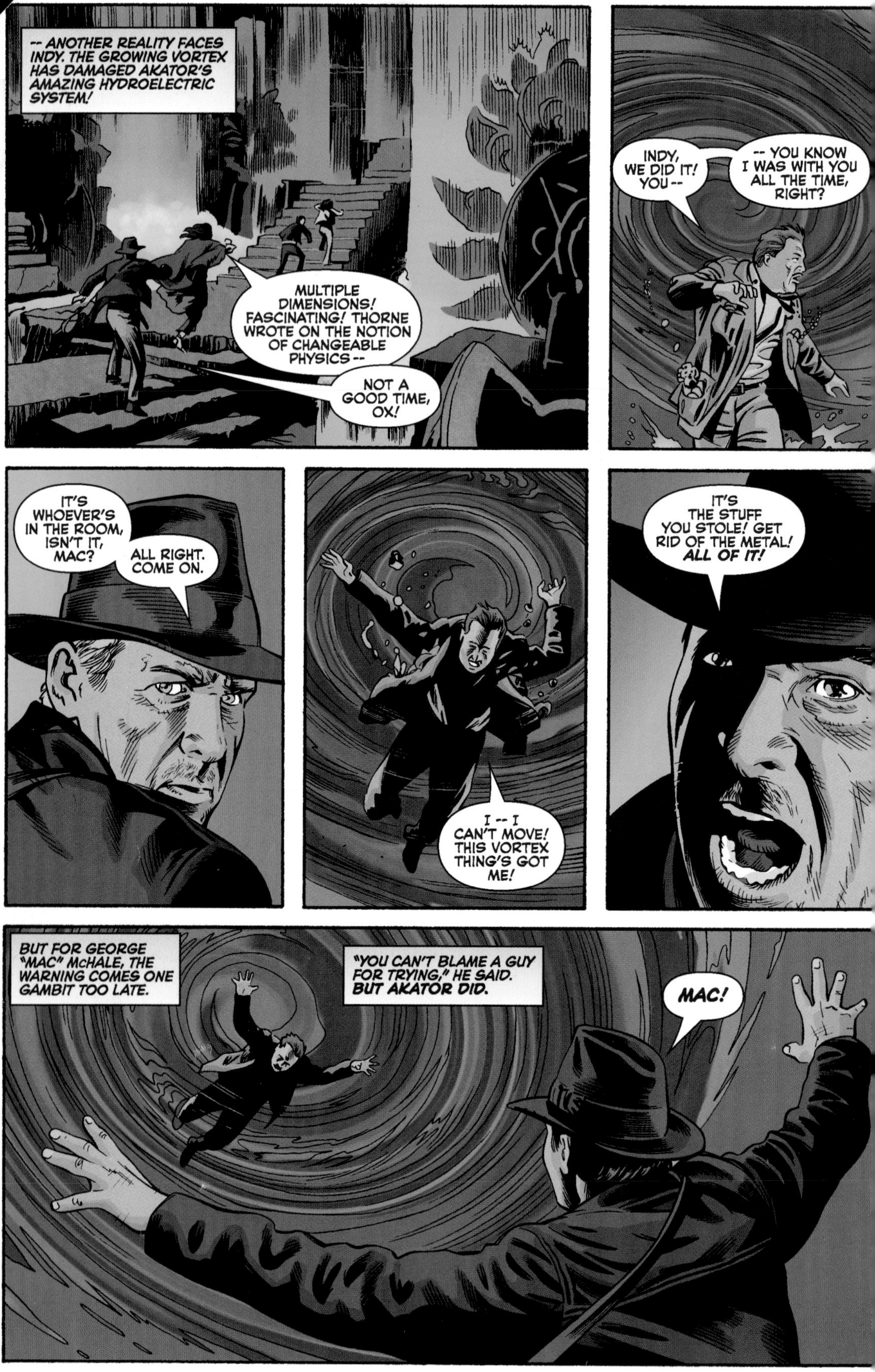
-- ANOTHER REALITY FACES INDY. THE GROWING VORTEX HAS DAMAGED AKATOR'S AMAZING HYDROELECTRIC SYSTEM!
MULTIPLE DIMENSIONS! FASCINATING! THORNE WROTE ON THE NOTION OF CHANGEABLE PHYSICS --
NOT A GOOD TIME, OX!
INDY, WE DID IT! YOU --
-- YOU KNOW I WAS WITH YOU ALL THE TIME, RIGHT?
IT'S WHOEVER'S IN THE ROOM, ISN'T IT, MAC?
ALL RIGHT. COME ON.
I -- I CAN'T MOVE! THIS VORTEX THING'S GOT ME!
IT'S THE STUFF YOU STOLE! GET RID OF THE METAL! ALL OF IT!
BUT FOR GEORGE "MAC" McHALE, THE WARNING COMES ONE GAMBIT TOO LATE.
"YOU CAN'T BLAME A GUY FOR TRYING," HE SAID. BUT AKATOR DID.
MAC!

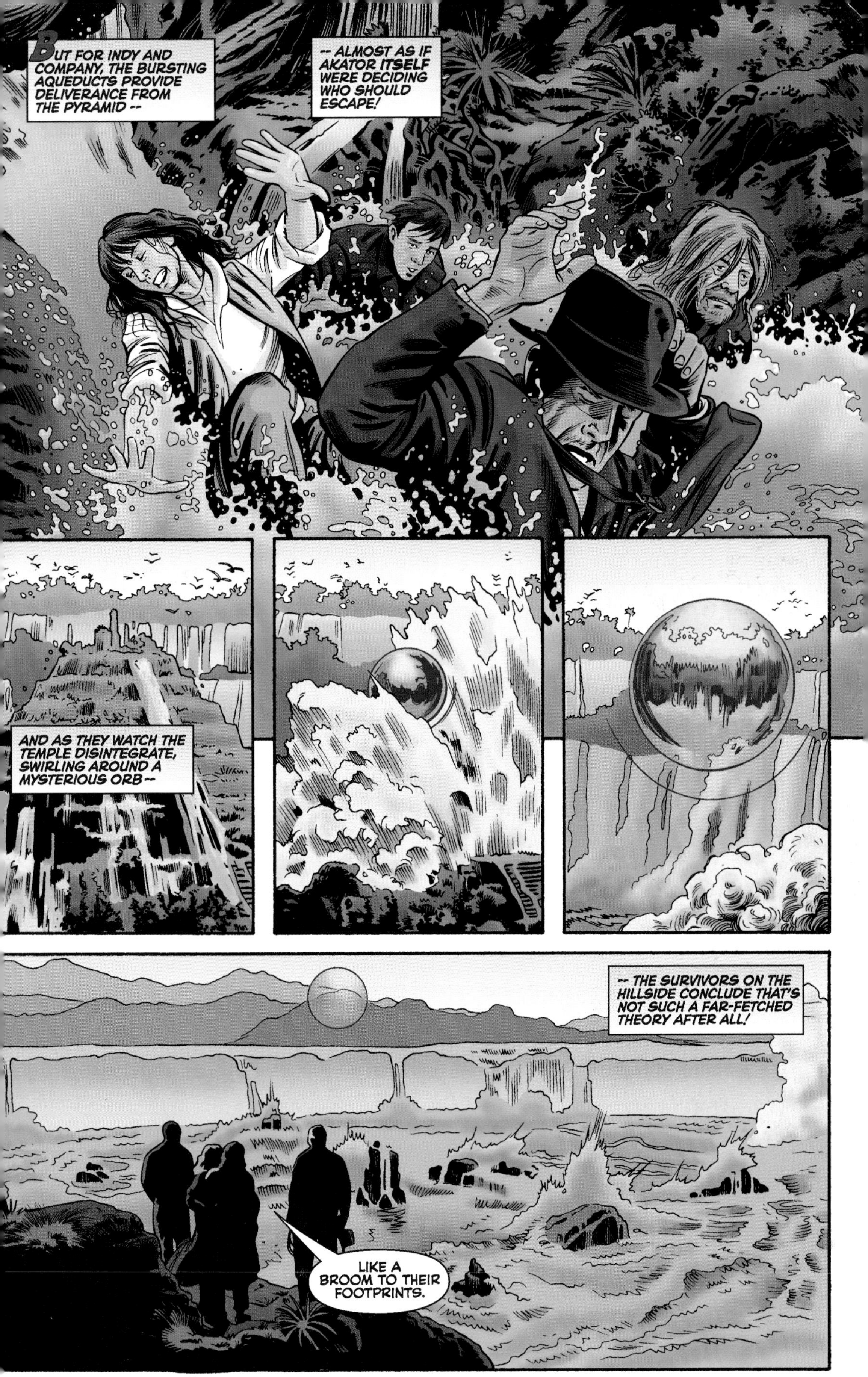
BUT FOR INDY AND COMPANY, THE BURSTING AQUEDUCTS PROVIDE DELIVERANCE FROM THE PYRAMID --
-- ALMOST AS IF AKATOR ITSELF WERE DECIDING WHO SHOULD ESCAPE!
AND AS THEY WATCH THE TEMPLE DISINTEGRATE, SWIRLING AROUND A MYSTERIOUS ORB --
-- THE SURVIVORS ON THE HILLSIDE CONCLUDE THAT'S NOT SUCH A FAR-FETCHED THEORY AFTER ALL!
LIKE A BROOM TO THEIR FOOTPRINTS.

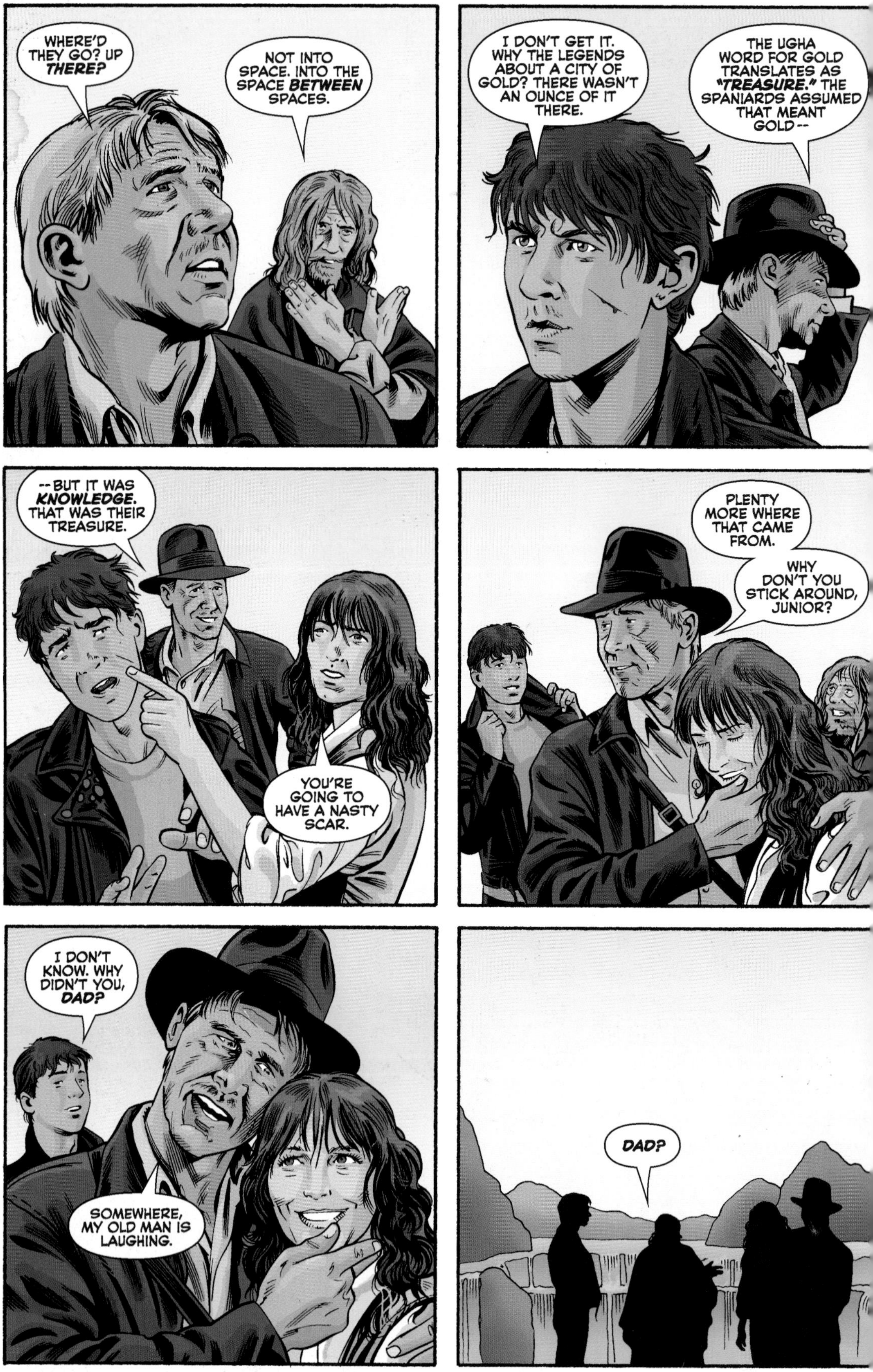
WHERE'D THEY GO? UP THERE?
NOT INTO SPACE. INTO THE SPACE BETWEEN SPACES.
I DON'T GET IT. WHY THE LEGENDS ABOUT A CITY OF GOLD? THERE WASN'T AN OUNCE OF IT THERE.
THE UGHA WORD FOR GOLD TRANSLATES AS "TREASURE." THE SPANIARDS ASSUMED THAT MEANT GOLD --
-- BUT IT WAS KNOWLEDGE. THAT WAS THEIR TREASURE.
YOU'RE GOING TO HAVE A NASTY SCAR.
PLENTY MORE WHERE THAT CAME FROM.
WHY DON'T YOU STICK AROUND, JUNIOR?
I DON'T KNOW. WHY DIDN'T YOU, DAD?
SOMEWHERE, MY OLD MAN IS LAUGHING.
DAD?

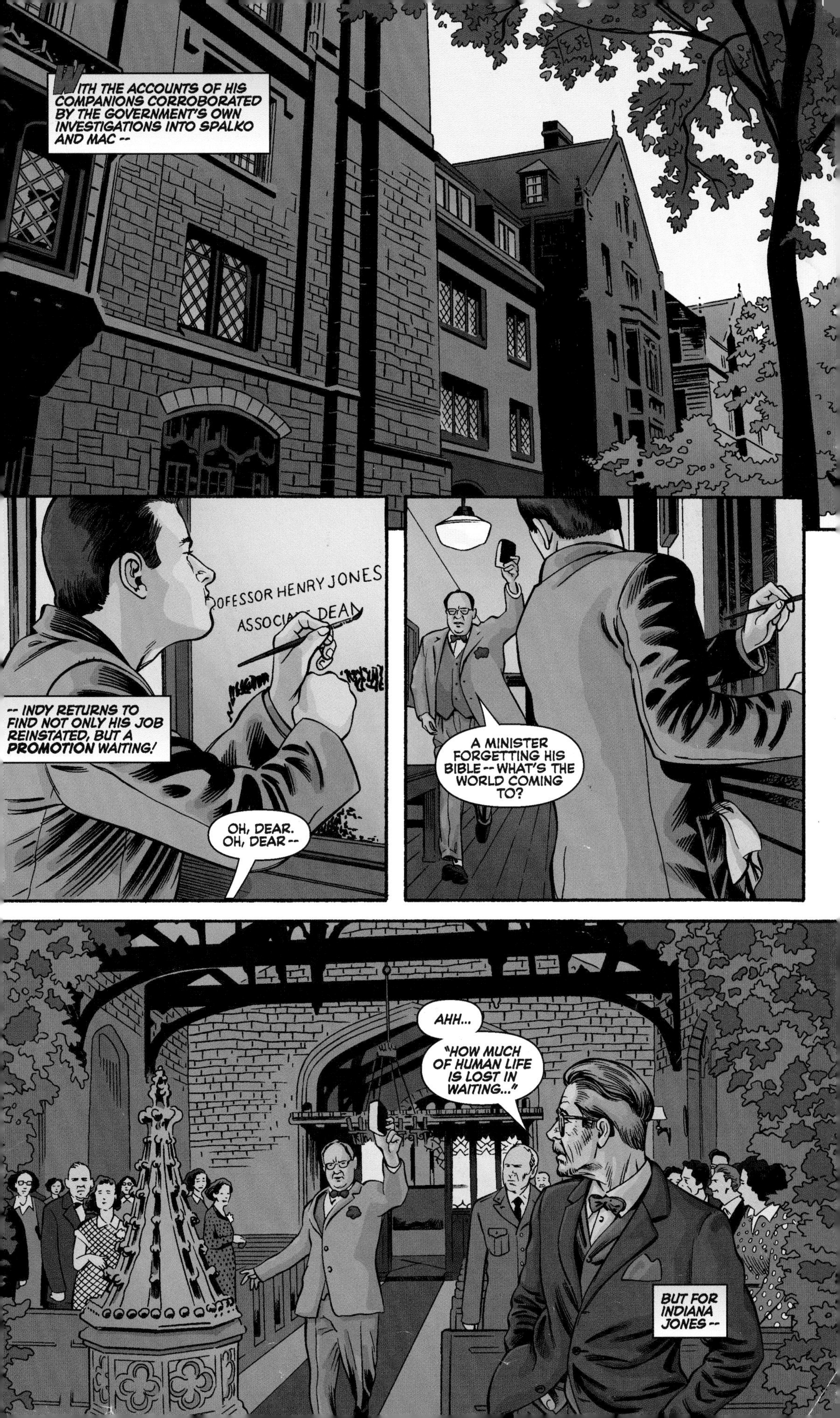
WITH THE ACCOUNTS OF HIS COMPANIONS CORROBORATED BY THE GOVERNMENT'S OWN INVESTIGATIONS INTO SPALKO AND MAC --
OFESSOR HENRY JONES
ASSOCIA DEAN
-- INDY RETURNS TO FIND NOT ONLY HIS JOB REINSTATED, BUT A PROMOTION WAITING!
OH, DEAR. OH, DEAR --
A MINISTER FORGETTING HIS BIBLE -- WHAT'S THE WORLD COMING TO?
AHH...
"HOW MUCH OF HUMAN LIFE IS LOST IN WAITING..."
BUT FOR INDIANA JONES --

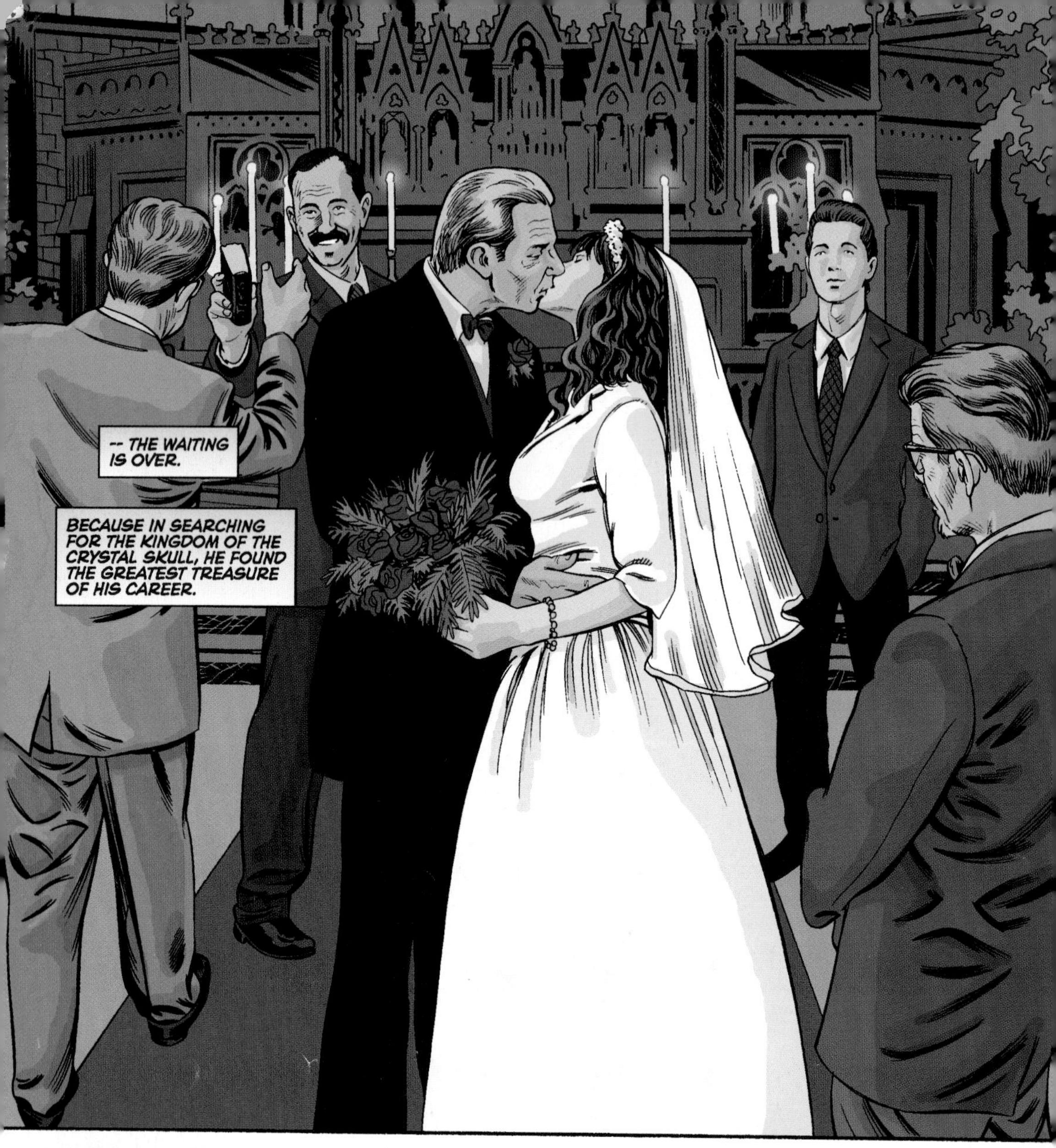
-- THE WAITING IS OVER.
BECAUSE IN SEARCHING FOR THE KINGDOM OF THE CRYSTAL SKULL, HE FOUND THE GREATEST TREASURE OF HIS CAREER.

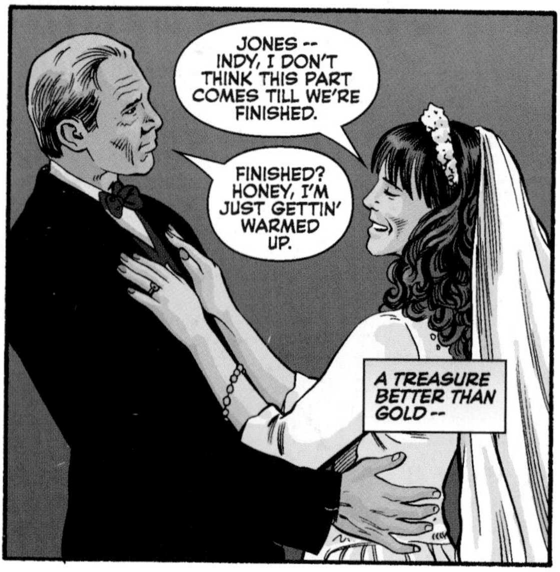
JONES -- INDY, I DON'T THINK THIS PART COMES TILL WE'RE FINISHED.
FINISHED? HONEY, I'M JUST GETTIN' WARMED UP.
A TREASURE BETTER THAN GOLD --

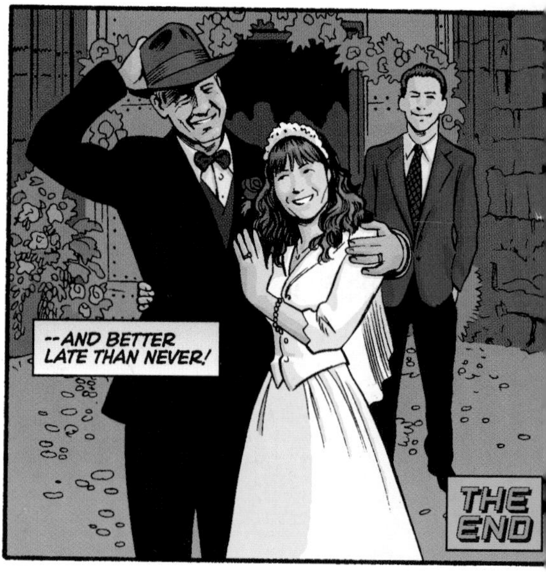
--AND BETTER LATE THAN NEVER!
THE END

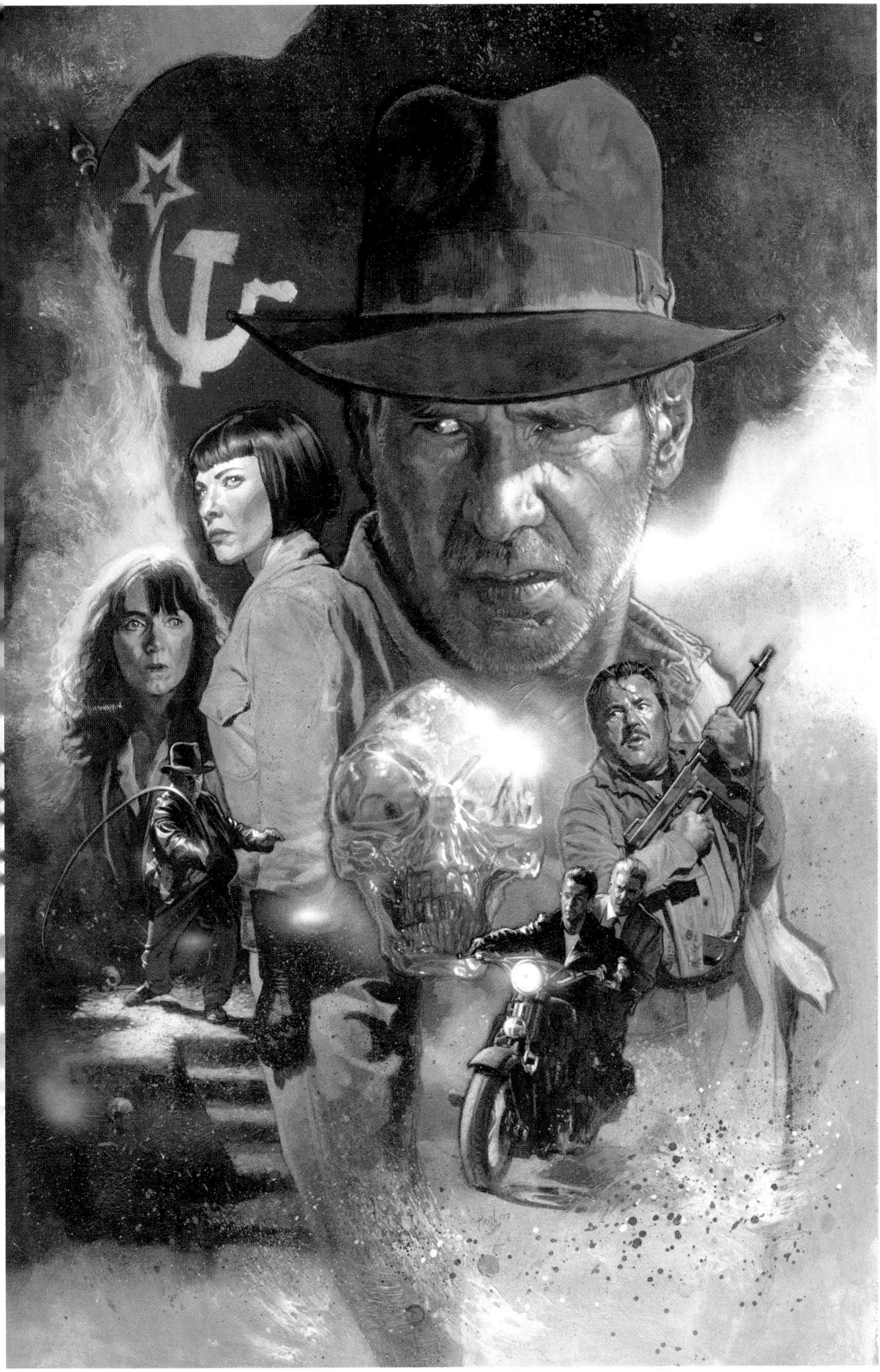

Illustration by Hugh Fleming

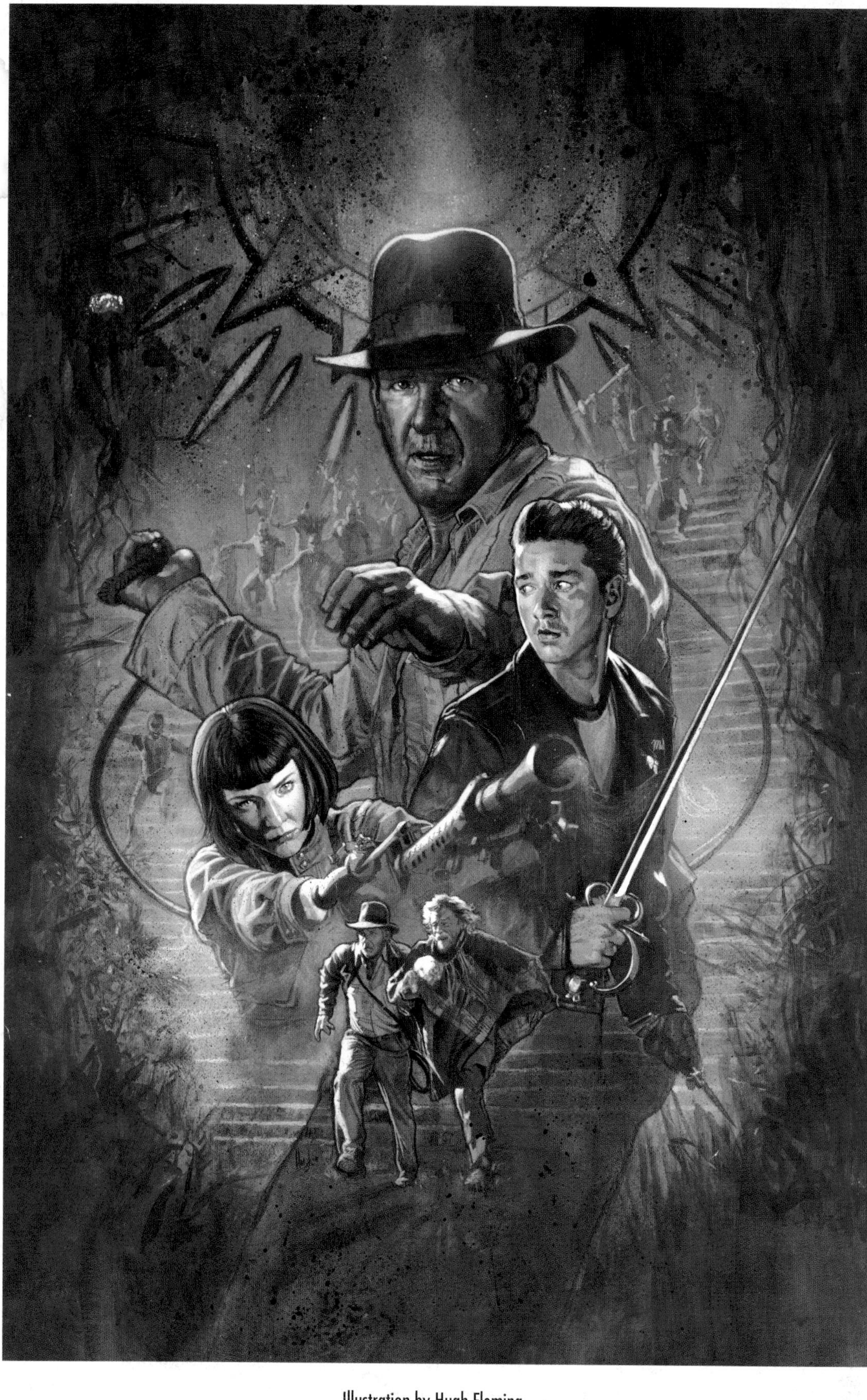

Illustration by Hugh Fleming

INDIANA JONES™

Indiana Jones is back in these massive omnibus volumes recounting several adventures from the career of the twentieth century's most adventurous archeologist! From Greece to Germany, the South Pacific to the seas of the Vikings, his race against the Nazis to recover artifacts like the Golden Fleece, the Philosopher's Stone, or the Spear of Destiny will run him afoul of legendary monsters, ancient cults, and armies of the undead!

Volume 1
ISBN 978-1-59307-887-4

Volume 2
ISBN 978-1-59307-953-6

$24.95 each!

Collecting many long-out-of-print stories in value-priced volumes, *Indiana Jones Omnibus* collections are a perfect jumping-on point for new readers!

READY TO TRY SOME OTHER GREAT STAR WARS® TITLES?

STAR WARS
REBELLION
Volume 1: MY BROTHER, MY ENEMY

REBELLION VOLUME 1:
MY BROTHER, MY ENEMY

Imperial officer Janek "Tank" Sunber makes a critical choice between his duty to the Empire and his loyalty to childhood friend Luke Skywalker in an explosive tale of Rebel spies, Imperial ambushes, and the dreaded Darth Vader!

ISBN: 978-1-59307-711-2 | $14.95

STAR WARS
LEGACY
VOLUME 1 BROKEN

LEGACY VOLUME 1:
BROKEN

The Jedi Temple is attacked, an Emperor is betrayed, and the Sith are born anew! A lot can happen in a hundred years, but that's just the beginning of the story!

ISBN: 978-1-59307-716-7 | $17.95

STAR WARS
KNIGHTS OF THE OLD REPUBLIC
VOLUME ONE
COMMENCEMENT

KNIGHTS OF THE OLD REPUBLIC VOLUME 1:
COMMENCEMENT

Thousands of years before Luke Skywalker would destroy the Death Star in that fateful battle above Yavin 4, one lone Padawan would become a fugitive hunted by his own Masters, charged with murdering every one of his fellow Jedi-in-training!

ISBN: 978-1-59307-640-5 | $18.95

STAR WARS
DARK TIMES
Volume One: THE PATH TO NOWHERE

DARK TIMES VOLUME 1:
THE PATH TO NOWHERE

Jedi Dass Jennir and his companion Bomo Greenbark survived the Clone Wars, but the fate of Bomo's wife and daughter remains a mystery. The two friends are determined to find them, but their path leads them from danger to darkness—where each of them stands to lose more than they may hope to gain.

ISBN: 978-1-59307-792-1 | $17.95

AVAILABLE AT YOUR LOCAL COMICS SHOP OR BOOKSTORE!

To find a comics shop in your area, call 1-888-266-4226.

For more information or to order direct visit darkhorse.com or call 1-800-862-0052 Mon.–Fri. 9 A.M. to 5 P.M. Pacific Time *Prices and availability subject to change without notice

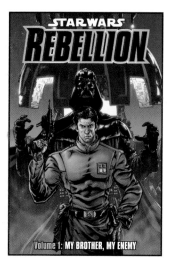

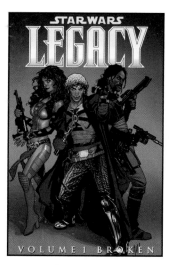

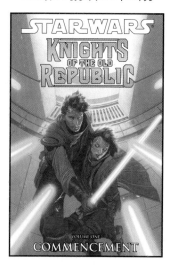

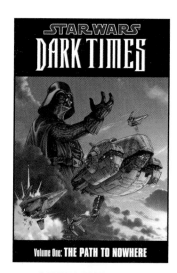